FIGURES *of* FREEDOM

FIGURES of FREEDOM
REPRESENTATIONS OF AGENCY IN A TIME OF CRISIS
Edited by Randy Laist & Brian A. Dixon

Fourth Horseman Press

Figures of Freedom
Edited by Randy Laist & Brian A. Dixon
Published by Fourth Horseman Press

First Edition, April 2024

All Materials Copyright © by the Individual Authors

Cover Artwork Based on "That Liberty Shall Not Perish…" (1918) by Joseph Pennell
Cover Designed by Brian A. Dixon

ISBN: 978-0-9883922-4-3

No part of this publication may be reproduced, stored in or introduced into a retrieval system, or transmitted, in any form, or by any means (electronic, mechanical, photocopying, recording, or otherwise), without the prior written permission of the copyright owner.

Fourth Horseman Press
http://www.fourthhorsemanpress.com/

TABLE OF CONTENTS

Introduction   17
Randy Laist

Section 1: What is Freedom?

"Becoming a WASP": *Mad Men* and   39
the Failure of the American Dream
Nicole Chrenek

At Apocalypse's Edge: The Paradox of   55
Freedom in Contemporary Popular
Science Fiction Films
Jasmine Tan Hui Jun

The Freedom of "the Endland of the   71
Convergence" or "the Long Soft Life"
in DeLillo's *Zero K*
Stephen Hock

Allegorical Tensions between "Freedom   91
to" and "Freedom from" in Jonathan
Franzen's *Freedom*
Peter Krause

"The Time for Expeditions was Over":   111
Infectious Collaborations, Multispecies
Justice, and Troubled Freedoms in Jeff
VanderMeer's *Southern Reach Trilogy*
Ashasmiti Das

Section 2: What Threatens Freedom?

"You Gave Up the World": Freedom and 143
Responsibility in Jenny Offill's *Weather*
and Lydia Millet's *A Children's Bible*
Claire P. Curtis

"Sometimes That's All It Takes to Save a World, 157
You See": Reading Freedom and the
Anthropocene in N. K. Jemisin's Writings
Katrina Newsom

The Shadow of the Pit: Freedom, Family, and 173
Neoliberalism in Meghan Lamb's *Failure to Thrive*
Jay Fraser

Can You Be Free If You're Not Real?: Emily 191
St. John Mandel on Freedom and the
Simulation Hypothesis
John C. Merfeld, Tom Richards, and Noah Stengl

Caught in the Web: Freedom and 211
Techno-Dystopia in *Mr. Robot*
Sony Jalarajan Raj and Adith K. Suresh

Section 3: Freedom for Whom?

Sonmi-451's Revolutionary Fight for 233
Freedom in David Mitchell's *Cloud Atlas*
Martha Zornow

Seeing Environmental Crisis: Reproduction, 249
Disability, and Climate Change in *Bird Box*
Tatiana Konrad

Freedom in *Toy Story*: Reading Woody's 261
Journey as a Post-Human Slave Narrative
Sutirtho Roy

"Those Who Deny Freedom to Others Deserve It Not for Themselves": Redefining the Content of Freedom in Colson Whitehead's *The Underground Railroad*
Beatrice Melodia Festa — 279

The Struggle at the End of the World: Black Freedom in Ta-Nehisi Coates's *Between the World and Me*
Sharmila Mukherjee — 295

INTRODUCTION

Randy Laist

In the immediate aftermath of the 2001 terrorist attacks on the World Trade Center and the Pentagon, George W. Bush framed the war on terror as a war between "freedom and fear." His most trenchant analysis of what motivated the 9/11 terrorists was the assessment that "they hate our freedoms," and this appraisal translated into the geopolitical policy of aggressively overthrowing tyrannical regimes to replace them with Western-style democracies, the ostensible guarantors of neoconservative freedom, in a worldwide series of military operations collectively labeled Operation Enduring Freedom. The Bush administration's "freedom" rhetoric became a hysterical symptom of post-9/11 anxiety, as french fries became "Freedom Fries," the new skyscraper planned for the World Trade Center became known as the "Freedom Tower," and patriotic Americans were continually reminded that "freedom isn't free." At the same time that this rhetoric dominated mainstream political and cultural discourse, however, the Patriot Act and other counterterrorism initiatives threatened the actual freedoms of Americans at home, while the Bush administration's military adventurism overseas enacted a patently oxymoronic project of enforcing freedom at the barrel of a gun, through a policy of "shock and awe."

Thus did the twenty-first century begin in America with a renewed appeal to the value of freedom, which had of course long been one of the oldest and most frequently invoked concepts in the rhetoric of American politics. The word "freedom" sits squarely in the middle of the First Amendment to the Constitution—protecting the "freedom of speech"—although this is actually the only appearance of the word "freedom" in either the Constitution or the Declaration of Independence. The Framers preferred the term "liberty," as in Jefferson's appeal to "life, liberty, and the pursuit of happiness," with its implication of a consensual socio-political structure that supports individual freedoms. Over the course of the last 250 years, however, the word "liberty" has receded into a kind of quaint nostalgia, while the term "freedom" continues to stir the blood and drive the campaign contributions of Americans across the political spectrum. This development tracks with a wider trend of individualism that has unfolded over the intervening centuries in Western culture, a trend which exists in complex interaction with the geopolitical ascendency of the United States itself. While "liberty" implies a collective freedom that has been deliberately engineered by a social structure of negotiations and compromises, "freedom" takes place at the level of the individual. It experiences itself as unbound by history or society. "Freedom of speech" is the archetypal American freedom in its focus on the scale of personal choice and agency. The spontaneous agency of the individual exerting "freedom of speech" is the lone gunman of the American imaginary, the American Adam (occasionally Eve) creating the world anew out of their own words and vision.

To be sure, the American infatuation with individual freedom has always been tinged with hypocrisy. The Framers of the Constitution were keenly aware of the internal contradiction between their political rhetoric of freedom and their economic identity as a slave society, which may explain why they were reluctant to use the word "freedom" in their founding documents. Since that time, the trans-generational project of shaming the United States into "living up to its ideals"—to become the freedom-loving nation it promised to be—has served as a powerful spur to social change. Throughout this same history, however, it is also easy to identify instances of the ideal of "freedom" being used as a justification for depriving other people of freedom, and it is also easy to find instances of the word "freedom" becoming trivialized as a marketing slogan for both political and commercial purposes. The Bush administration's blatant appropriation of the word "freedom" to market its war on terror has paved the way for further and more transparently self-serving applications of the word, especially in conservative circles, to entities such as the House's "Freedom Caucus," the protest by truck drivers against Covid restrictions that were described as "Freedom Convoys," and planned urban developments proposed by Donald Trump as "Freedom Cities." The left, meanwhile, aware of the power of "freedom" as an American shibboleth, has tried to assert their own claim to the word, as in Joe Biden's first 2024 reelection campaign television ad, which uses the word "freedom" seven times in 90 seconds and which identifies "defending our basic freedoms" the "cause of his presidency." Biden also articulated the argument for providing military support for Ukraine and Israel with an appeal to America's global-historical mandate to defend "the cause of freedom" ("Biden's remarks"), speaking in terms that clearly circled back around to the post-9/11 rhetoric of the Bush administration.

It would be easy to dismiss all this political bandying-about of the word "freedom" as empty rhetoric, but twenty-first-century freedom rhetoric in political discourse parallels socio-historical trends that have cast classical conceptions of freedom into new registers of complexity. To be sure, the war on terror supported a robust discourse in the fraught question of how a society balances the values of freedom and security, a perennial debate that takes on added urgency in a time of cellular communications, video surveillance, and digital data. Although the specter of terrorist attacks dwindled in the Obama years, questions about how big tech simultaneously enables and imperils freedom continued to stir debate and to influence perceptions of social media, screen time, and artificial intelligence. Indeed, in addition to the question of digital surveillance, people's daily experience of relying in so many ways on their phones provides daily object lessons in the way that a person's free will can become absorbed into behavioral-neurological patterns of addictive pleasure-response.

The debate about the addictive quality of social media and screen time itself tends to express a brain-based perspective that has largely supplanted "deep psychology." The scientific language of neurotransmitters and synaptic configurations has replaced humanist psychological paradigms of personality in a way that marginalizes the emphasis that mid-twentieth-century psychologists placed on freedom and agency. In the 2020s, the startling emergence of generative AI chatbots reinforced a perception that language and perhaps even consciousness itself are systemic effects of digital data, and that, rather than being grounded in some metaphysical principle that might have underwritten a claim to freedom, conscious experience can be explained as the outcome of an algorithm. Indeed, the rise of "nones" as the fastest-growing religious affiliation throughout the twenty-first century diminishes the prevalence of "faith-based" conceptions of human freedom as a heavenly gift, situating human identity within the context of chemical and physical forces.

The mapping of the human genome has facilitated an understanding of the genetic underpinnings of our bodies and minds, while the rise of ecology and climate science has revealed the extent to which we are embedded in systems that overwhelm our ability to understand them or, in many cases, even to perceive them. LGBTQ+ and Trans Rights advocates have drawn attention to the extent to which sexual preference and gender identity are in-born traits rather than free choices, while the Black Lives Matter movement and the 1619 Project have revealed the extent to which racial discrimination persists in unconscious or "implicit" forms. Meanwhile, the emergent climate crisis reanimates the debates from the Bush years about how consumerist freedom should be balanced against ecological security, and the war in Ukraine has reanimated America's Cold War era identity as beacon of the "free world," even as Trump's reelection campaign promises to institute authoritarian rule at home.

This summary encompasses a wide span of diverse trends, but one thing that ties them all together is the question of freedom: what it means to be free in the twenty-first century, and even whether the concept of freedom itself might be anachronistic. Reaction against this underlying anxiety may explain why the word "freedom" has reemerged in political discourse as such a potent motto. Ritualistic intonation of the word may serve to offer a kind of magical protection from the loss of the actual experience of mobility, self-efficacy, and possibility that the word supposedly signifies.

The prevalence with which twenty-first-century trends foreground questions of freedom, frequently complicating classical conceptions of freedom as a transcendent value, has not gone unnoticed by cultural commentators, who have produced a number of significant works dedicated to reassessing the state of contemporary freedom. Wendy Hui Kyong Chun's *Control and Freedom* (2006) examines the meaning of the fact that many of the ways that human beings express their freedom, even their prototypical "Freedom of Speech," rely on what she calls "control technologies" such as fiber-optic networks, software programs, and the Internet, resulting in a condition in which "power now operates through the coupling of control and freedom" (1).

Similarly, Byung-Chul Han's *Psychopolitics* (2017) argues that the specters of Big Data, corporate surveillance, and self-help culture create a cultural condition in which "freedom itself, which is supposed to be the opposite of constraint, is producing coercion," as "everything that belongs to practices and expressive forms of liberty—emotion, play and communication—comes to be exploited" in the interest of creating a society of "neoliberal slave[s]" (2-3).

Other writers have reassessed the master narrative of American history to excavate the degree to which the institution of literal slavery served as the "primal scene" out of which America's national preoccupation with freedom originally arose. For at least some of the Founding Fathers, the American freedom most worth preserving was the freedom to own other people, and the revolutionary rhetoric of resisting monarchical "slavery" derived its urgency from white Americans' insistence on asserting their superiority to the Black people enslaved under their laws. Tyler Stovall argues that "the coexistence of racism and freedom in the modern world is less a contradiction than the articulation of the variegated nature of both concepts and their manifold interactions over time" (24), and that what American political rhetoric has historically identified as "freedom" is actually "white freedom"—"the belief (and practice) that freedom is central to white racial identity, and that only white people can or should be free" (11).

In *Freedom's Dominion* (2022), the historian Malcolm Cowrie conducts a close reading of the history of Barbour County, Alabama, that illustrates how "appeals to American freedom so often serve as an ideological motor for practices of domination of other people's land, labor, and political power," and the historical progression whereby "racialized anti-statism became a core aspect of American freedom" (5). Although Cowrie's book examines the deep history of the nineteenth and twentieth centuries, his final chapter notes that the Trump supporters who stormed the Capitol in January of 2021 "were, in fact, not wrong to call themselves 'freedom fighters' within a deeply flawed American creed" (414).

INTRODUCTION

Linda M. G. Zerilli's *Feminism and the Abyss of Freedom* (2005) provides a critique of a masculinist rhetoric of a style of freedom that is defined as "a phenomenon of the will, a property of the subject, and a means to an end whose name is sovereignty" (93), and she proposes a counter-definition of a freedom that "requires a certain kind of relation to others in the space defined by plurality" (19).

In an influential 2012 book, Mimi Thi Nguyen critiques *The Gift of Freedom*, an exchange that involves a ceremonial bestowal of "freedom" on refugee populations that is simultaneously the creation of a "debt" that "preclude[s] the subject of freedom from being able to escape a colonial order of things" (5).

Amid this microgenre of freedom-oriented cultural studies analyses, one of the most sweeping is Elisabeth R. Anker's *Ugly Freedoms* (2022), which distinguishes between two kinds of "ugly freedom." On the one hand, there is the "ugly freedom" that encompasses "control over nature, individual sovereignty, human exceptionalism, uncoerced will, and private ownership" (33), the definition of freedom that provides justification for any act from slave-owning to genocide to ecocide that expresses the ability of the individual to exert mastery of its environment. But Anker is even more interested in a second "valence" of the term "ugly freedom," describing "practices of freedom in the discarded spaces and disparaged practices of the freedoms reflexively deemed ideal" (14), forms of freedom that are considered "ugly" because they are performed by marginalized people in imperfect, muddled, and tentative ways.

Taken together these writers emblematize Slavoj Žižek's conclusion in a 2014 video commentary, "What is Freedom Today?", that "true freedom means looking into and questioning the presuppositions of everything that is given to us by our hegemonic ideology... including the notion of freedom itself."

While philosophers and cultural studies scholars have contributed rich critical insights into the discourse about contemporary freedom, the most profound and impactful expressions of the problematics of the twenty-first century have certainly been those represented in imaginative literature. Indeed, narrative art has always been a medium through which human beings have explored the nature of freedom, concocting imaginational spaces in which hypothetical humans experiment with the possibilities, perils, and paradoxes of freedom. Storytelling is itself inseparable from questions of the possibilities and the limits of human freedom in its dramatization of characters who exist in a tension between their free agency as individuals and the constraints they face within the context of their stories. Simultaneously, storytelling is also an expression of the free creative artistry of the storyteller, as well as the interpretive freedom of the audience of a narrative, who is always free to either turn into or away from the quasi-captive trance woven by the narrative, and also to arrive at their own free judgements about the narrative itself. The stories that a culture tells itself are more compelling barometers of the way that that culture understands the nature of human freedom than the speeches of politicians or even the theories of philosophers. As Anker insists, "How we tell stories of freedom matters" (29), not only because popular narratives reveal cultural attitudes about the nature of freedom, but also because stories shape cultural attitudes, serving as a model of human reality that influences the expectations and perceptions of mass-audiences.

As one of the most familiar vectors of narrative, television serves as a compelling mirror in which to view representations of human freedom. The series that did more than any other to establish the tone of the televisual landscape for the twenty-first century is certainly *Survivor*, which debuted in America on CBS in May of 2000. In the logic of *Survivor*, confinement on an island becomes an opportunity for the contestants to enact their free individualism—casting off the expectations and regulations of society and making themselves over as lone Crusoes. The freedom of *Survivor*'s contestants is enabled but also circumscribed by the island itself and the condition of scarcity, as well as by the rules of the show. But even this circumscribed freedom is further embedded within a surveillance society, where the "free" individuals are subject to the judgements of their fellow islanders, the viewers at home, and the television producers. Indeed, the televisual apparatus of cameras, hidden microphones, interpretive editing, and global broadcast constitutes yet another, globally totalizing frame that dwarfs the performative depictions of freedom staged by the show's contestants. The contestants come and go, more or less interchangeably, but the apparatus of control—the show itself—has remained on the air as one of the most definitive representations of the state of freedom in the twenty-first century.

Survivor's success reshaped television in the 2000s, spawning a generation of reality show clones that not only marginalized what came to be retronymically known as "scripted television" on the major networks, but proliferated into cable as well until countless cable channels became reality television channels, applying the *Survivor* template of performative freedom within the bell jar of global surveillance to "mainland" activities such as home improvement, cooking, dieting, dancing, dating, and drag shows. The immersive effect of this phenomenon conveys the impression that all of human life is some version of *Survivor*, with the spectacle of human freedom exhausting itself inside an architecture of control.

This impression became the foremost theme of *Lost* (2004-2010), a "scripted" drama series that applied the Survivor model of reality to its fictional characters not only by stranding them on an island but also by "eliminating" them on a regular basis (killing them off) and by its dramatization of a meta-architecture containing, shaping, and even exploiting what they thought was their free will. *Lost*, in turn, can be considered as a "hinge" between the reality shows of the 2000s and the renaissance of scripted television in the 2010s. *Lost* became the model for a generation of "prestige" television series such as *The Wire*

(2002-2008), *Game of Thrones* (2011-2019), and *The Walking Dead* (2010-2022), serialized dramas featuring multi-dimensional characters whose fates and relationships evolve over many episodes and often many years of interrelated incidents. Despite the enormous variety of this genre of television, one of the qualities that all these serialized dramas have in common is their dramatization of the ambiguous relationship between the characters' existence as free individuals and their embeddedness within a vast ensemble of other characters and events, as well as the extent to which their fates are tied to the generic conventions of serialized television itself. In this sense, both major television trends of the twenty-first century, reality shows on one hand and intricately scripted serialized dramas on the other, represent a similar anxiety about the manner in which contemporary freedom plays out against a background of invisible but omnipresent coercion.

Many of the most conspicuous trends in twenty-first century film have also foregrounded the theme of freedom. In a time of ecological crisis, it is not surprising that one of the prevailing genres of the first quarter of the century has been postapocalyptic narratives. The conditions represented in postapocalyptic movies such as *Children of Men* (2006), *The Road* (2009), and *A Quiet Place* (2018) echo those faced by the contestants on *Survivor*, dramatizing the sense in which the conditions of survivalism both constrict the scope of characters' freedom while also opening up possibilities for new kinds of freedom, reflecting both hopeful possibilities for remaking human society as well as lawless Hobbesian fantasies, visions of what Žižek refers to as "obscene freedom." Postapocalyptic fiction illustrates a certain kind of freedom—a particularly American kind—a "freedom from" governance, typically dramatizing how terrifying and dehumanizing such a freedom might be.

One of the most prominent subgenres of postapocalypse fiction has certainly been zombie stories, the zombie serving as a kind of mascot for twenty-first century anxieties. While the zombie figure originally evolved in a

INTRODUCTION

twentieth-century context, it has shambled (and often sprinted) into this century with a vengeance, proliferating into novels, videogames, television, memes, and, of course, movies like *28 Days Later* (2002), *I am Legend* (2007), and *Zombieland* (2009). Zombie fiction iterates the *Survivor* trope while also populating it with a figure, the zombie, who emblematizes a human body altogether devoid of freedom. Zombies have no freedom—they are creatures of pure impulse—and the comparatively free human beings who fight them are continually threatened not only by the possibility that they might be helplessly assimilated into the zombie's condition of unfreedom but also the possibility that the fight against the zombies itself might have the effect of dehumanizing or zombifying them, rendering them unfree.

Like the zombie, the superhero is another "figure of freedom" who originated in the twentieth century but who has been reinvented to reflect the mood of the twenty-first. Whereas twentieth-century Superman was a utopian figure of transcendent power, 2006's *Superman Returns* portrays a Superman who is alienated and out-of-place. 2013's *Man of Steel* involves a plot to use Supes's genes to found a society of "racial purity," and his climactic battle against General Zod is so destructive that it convinces the Batman of *Batman v Superman* (2016) that Superman is actually an existential threat to humanity. The character of the "conflicted" superhero presents twenty-first-century audiences with depictions of the dangers and anxieties associated with superheroic freedom, and Batman himself is the superhero who most deliberately embodies this tension, explaining perhaps why Christopher Nolan's Batman trilogy holds a privileged place in the crowded gallery of modern superhero movies. Batman's wealth, intelligence, and strength give him unlimited freedom, but he wields this freedom in a state of angst, trauma, and masochism. Even the more carefree antics of Marvel's *Avengers* movies grapple with the question of whether the Avengers need to be regulated by a U.N. Committee. The series *WandaVision*

(2021), among the more thoughtful Marvel productions, portrays a superhero so powerful that she is spellbound by her own ability to distort reality; the phantastic freedom of Wanda Maximoff's ability to fulfill her own wishes comes to constitute a mental prison in which she is both transcendentally free and abjectly enslaved.

The twenty-first-century popularity of both zombies and superheroes can be considered within the scope of the wider trend of "reboots" of twentieth-century franchises. On the one hand, the ubiquity of these reboots suggests a sense of cultural enslavement to a vanished past, as if the creative freedom of the cultural imagination has been hobbled and reduced to stuttering repetitions of old stories. At the same time, however, many twenty-first-century reboots enact critiques and reinventions of their familiar narratives. Although it is not itself a reboot, the first *Shreck* movie (2001) may be identified as an early example of this trend in the way that its "fractured" approach to familiar fairy tale narratives simultaneously recounts these old stories and subverts them. Disney conducts a similar deconstruction of the biases of its twentieth-century productions when, in *Frozen* (2013), the princess is saved by the true love not of the man in the story but that of her sister. The reboots of the *Star Wars*, *Ghostbusters*, *Rocky*, and *Karate Kid* franchises also articulate critiques of the variously patriarchal, jingoistic, and white-supremacist assumptions retrospectively evident in their original incarnations. In this way, these so-called "woke" reboots of familiar franchises aim to free us from the perceptual limitations that bound previous generations of filmgoers. This trend parallels a common theme in twenty-first-century children's movies such as *Encanto* (2021), *Raya and the Last Dragon* (2021), *Sea Beast* (2022), and *Nimona* (2023), in which the story revolves around the discovery that a privileged master-narrative of the past has been deliberately deceptive. Such narratives highlight the manner in which narrative itself can act to both delimit freedom, when stories are used to manipulate listeners and distort the past, as well as to free us from our own controlling narratives.

The relationship between narrative and freedom is also one of the most prominent themes among twenty-first century novels as well. Richard Powers's *The Echo Maker* (2006) centers around a disturbing psychiatric condition, Capgras syndrome, that haunts the book's characters with a sense of the degree to which our identities are woven out of narratives, and to which these narratives themselves are subject to neurological, evolutionary, and chthonic forces that defy our understanding. The characters come to doubt their own ability to control their desires, their behaviors, and even their own identities, but the story leads up to Karin's epiphany regarding a kind of freedom to be found in the chaos of this radical skepticism: "If all forged, then all free. Free to play ourselves, free to impersonate, free to image anything. Free to weave our minds through what we love" (426).

Throughout Margaret Atwood's influential *MaddAddam* trilogy, the power of narrative coexists alongside genetic engineering as a means of trying to shape reality, even as the mutations inherent in both storytelling and genetics offer new possibilities for freedom. In the first book, Crake's genetic design of the crakers is complemented by the stories Oryx tells them as a way of instilling them with a coherent culture. In their post-apocalyptic freedom, however, Snowman and then Toby elaborate the crakers' mythology in ways that both protect them from difficult realities and help them come to terms with the new world they are inheriting. In the final book of the series, the crakers begin to tell their own stories, facilitating new kinds of interspecies affinities among humans, crakers, and pigoons.

Jennifer Egan's *A Visit from the Goon Squad* (2011) and George Saunders's *Lincoln in the Bardo* (2017) both represent characters who become trapped in their own narratives to such an extent that they become grotesque caricatures of themselves.

FIGURES OF FREEDOM

In Viet Thanh Nguyen's *The Sympathizer* (2015), the unnamed narrator's act of narrating his winding and complex "confession" leads him to find a new meaning hidden in Ho Chi Minh's motto, "Nothing is more important than independence and freedom." The agonizing ordeal of Vietnam's wartime experiences, fought on all sides in the name of "freedom," convinces the narrator of the validity of the counter-truth that *nothing* is more important than freedom; that the existential space of nothingness itself provides a refuge where one can be free from the violence perpetrated in the name of "freedom." In keeping with the bivalent poise of the whole novel, the two interpretations of this phrase remain in tension with one another, "freedom" and "nothing" both suspended in a complex balance that acknowledges the necessity of freedom while also relativizing this necessity, tempering the tendency of this powerful idea to overload the moral imagination.

This list of fictional representations of the theme of freedom could be expanded indefinitely. Every story is about freedom in one way or another, and every representation of freedom inevitably negotiates the dynamic questions involved in what it means to be free, who gets to be free, what one should do with one's freedom, the risks of freedom, and how one can even know how free they are, or how unfree. Indeed, such questions might only be answerable through the language of storytelling, since they are intimately connected to the lived experience of time, context, and consciousness. It may well be that one of the cognitive functions that narrative fulfills for human societies is its ability to help us think through the imponderable questions of human freedom. There are so many narratives that suggest fruitful insights about these questions, and so many ways that these narratives express and interrogate the theme of freedom, that the inquiry into this topic benefits from a multi-perspectival approach that brings together international scholars from around the world to examine novels, films, and television shows for

INTRODUCTION

what they have to teach us about the state of freedom in America and the world in the first quarter of the twenty-first century. The contributors to this book share this critical mission, and, together, their chapters constitute a diverse but interconnected exhibit of the "figures of freedom" that populate our cultural imagination.

The chapters in this book approach the question of freedom from a wide range of interrelated perspectives. The chapters in the first section examine philosophical and existential questions of the nature of freedom as it is conceptualized and represented in contemporary fictional texts. In "'Becoming a WASP': *Mad Men* and the Failure of the American Dream," Nicole Chrenek traces the emergence of the late-twentieth-century brand of white, middle-class freedom, and considers the manner in which a popular television series critiques the shortcomings of this traditional definition of freedom from a twenty-first-century perspective. Jasmine Tan Hui Jun's chapter, "At Apocalypse's Edge: The Paradox of Freedom in Contemporary Popular Science Fiction Films," considers the dynamics of freedom as they operate within apocalyptic contexts that dramatize only slightly disguised representations of our own historical moment. Stephen Hock's "The Freedom of 'the Endland of the Convergence' or 'the Long Soft Life' in DeLillo's *Zero K*" and Peter Krause's "Allegorical Tensions between 'Freedom to' and 'Freedom from' in Jonathan Franzen's *Freedom*" both map out the ways that two celebrated novelists have illustrated competing definitions of freedom that motivate their characters' decisions. Ashasmiti Das, meanwhile, in "'The Time for Expeditions was Over': Infectious Collaborations, Multispecies Justice, and Troubled Freedoms in Jeff VanderMeer's *Southern Reach Trilogy*," meditates on a haunting vision of a landscape where all definitions of freedom dissolve along with the anthropocentric biases that supported them.

The chapters in the second section of *Figures of Freedom* consider the various ways that emergent economic, ecological, and technological conditions of the twenty-first century inflect conventional perceptions and practices of freedom. Claire P. Curtis, in "'You Gave Up the World': Freedom and Responsibility in Jenny Offill's *Weather* and Lydia Millet's *A Children's Bible*," conducts a reading of this pair of novels that investigates the impacts that the threat of climate change has on characters' perception of their own freedom. Katrin Newsom's chapter, "'Sometimes That's All It Takes to Save a World, You See': Reading Freedom and the Anthropocene in N. K. Jemisin's Writings," considers similar new disruptions and possibilities in posthuman freedom within the context of a world where climate catastrophe has become all-pervasive. On a more intimate scale, Jay Fraser's chapter, "The Shadow of the Pit: Freedom, Family, and Neoliberalism in Meghan Lamb's *Failure to Thrive*" looks at Lamb's novel as a parable about how hardships associated with contemporary economic conditions diminish the characters' sense of their own agency and mobility. In "Can You Be Free If You're Not Real?: Emily St. John Mandel on Freedom and the Simulation Hypothesis," John C. Merfeld, Tom Richards, and Noah Stengl read Mandel's novel *Sea of Tranquility* (2022) to examine the implications of the simulation hypothesis for the conceptualization of human freedom, while Sony Jalarajan Raj and Adith K. Suresh, in "Caught in the Web: The Illusion of Freedom and the Techno-Dystopia in *Mr. Robot*," analyze a popular television series in terms of its representations of the challenges that digital technologies pose to classical conceptions of human freedom.

The final series of chapters in this book considers the ways that possibilities for freedom have been experienced from the perspective of certain marginalized populations, populations traditionally excluded from mainstream discourses of freedom. Martha Zornow performs a reading of "Sonmi-451's Revolutionary Fight for Freedom in David Mitchell's *Cloud Atlas*" that considers the question of freedom from the perspective of a socio-economically disadvantaged female fabricant. Tatiana Konrad examines the unique ramifications that an apocalyptic monster outbreak has for mothers and persons with disabilities in "Seeing Environmental Crisis: Reproduction, Disability, and Climate Change in *Bird Box*." The final three chapters in this book evaluate the unique resonance that the idea of freedom has with regard to African American history and identity. Sutirtho Roy's "Freedom in *Toy Story*: Reading Woody's Journey as a Post-Human Slave Narrative" and Beatrice Melodia Festa's "'Those Who Deny Freedom to Others Deserve It Not for Themselves': Redefining the Content of Freedom in *The Underground Railroad*" discuss a children's movie and a Pulitzer Prize winning novel, respectively, to revisit the history of American slavery to discover what it has to teach us about the perils and possibilities of freedom. Sharmila Mukherjee's chapter, "The Struggle at the End of the World: Black Freedom in Ta-Nehisi Coates's *Between the World and Me*," concludes *Figures of Freedom* with a series of deeply personal reflections on the ways that American rhetorics of freedom too often act as cover for practices of oppression.

Taken together, these writers' perspectives push and pull the idea of freedom into new shapes that allow it to map onto the emergent geographies of our anxious century. In its many permutations, freedom remains one of the most powerful ideas in the human lexicon, and, while, like all powerful things, it can be wielded in destructive ways, it can also help guide us to invent new possibilities, new solutions, and new stories for a shared human future.

Works Cited

Anker, Elisabeth R. *Ugly Freedoms*. Duke University Press, 2022.

"Biden's Remarks on Wars in Ukraine and Israel." CNN, 19 Oct. 2023.

Chun, Wendy Hui Kyong. *Control and Freedom: Power and Paranoia in the Age of Fiber Optics*. MIT Press, 2006.

Cowrie, Malcolm. *Freedom's Dominion: A Saga of White Resistance to Federal Power*. Basic Books, 2022.

Han, Byung-Chul. *Psychopolitics: Neoliberalism and New Technologies of Power*. Translated by Erik Butler, Verso, 2017.

Nguyen, Mimi Thi. *The Gift of Freedom: War, Debt, and Other Refugee Passages*. Duke University Press, 2012.

Nguyen, Vieth Thanh. *The Sympathizer*. Grove Press, 2015.

Powers, Richard. *The Echo Maker*. Farrar, Straus and Giroux, 2006.

Zerilli, Linda M. G. *Feminism and the Abyss of Freedom*. University of Chicago Press, 2005.

Žižek, Slavoj. "What is Freedom Today?" *The Guardian*, 3 Dec. 2014.

SECTION 1
What is Freedom?

"Becoming a WASP":
Mad Men and the Failure of the American Dream

Nicole Chrenek

Mad Men's (2007-2015) pilot episode ends with a twist reveal: after meeting with Greenwich Village artist Midge (Rosemarie DeWitt) at lunch and joking about getting married to her, the show's anti-hero protagonist, Don Draper (Jon Hamm), returns home to Ossining, where he lives with his wife, Betty (January Jones), and their two children. This ending sets up the predominant theme of the entire series: that Don Draper is not who he seems to be, and that he must constantly work in order to keep up this façade.

Don—birth name Dick Whitman—has stolen his name from a fellow soldier in the Korean War in an effort to escape his Pennsylvania upbringing and abusive father.[1] In faking his own death, he gives birth to his new identity— Don Draper, ad man. Of course, this identity takes years of careful curation. He placates, and eventually befriends, the real Don Draper's wife, and earns a spot at Sterling Cooper by getting Roger Sterling (John Slattery) drunk at lunch. By 1960, the year in which *Mad Men*'s pilot takes place, Don has used the "fake it 'til you make it" method to his advantage: he has a high creative position at a respected agency, a house in the suburbs, a beautiful former model for a wife, and two children. Don's identity theft has allowed him to achieve the American Dream, but this comes with high risk: he must always be ready to leave it all at a moment's notice, should his crimes be discovered. Don is constantly running from his past towards an unattainable future. He is always trying to become the man that he has created. When, at the end of the show's first season, Pete Campbell (Vincent Kartheiser) threatens to reveal Don's real identity, Don tries to convince his mistress, Rachel Menken (Maggie Siff), to pick up everything and leave the city with him in order to start a new life together. Shocked by his urgency, she realizes that this is not the romantic getaway he framed it to be: "You don't want to run away with me. You just want to run away," she says, dismayed (S1E13).

In a *Paris Review* interview, series creator Matthew Weiner states that "I've always said [*Mad Men*] is a show about becoming white. That's the definition of success in America—becoming a WASP. A WASP male" ("The Art of Screenwriting"). This chapter analyses Don Draper's idea of freedom—its roots in Don's striving for the American Dream, and how freedom, to Don, is the freedom to move forward, leaving the past in the rearview mirror. It then moves to an analysis of how Don pursues this idea of freedom at all costs, making significant sacrifices to become the person he has lied about being all along. Finally, it examines the failure of Don's American Dream, and how this leads to the fate he meets at the end of the series. The rise and fall of Donald Draper are all a result of the shaky foundation upon which he has built his conception of freedom.

In the introduction to *The American Dream: A Short History of an Idea That Shaped a Nation* (2003), Jim Cullen notes that

> However variegated its applications—which include the freedom *to* commit as well as freedom *from* commitment—all notions of freedom rest on a sense of *agency*, the idea that individuals have control over the course of their lives. Agency, in turn, lies at the very core of the American Dream, the bedrock premise upon

which all else depends. To paraphrase Henry David Thoreau, the Dream assumes that one *can* advance confidently in the direction of one's dreams to live out an imagined life. (10)

Don's idea of freedom, of course, rests particularly on what Cullen specifies as "freedom *from* commitment." For as long as he can, Don resists signing a contract at Sterling Cooper in order to avoid being held down. He wants the option to run at a moment's notice, should his true identity be discovered. Philip Slater identifies running away as quintessential to the American Dream: "This nation was settled and continually repopulated by people who were not personally successful in confronting the social conditions in their mother country, but fled in the hope of a better life... Escaping, evading, and avoiding are responses which lie at the base of much that is peculiarly American" (qtd. in Hauhart and Sardoč 4).

For Don, freedom relies on a feeling of agency; as soon as he feels that he does not have control over where he goes, what he does, and at what time, according to his own whims, he feels as if he has lost his freedom. When Roger Sterling attempts to convince Don to sign a contract at the agency, Don refuses—likely as a safety precaution, should his true identity be discovered, especially since Pete Campbell and Bert Cooper (Robert Morse) already both know the truth.[2] Roger phones Betty and explains the situation to her, in a somewhat scummy but ultimately successful move to get Don to sign the contract. When Betty confronts Don about not signing the contract, he lies to her about his reasoning for not signing: "No contract means I have all the power. They want me, but they can't have me" (S3E7). What he tells her is somewhat true. In an earlier episode, when Puttnam, Powell, and Lowe take over the company, Don is able to threaten them with leaving the company without being in breach of his contract. This move ultimately proves successful for him, as Duck (Mark Moses), who proposes changes to the company structure that Don disagrees with, is ousted from the company. Don's motivation for not signing a contract, however, is not a move of corporate power. Betty sees through it and asks: "It's three years, Don. What's the matter, you don't know where you're going to be in three years?" (S3E7).

Don's concept of freedom as agency is demonstrated even on the smaller scale. Don does not necessarily just want to be able to flee should he be discovered—he also wants to do whatever he wants, whenever he wants. He constantly leaves the office at lunchtime, often to meet with his mistresses—and when he isn't meeting with his mistress, he is at a bar getting drunk. In the show's seventh season, when Don returns to the office on probation, he throws a fit, no longer able to navigate the office however he pleases. When Peggy (Elisabeth Moss)—until this point Don's protégé—effectively becomes his boss and gives him the task of coming up with taglines—a job reserved for lower-level copywriters, and one he previously assigned to her many times—he throws his typewriter off his desk, frustrated with his lack of mobility.[3] In several of the show's season finales, Don leaves the office without warning and without notifying anyone when he will return. At the end of the second season, Don abandons Pete in California during a work trip, and in the show's final episodes, he runs away once more, again to California.[4] When he returns to New York from his first impromptu visit to California, he apologizes to Betty for his time away: "I had to have some time to think about things," he tells her. "Must be nice," she says, "needing time and just taking it, all on your own terms" (S2E13). To Don, freedom means taking time away, on his own terms, without, to Betty's lament, "wondering what anybody thinks."

The American Dream is founded not only on mobility and freedom from commitment but also on the ideal that can be achieved, supposedly, through hard work and dedication, regardless of background. At the beginning of the series, Don lives with Betty, his young, beautiful, ex-model of a wife, and their two children. They live in a house in Ossining that does not literally have a white picket fence, but may as well. Suburbia is a large part of the American Dream, according to David R. Coon in *Look Closer: Suburban Narratives and American Values in Film and Television* (2013), epitomized by "a variety of social values and ideals, including the importance of tradition, the centrality of the nuclear family, the desire for a community of like-minded neighbors, the need for clearly defined gender roles, and the belief that with hard work and determination anyone can be successful" (3-4). An essential part of the American Dream is service to the country; former Army members are still, today, saluted as heroes, just as Don is in Season 2, Episode 6, "Maidenform." In this scene, Betty looks up at him in equal admiration and curiosity, revering him as a hero while completely unaware of what his service entailed due to his hesitation to talk about his time in the Korean War.[5] Edward Humes discusses how the G.I. Bill of 1944 permanently changed the American Dream:

> A nation of renters would become a nation of homeowners. College would be transformed from an elite bastion to a middle-class entitlement. Suburbia would be born amid the clatter of bulldozers and the smell of new asphalt linking it all together. Inner cities would collapse... there was never anything like it before. (12)

At the beginning of the series, Don appears to have it all: the perfect family, the perfect suburban home, and a Purple Heart from his service in the war. But *Mad Men* quickly dissolves this illusion. As the show progresses, viewers discover that the symbols of the perfect American life he has accrued are hollow and false.

In the fifth episode of the first season, "5G," Don's younger half-brother Adam Whitman (Jay Paulson) finds Don after seeing his photo in the newspaper. Adam merely wants to have a relationship with Don; he wants to hear about Don's life since faking his death in Korea and meet

Betty and the children. Don refuses to form a relationship with Adam in the fear that doing so would make it more likely that someone—likely Betty—would discover the true nature of their relationship and, consequently, Don's past. He bribes Adam with five thousand dollars—the origin of the episode's name, "5G," which is also Adam's hotel room number—to leave New York and never contact him again. "I have a life, and it only goes in one direction," he tells his brother, "Forward" (S1E5). Adam kills himself only a few episodes later. He dies with the small fortune left to him by his half-brother, but no family.

Adam's death is not even the first that occurs in Don's pursuit of freedom, nor is it the last piece of collateral damage from Don's destructive mission for an American Dream that is impossible to achieve. The birth of Don Draper was only possible through the death of Don Draper—the "real" one, that is. That Don Draper as we see him in the series's first episode is born out of a wartime casualty illustrates the futility of the American Dream he wants so badly to embody. What he originally views as a "new" start cannot be further away from that—he has taken the name of the man whose death he has inadvertently caused, laden with the baggage of his past life. Every time someone calls Don by his "new" name, he is reminded of its origin. The "real" Don Draper is not just someone who was killed in a freak accident but a soldier killed in the Korean War, the inciting event of the Cold War.

American Cold War politics framed communism as a threat to individualism and upheld capitalist societies as the standard for freedom. Of the Korean War, Hong-Kyu Park writes that "Truman made the United States a policeman of communism" (258). American politics framed the Korean War as a battle between right and wrong, in which America's capitalistic values were representative of freedom. Don's taken name bears the baggage of its origin as a name taken from a man who was days away from finishing his service in a war fought in the name of capitalism.

Through depicting significant events that took place during the time period in which *Mad Men* takes place, the show traces the progress of political change that upturned America throughout the decade. *Mad Men*'s temporal setting is the perfect one in which to depict the decay of the American Dream; it's the period during which the Civil Rights movement, the Vietnam War, the Kennedy assassination, and the Kent State shooting all occur, to name a few of those events depicted in the show. The series's first episode begins with a title card that reads: "MAD MEN: a term coined in the late 1950s to describe the advertising executives of Madison Avenue. They coined it" (S1E1). By 1960, the year in which the first episode of *Mad Men* takes place, the age of the "mad men" of Madison Avenue is already coming to a close. While *Mad Men* opens with the premise that it will depict the wild, glamourous lifestyle of 1960s "mad men," it is really a series about the decline of this era.

As Don falls further, his younger, more progressive counterparts—such as Peggy Olson and Pete Campbell—rise through the ranks of Sterling Cooper. Don's downfall runs in parallel with the growing disillusionment with the American Dream that gradually took place during the 1960s. Don's façade cracking and, finally, shattering, is symbolic of the fracturing of the American Dream throughout the era in which *Mad Men* takes place. This is first evident in the first season's finale, "Nixon vs. Kennedy." As the 1960 election comes to a close, Pete confronts Don about his real identity and threatens him with revealing his secret in an attempt to gain leverage for a promotion within the company. As Matt Zoller Seitz has pointed out in *Mad Men: Carousel* (2015), the episode's title signifies, of course, the battle between the two presidents, but also a battle between old and young, Don and Pete. Don says, "[when I look at] Nixon, I see myself"—a parallel sustained throughout the series (S1E12). Don is Nixon, with his rough upbringing and self-made attitude, and Pete is Kennedy, with his rich parents and easy lifestyle. The episode ends with Nixon losing, and Don's identity revealed to Cooper. While Don does not face any immediate consequences once his boss finds out about his true identity, this season finale is a loss for Don on two levels: his candidate, with the rough, self-made, pick-yourself-up-by-the-bootstraps image, has lost the election, and now at least two people at his agency know about his true identity.

A few years later, another Kennedy event parallels personal loss in Don's life. In the penultimate episode of the third season, "The Grown Ups," Don's divorce coincides with the Kennedy assassination. It is no coincidence that Don's marriage finally crumbles the day after the American population sees their president shot and killed on live television. On both the small and the large scale, this is the death of the American Dream. Betty is deeply affected by Kennedy's death, crying on her couch in mourning, when she suddenly witnesses the subsequent televised assassination of Oswald. "What is going *on*?" she asks, in visible distress, after the shooting (S3E12). In *Mad Men: Carousel*, Seitz discusses the parallels between the personal and the political in "The Grown Ups":

> The script is full of sentences and phrases that seem as though they could refer to the assassination as well as to whatever personal drama the characters are going through, such as Henry's "I'm not in love with the tragedy of this thing," and Don's statement to Betty, "You're very upset, I understand. I know it's painful, but it's going to pass." The latter occurs in the scene in which Betty returns from her meeting with Henry and tells Don she doesn't love him anymore. When Don says, "I know it's painful," he's referring to this grim phase of their marriage, but he's gesturing at the TV, which shows live coverage of JFK's burial at Arlington Cemetery. (185)

Don is incapable of understanding Betty's distress in response to the Kennedy assassination, and this reflects their larger dynamic: Don never understands Betty's emotions and rather dismisses them. In addition to this emotional miscommunication, Betty realizes her husband is not the all-American hero she previously thought he was—while the rest of the country faces the gruesome murder of their beloved president. "All this time, I thought you were a football hero who hated his father," she tells him. Her image of him as the football star who fought in the war for her country's freedom—the persona Don thought that inhabiting would bring him freedom and mobility—has inevitably crumbled, costing him his marriage (S3E12). The breakdown of Don and Betty's marriage runs in parallel to the Kennedy assassination because both events entail the loss of a certain patriotic hope and naïveté. The cracks in the façade of the Don Draper persona, born out of a patriotic hope to achieve the American Dream, are a symbolic representation of the collective loss of faith in the American Dream that took place during the significant social and political change of the 1960s.

When audiences were first introduced to Don Draper, they saw, like Don's awestruck clients, a cool, suave man—the image of the ideal man in 1950s America. Don Draper is often heralded as a shining image of calm, collected masculinity. A *GQ* article on Don Draper's fashion stated: "'You shouldn't be lionizing this guy or at least holding him up as a paramount of virtue,' Jon Hamm told *The Guardian* in 2013... but a lot of us did" (Renwick). But the trajectory of *Mad Men* depicts how Don falls from this state—how, in fact, he never was the image of success that he always tries so hard to project. Don first appears to the audience facing away from the camera, in a room full of smoke. The first episode's title, "Smoke Gets in Your Eyes," takes its name from a 1958 song by the Platters, originally written by Jerome Kern and Otto Harbach, but is also an indication of Don's status as a fraud. The song's lyrics make reference to the blindness experienced by those unwilling to see or incapable of seeing someone's flaws:

> They say one day you'll find
> All who love are blind
> When your heart's on fire, you must realize
> Smoke gets in your eyes. (Kern and Harbach)

Don Draper's cool demeanor is a façade—a smokescreen. When the audience first sees him, the haze that surrounds him makes him difficult to read. He seems impenetrable. Even his coworkers, who have known him for years, make reference to how secretive he is: "Draper? Who knows anything about that guy. No one's ever lifted that rock. He could be Batman for all we know," says Harry Crane (Rich Sommer) (S1E3). But *Mad Men*'s narrative arc gradually breaks down this façade by revealing the cracks in Don's act.

Most notable of these moments in which Don's persona crumbles—not only for viewers, but also for the people around him—is when he reveals during a pitch to Hershey that the sickly-sweet, good-old-American story he has just told them, in which his father took him to the drugstore to pick out any candy he wanted as a child, was a lie. "I was an orphan. I grew up in Pennsylvania, in a whorehouse," he starts, to the horror of his colleagues (S6E13). He describes reading about the Milton Hershey School and dreaming of the alternate future he could have had there, as opposed to the cruel childhood he had with his abusive father.[6] He describes eating a Hershey bar as a child, "feeling like a normal kid" (S6E13). Everyone at the conference table is shocked at Don's revelation and, of course, the agency does not win a contract with Hershey.[7] The true story Don has presented them with is crushing and real—nothing like the sterilized, cookie-cutter narrative they want to sell to their customers. Here, Don reveals not only his true past, which does not fit the ideal narrative of the American Dream, but also his yearning to live the life he sees in advertising: that of the pure, white picket fence, all-American nuclear family.

Don chastises Rachel Menken for believing in love in the series's first episode: "The reason you haven't felt [love] is that it doesn't exist. What you call 'love' was invented by guys like me, to sell nylons," he tells her (S1E1). But Don's breakdown during the Hershey pitch shows that he is just as susceptible to advertising as the foolish American consumer he often ridicules. He has spent his entire life yearning for an American Dream that is unattainable because it doesn't exist. It was invented by guys like Milton Hershey, to sell chocolate bars.

Donald Draper has been emblematic of suave masculinity since *Mad Men* first appeared on the air. The name instantly connotes a smooth-talking ad man with a glass of whiskey in his hand and a cigarette dangling from his lips. Yet the show does not call for the audience to identify with Don, nor does it endorse any of his actions. You're not supposed to want to be Don, because he is not a good person. There is another reason for why nobody should want to be Don Draper: nobody *can* be Don Draper—not even Don Draper himself. Don's enlistment in the Korean War was meant to be an escape from his bleak Pennsylvanian upbringing. Instead, it was the birth of an identity with a past from which he is constantly running away. Even after years of curating his identity and building a Don Draper that exemplifies American mid-century ideals, he still cannot become the man he has convinced everyone that he is: "I took another man's name and made nothing of it," he tells Peggy in the series finale, "Person to Person" (S7E14). Don's vision of freedom was unattainable from the moment it was conceived; even before he took Don Draper's name, he went off to war in the pursuit of freedom from his abusive father.

While his phone call with Peggy implies that he may be about to commit suicide—implied, as well, by the series's opening credits, which depict a suited man falling from a skyscraper—Don does not kill himself but rather returns to the world of advertising after peaceful meditation at a retreat in California. Don's "enlightenment" at the end of the series results in his finding peace being part of the advertising machine, and the series implies that he goes on to create the iconic "I'd like to buy the world a Coke" ad. Don embraces the countercultural aesthetics he has previously felt alienated from in order to create, presumably, an endless swill of soulless advertisements. Don has a sense of superiority for not being susceptible to advertising; as an ad man, he believes himself immune to it. "I hate to break it to you, but there is no big lie," he tells a Greenwich Village artist (S1E8). From the beginning, however, he has been deceived by American propaganda. One could say that Don has become the perfect ad man; he has convinced even himself. What he believed to be a pursuit of freedom has actually trapped him, precisely because his concept of freedom was built upon the American Dream. By depicting the slow, crumbling breakdown of Don Draper, *Mad Men* illustrates the breaking down of the American Dream in the 1960s and the need for a new freedom, with different roots, that ushered in the age of the 1970s. Unable to change, Don finds peace in stasis. His dream, from the beginning—which Jim Hobart (H. Richard Greene) tempts him with at multiple points throughout the series—is to create an advertisement for Coca-Cola, which he finally does in the series finale. Don's dream is to sell a big-name product, a corporate aspiration born out of the capitalist nature of America. Don only achieves peace by recognizing the hollow nature of his American Dream.

Modern audiences are captivated by *Mad Men* because of its sharp analysis of a period of major change in American history. While the series is a period drama, deftly handling historical events particular to the 1960s, it is in part so beloved because it speaks to a contemporary American experience. The Sixties fascinate us today because they were a period of dramatic social and political change. Viewers are entranced by a bygone era that should seem foreign to them half a century later—but, somehow, it doesn't. While the temporal setting of *Mad Men* isn't one most viewers are familiar with, the emotional atmosphere—the tension between those who long for change and those who fear it, growing disillusionment with the American Dream—is one they know all too well. *Mad Men*'s temporal setting allows for its commentary on contemporary America. Don is a man spending his entire life trying to be someone he can never become. Is this not a predicament we are all too familiar with, in an era of social media, its façades, and the unattainable standards it creates? Even outside of the internet, we are all trying to be people we are not. We lie on our CVs, we buy clothes because our favorite celebrities wear them, we curate ourselves in order to appeal to others. We are all Don Draper, creating personas we can never live up to. He appeals to us not because of his suave demeanor but because when we look at Don, we see ourselves. While Don's inability to adapt to change leads to his finding happiness in stasis, we tell ourselves that maybe—hopefully—we will meet a different fate. We convince ourselves that Don's failure does not predict our own, that our contemporary values can save us from the American Dream. This conviction is all we have—and we hope that it can save us.

Notes

1. While "Dick" is, technically, short for Richard, it's more the case that "Richard" is long for Dick. Season 3, Episode 1, "Out of Town," reveals that the name comes from a promise Don's birth mother never lived to keep; when Don's father convinces her to sleep with him, she says that if she gets pregnant, she will "cut his dick off and boil it in hog fat" (S3E1). When she gives birth to the child they conceived as a result of that night, she repeats the promise, this time while dying in childbirth. Don's birth name is a constant reminder of where he has come from; all the more reason to try and rid himself of it.

2. When he finally convinces Don to sign the contract, Cooper asks Don: "After all, who's really signing this contract anyway?"—

subtly reminding Don that he could choose to reveal his identity, should he refuse to sign the contract.

3. Don is, of course, also frustrated with the reversal of gender dynamics. As supportive Don is of Peggy, it is still clear in this scene that the fact that he is now working for a woman infuriates him.

4. California, and the West in general, is a mythical place in *Mad Men*. Its artistic, bohemian nature is presented in stark contrast to New York's heavily corporate atmosphere. Employees of Sterling Cooper speak of California as a land of opportunity, embodying an attitude of Manifest Destiny—Stan Rizzo, a member of the Creative department, says, "It's the frontier. I don't even need running water. Just let me set up the homestead" (S6E13).

5. In "Red in the Face," Betty laments Don's refusal to talk about his service: "Don never talks about the war," she tells Roger (S1E7). She doesn't know this, but it's because it was so short.

6. Formerly known as the Hershey Industrial School, the Milton Hershey school was a boarding school that took in orphans in order to give them an education.

7. After this horrific meeting, Don is placed on mandatory leave.

Works Cited

Coon, David R. *Look Closer: Suburban Narratives and American Values in Film and Television*. Rutgers University Press, 2013.

Cullen, Jim. *The American Dream: A Short History of an Idea That Shaped a Nation*. Oxford University Press, 2004.

Hauhart, Robert C., and Mitja Sardoč. *The Routledge Handbook on the American Dream*. Vol. 1, Routledge, 2022.

Humes, Edward. *Over Here: How the G. I. Bill Transformed the American Dream*. Diversion Publishing Corp., 2006.

Kern, Jerome, and Otto Harbach. "Smoke Gets in Your Eyes." *Remember When?* Mercury, 1958.

Park, Hong-Kyu. "American Involvement in the Korean War." *The History Teacher*, vol. 16, no. 2, Feb. 1983, pp. 249-63.

Renwick, Finlay. "15 Years on from *Mad Men*, the Don Draper Effect Is Dead in Menswear." *British GQ*, 25 July 2022. *https://www.gq-magazine.co.uk/fashion/article/mad-men-anniversary-don-draper-suit*.

Seitz, Matt Zoller. *Mad Men: Carousel*. Abrams Press, 2015.

Weiner, Matthew. "The Art of Screenwriting No. 4." Interview by Semi Chellas. *The Paris Review*, no. 208, Spring 2014. https://www.theparisreview.org/interviews/6293/the-art-of-screenwriting-no-4-matthew-weiner.

——, creator. Mad Men. Lionsgate Television, 2007-2015.

Nicole Chrenek is a writer and scholar currently residing in London, United Kingdom. Originally from Grande Prairie, Alberta, she completed her Bachelor of Arts and Master of Arts in English Literature at McGill University before moving to London to pursue a Master of Arts in Creative Writing at Royal Holloway, University of London. She previously received the Margaret Gillett Fellowship for Research on Women at McGill University in both 2021 and 2022. Her research interests include the uncanny, the domestic, motherhood, and lesbian anxieties. She has previously presented work at ACCUTE, NeMLA, and the LCIR.

At Apocalypse's Edge:
The Paradox of Freedom in Contemporary Popular Science Fiction Films

Jasmine Tan Hui Jun

The year is 2013. In *Pacific Rim* (2013), Godzilla-like aliens called the Kaiju enter our world through the Breach, swimming up from the depths of the Mariana Trench to attack human civilization. The year is 2015. In *Edge of Tomorrow* (2014), aliens called the Mimics arrive on Earth via an asteroid and begin conquering our planet one continent at a time. The year is 2048. In *The Tomorrow War* (2021), aliens called the White Spikes have driven humanity towards the brink of extinction. Prior to the alien invasion, humans had no natural predators. Secure at the top of the food chain, humanity is segregated into different nations, races, genders, and beliefs, factors that are socially constructed rather than based on biological difference. In fact, this pursuit of individual freedom at the cost of others is humanity's hamartia that ultimately results in humans being on the losing side of the war in all three of these films.

Aliens are "*dei ex machina*, external elements that enter to disturb the equilibrium... that unlock doomsday" (Sardar 5). As a trope in the science fiction genre, aliens function as an indicator species, establishing "what is not human to better exemplify that which is human" (6). Yet, for all their otherness, aliens are so pivotal to the construction of the apocalypse because they represent the unity that eludes humanity. In the aforementioned films, human society is destabilized by the aliens' ability to achieve complete cooperation, a characteristic that is encoded into their monstrous bodies by biological design.

To fight the Kaiju, "the world came together, pooling its resources and throwing aside old rivalry for the sake of the greater good." To fight the Mimics, "over seventeen nations have joined the United Defense Force" in a global war. To fight the White Spikes, "for the first time in human history, the armed forces from every nation are united against one enemy." Yet, an apocalypse should not have been a prerequisite for humanity to understand our continuous failure at realizing that our individual freedom is contingent on the universal freedom of our fellow humans. Why do humans only unite as a species when we have a clear biological enemy? In other words, why does an apocalypse need to happen for humanity to realize that our fate is a shared one? Ironically, the greatest threat to humanity's existence is not an external alien force but the continued insistence of our self-imposed differences. In asserting our own otherness from each other, we sabotage our own survivability and imperil our own freedom.

The apocalypse is formulated in conjunction with the limitations of freedom; freedom cannot occur without constraint, biological or otherwise. The illusion of freedom already existed before the apocalypse; the arrival of the aliens only serves to expose this illusion. The apocalypse, as David Ketterer suggests, may be codified into a "moment of juxtaposition and consequent transformation when an old world of mind discovers a believable new world of mind, which either nullifies and destroys the old system entirely or... makes it part of a larger design" (qtd. in Pitetti 13). Freedom exists in a dichotomy. In order to attain any form of freedom (individual or collective), there need to be constraints, like an alien apocalypse. Crucially, the biology of these alien creatures promotes cooperation, a quality that is rarer in human society with its self-imposed differences. This war with the aliens catalyzes a paradox of freedom whereby humans realize that they need to first renounce personal freedom through individual self-sacrifice in order to attain universal, collective freedom. The paradox of freedom is not a novel concept, but the manifestation of this paradox continues to prevail throughout science fiction films. According to Byung-Chul Han, "freedom itself, which is supposed to be the opposite of constraint, is producing coercion" (1). Han outlines how concepts like freedom are defined by their dialectical opposites, which in this case is constraint. While it is tempting to regard freedom as *a priori*, in reality, it is *a posteriori*, determined by individual experience.

By exploring the organization of alien biology and contrasting it with the biology and social hierarchy of humans, this chapter aims to examine how the individual's relationship to the whole of society is negotiated in the films. Any social system depends on some form of order, and this order is fundamentally at odds with the chaos that a cataclysm brings. This principle of ordering is one that is reflected in the taxonomy of alien biology. This chapter will have two main linchpins: namely, alien biology and sacrifice. In terms of ensuring our survival as a species, the biology of the Kaiju, Mimics, and White Spikes generally emphasizes sameness, whereas humans privilege difference. The paradox here is that the biological traits that allowed the aliens to be on the winning side of the war at the beginning of the films are ultimately the very weaknesses that humanity exploits to triumph and ensure our survival.

The Kaiju of *Pacific Rim* are initially classified into five categories by humans, but later in the film, Dr. Newton Geiszler (Charlie Day) finds out that, although each Kaiju looks different from each other, they actually share the same genetic code and are clones of each other. This is reflected in the name "Kaiju" itself, which has no plural form; both individuals and species bear the same name.

Geiszler's discovery disrupts prior notions that the monsters are acting on an animalistic urge. Instead, the Kaiju are more intelligent than humans first thought. They have two brains, a primary and secondary one, to process the stimuli around them. More importantly, the species is connected by a hive mind where individual organisms are subsumed into the collective organism. The aliens are stronger together because of their interconnected minds, and the individual Kaiju (whether hound or exterminator) do not act independently but work together towards the common goal of exterminating the "vermin," after which, "the new tenants will take possession." The use of the word "vermin" here to denote humans suggests that the world does not inherently belong to humanity. This is ironic, considering that our failures in our management of the planet position the alien "colonists" to become the new stewards for Earth. The White Spikes of *The Tomorrow War* have likewise been ushered into taking over Earth by anthropogenic climate change, the aliens being released from their icy spaceship prison with the melting of glacial ice.

While having the same DNA as each other might have initially enabled the individual Kaiju to function better as an extension of the entire species and given them a biological edge, humanity's plan to destroy the Breach and eliminate the Kaiju threat hinges on genetics. Scientists Dr. Geiszler and Dr. Hermann Gottlieb (Burn Gorman) tell the protagonists Raleigh Beckett (Charlie Hunnam), Mako Mori (Rinko Kikuchi), and Stacker Pentecost (Idris Elba) that "the Breach genetically reads the Kaiju like a barcode at the supermarket and lets them pass." The solution to *Pacific Rim*'s apocalypse lies in having to "fool the Breach into thinking you have the same [genetic] code." Once the Jaeger *Gipsy Danger* uses a Kaiju carcass to enter the Breach, we see the layers of the Breach unfurling. Despite *Gipsy* no longer holding on to the Kaiju's body past the breach of the first barrier, the Breach continues to open up, almost as if the mechanism is too careless with its hubristic belief in the infallibility of the Kaiju's genetic signature. There was no biological failsafe or contingency to prevent *Gipsy* from infiltrating the heart of Kaiju society and detonating.

Nonetheless, the Kaiju are not the only ones who share a hive mind. Raleigh says in a voiceover at the start of the film that "to fight monsters, we created monsters of our own: the Jaeger program was born." Jaegers are large, mechanized, Transformer-esque machines that combine man and metal. Similar to the Kaiju's hive mind, the Jaegers cannot be piloted alone. Because "the neural load to interface with a Jaeger proved too much for a single pilot, a two-pilot system was implemented." While two pilots are far from a hive, there is still a sense that humans are stronger together than apart. Even the Drift Compatibility required for the Jaeger pilots' neural handshake is an exercise in vulnerability and intimacy, since mind-melding between the pilots is necessary for them to pilot the Jaeger's body as a single entity. According to Raleigh, "the deeper the bond, the better you fight." Here, the individual does not exist. They are part of a larger whole with the other pilot and the Jaeger machine itself. This relinquishing of individual freedom of mind is what allows the Jaeger to be effective in combat with the Kaiju.

Similar to the Kaiju, the Mimics can also be thought of as one entity. In *Edge of Tomorrow*, William Cage (Tom Cruise) learns that he is "not fighting an army. You have to think of [the Mimics] as a single organism." Each Mimic has a specific role to play, with the common drones behaving like claws, the rare Alphas serving like a central nervous system, and the Omega acting as its brain. On the frontlines of Operation Downfall, Cage kills an Alpha, triggering the Omega's self-preservation mechanism, starting the day over again to give the Mimics a tactical advantage to study their human enemy further. This time loop is a double-edged sword because, while it allows the Omega to "remember what's going to happen" and to know "exactly what [humans are] going to do before we're going to do it," it also grants Cage with the power to reset the day. The aphorism "an enemy that knows the future can't lose" holds true for both sides, giving the humans and aliens an equal chance of turning the tide of the war. Dr. Noah Carter (Noah Taylor) tells Cage that despite the film's presentation of the Mimics as "a perfectly evolved world-conquering organism," like "a virus" in the cosmos, "its only vulnerability is humanity." Cage's newfound ability to—quoting the film's tagline—"Live. Die. Repeat." is one that is paid for in blood. The Alpha's blue blood mixes with Cage's when he kills it and the price for humanity's freedom is paid for daily with Cage's death. The film shows a montage of the ways in which Cage and Rita Vrataski (Emily Blunt) die in their successive attempts to get off the beachfront battle and find the location of the Omega. The Omega tries to trap Cage by feeding him false information on its location, and Cage overcomes this deception by using a transponder to connect to the Omega's wavelength, turning the Mimics's biological power into its downfall.

Time is also a key motif in *The Tomorrow War*. Instead of a time loop, the future war is facilitated by a temporal displacement device called the Jump Link. This disruption of linear time is portrayed as the film begins, with *Tomorrow*'s apocalypse *in medias res*, when soldiers from the past—including the film's protagonist, Dan Forester (Chris Pratt)—are falling from the sky to their deaths. The sky is tinted red, and the city of Miami is in literal and figurative ruins. The film employs the pathetic fallacy. The apocalyptic mood is conveyed through the color red, representing the spilled blood of civilians turned soldiers. Later in the film, Dan's adult daughter in the future tells him that "we [humanity] are literally living on borrowed time," echoing Ziauddin Sardar's assertion that "science fiction is a time machine that goes nowhere… the fiction of mortgaged futures" (1). Time and time again, science fiction films return to the locus of the apocalypse, the pivotal point when the future of freedom and fate of humanity is decided.

Like the Kaijus and Mimics before them, the White Spikes are brutal in their decimation of humanity. While the Kaiju and Mimic do not differentiate between male and female aliens, the White Spikes do. The female White Spikes are shown to be rarer and more aggressive than the males, with the males being willing to "die to defend" the females because "all they seem to care about is the survival of the species." This will to survive is a sentiment shared by humans in all three of the films. The female White Spike parallels the Alpha mimic in terms of her rarity in their alien population but also for her additional adaptations that separate her from the rest of their species. The remaining human population, led by Dan Forester's adult daughter, Muri Forester (Yvonne Strahovski), have bioengineered a toxin that can kill the male White Spikes but not the female, whose genetics are similar to the males but whose body enables faster metabolism and detoxification. Muri emphatically states that "[female White Spike] physiology is the key to their extinction." Eventually, Muri does succeed in synthesizing a toxin to kill the female White Spike, using the aliens' biology against them.

Moreover, even as humans designate aliens as the consummate "other," both species are not as different as they appear upon closer inspection. The depiction of aliens as an invasive species aiming to eradicate humanity creates a false dichotomy between human and "other" and between friend and foe while neglecting the similar motivations of both species. The desire for freedom is not a trait that is distinctly human, neither is it limited to humanity. Aliens and humans may be opposites on the battlefield but they are driven by the same intrinsic desire to persist and avoid the extinction of their species. The emphasis on invasiveness suggests that this survival will come at a cost to the other species. While the aliens seem to possess a biological edge over humans, they are not exactly a perfect species because they also are constrained by their own hive minds. Because their actions are guided entirely by rationality, they fail to account for humanity's emotional choices.

Each individual alien acts in concert with each other. They are aware of their roles as parts within a larger whole, but the choices that they make contribute to the survival of the whole community. The aliens' choices are in alignment with their roles. Ironically, the world is saved because the protagonists do not play their ascribed roles. This discrepancy is perhaps an antidote to the biological determinism that pervades alien biology, because human beings still have the capability to rebel and do the unexpected. Although humans need to band together in order to survive, the individual still has the responsibility to think for themselves and for the rest of society.

At the sacrificial altar of freedom, "the self must cling to the total premise of its own freedom at the expense of the world" (Cubitt 26). This paradox is further highlighted by Frank Kermode on philosopher Jean-Paul Sartre's "anguish of freedom… when a man commits himself to anything, fully realizing that he is not only choosing what he will be, but is thereby at the same time a legislator deciding for the whole of mankind" (143). This raises the issue of obligation among individual humans to the rest of humankind and vice versa. The question of how this duty to each other is enacted does not have a biological basis: "the idea that we are entitled to make demands on our fellows, and that we also have obligations to them, is solely in the human dimension" (Barnett 299). Thus, freedom seems to be a human imperative, not a biological one. Paradoxically, the pursuit of freedom is not unique to humans, but freedom seems to hold more value for humanity.

Interestingly, the cancellation of the Apocalypse (in Pentecost's words) is regarded as a restoration of the world in the films, but it is not a return to the world as humanity once knew it. In *Pacific Rim*, the world rights itself to its former state before the apocalypse began. There are no Kaiju and no Jaegers. Pentecost reminds us in his rousing last stand speech that, "At the edge of our hope, at the end of our time, we have chosen not only to believe in ourselves, but in each other. Today, there's not a man nor woman in here that shall stand alone. Not today. Today we face the monsters that are at our door and bring the fight to them."

Pacific Rim reiterates that humanity's salvation lies in the collective human consciousness and in our solidarity as a species. Pentecost, in particular, exemplifies this self-sacrifice and lives up to the utilitarian formula, "the needs of many outweigh the needs of the few." He belongs to the first generation of Jaeger pilots and suffers from radiation poisoning after being exposed in the Mark 1s. In the early days of Jaeger technology, the safety of Jaeger pilots meant less than the lives of the rest of humanity, but Pentecost never questions his own sacrifice, deeming it necessary. Even though stepping into a Jaeger again would kill him, Pentecost suits up without hesitation when fellow pilot Hercules "Herc" Hansen (Max Martini) is injured and can no longer pilot *Striker Eureka*. He hides his illness from everyone, telling Raleigh, "All I need to be to you and everybody on this dome is a fixed point, the last man standing." This idea of a fixed point is significant, because Pentecost willingly subjects himself to pain a second time, telling Mako that "not getting into [a Jaeger] will kill us all." During the final mission, there is an implicit understanding between the four Jaeger pilots (Pentecost, Chuck, Raleigh, and Mako) that they would die, without hesitation to destroy the Breach. Raleigh gives Mako his oxygen when she falls unconscious, sparing her life and finishing the mission to detonate *Gipsy*'s nuclear reactor by hand even though there is no guarantee that he will survive the blast.

In *Edge of Tomorrow*, self-sacrifice is enacted for the sake of the greater good and romantic love in equal measure. Cage is initially depicted as selfish and looking out for his personal safety. He has no problem convincing others to join the war and to put themselves in harm's way, but he won't even consider helping to film these sacrifices. He values his own life above the lives of others, and the film charts his character development until his eventual sacrifice. This recapitulates Master Sergeant Farell's (Bill Paxton) belief that "battle is the great redeemer, the fiery crucible in which the only true heroes are forged, the one place where all men truly share the same rank." Here, the alien apocalypse is a metaphorical trial-by-fire that elevates individuals to the shared rank of human. He meets Rita, the Angel of Verdun, who teaches him about the Alpha's power and trains him to fight in the Exosuit. Over time, Cage is forced to witness Rita die repeatedly and is helpless to save her. This mirrors Rita's experience having to watch the man she loved, Hendricks, die three hundred times at Verdun. Cage's reticence to sacrifice Rita is punctuated by their chagrin at having to know each other under such apocalyptic circumstances. He and Rita both end up sacrificing their lives to kill the Omega in the Louvre. As Cage jumps into the water and swims toward the submerged Omega, the imagery of it unfurling is reminiscent of the Breach opening in *Pacific Rim*. Cage detonates the explosives, destroying the Omega and also an Alpha whose blood resets the timeline to the day before Operation Downfall. But sacrifice is not just limited to the protagonists. Even J Squad, who was previously antagonistic towards Cage, "take a hit for the team," with Griff (Kick Gurry) and Skinner (Jonas Armstrong) buying time for Cage and Rita. The end of the apocalypse is achieved by a group of unsung soldiers whose heroic sacrifice, while not overturned, will never be recognized or lauded.

Similarly, in *The Tomorrow War*, the central self-sacrifice in the film is done out of familial love rather than to save humanity. Dan rejects the title of "hero," saying, "If I got to save the world to save [Muri], then I'm damn sure going to do it." The film suggests that the greater good is incidental and ancillary. Dan's choice to be a father over humanity's hero is what ultimately wins the war. Danny Fingeroth argues that superheroes, or heroes in this case, are the "idealized vision the entire world has of itself" (25). But as with all ideals, he also asks, "Is the idea of freedom a mass delusion?" (71). Perhaps the world puts too much faith in these more-than-human superheroes, and, when it comes down to it, Dan's admission that his self-sacrifice is not altruism on behalf of humanity is a more realistic portrayal of freedom. Because the film focuses on familial sacrifice, it brings a biological element into the narrative whereby the loved ones who share DNA with the heroes may be understood as a perpetuation of the self. Adult Muri's sacrifice at the Deepswell-9 Jump Link facility that allows Dan to travel back to the past is once again shrouded in red, a visual parallel to the beginning of the film. Before Muri falls into the ocean of aliens, she implores Dan to leave her to die in the future, using the words he used to tell her as a child, that one has to "do what nobody else is willing to do." The scene where she falls depicts her descent in slow motion; the frame of her suspended in the air between her father and the White Spikes evokes a descent into Dante's hellish inferno. The red bleeds into the past when Dan teleports back to 2022 only to find out that the Jump Link is broken and that there is no way to travel to the future to save Muri. Haunted by this failure, he figures out a way to prevent the future war from happening in his own time. On an illegal, unsanctioned trip to a Russian glacier, Dan and his father James (J. K. Simmons), Charlie (Sam Richardson), Dorian (Edwin Hodge), and a team of soldiers from the future find the White Spike spaceship buried under the ice. The inside of the spaceship is bathed in the same reddish hue that marked the apocalyptic scenes of the future war, implying that the war has now shifted to the present. Dorian, who has terminal cancer, blows up the ship with a colony of White Spikes, shouting, "If I'm going to die, I'm going to die my way." Here, self-sacrifice is a form of freedom, too. Even if the outcome is the same, Dorian defines the terms and parameters of his own sacrifice.

Freedom comes in many forms and is connoted by a wide range of terms, including words like agency, autonomy, and liberty. But at the core of its DNA, etched into all its synonyms, freedom means having a choice. It is not always a choice born out of good options, because sometimes bad options are all one has. Rather, this choice has to be a deliberate one, allowing decisions that span the spectrum from selfishness to generosity. This is what emphasizes the enormity of the sacrifice that each character makes, because they knowingly choose to risk their lives, sacrificing their personal safety to ensure the safety of others. By privileging the whole of humankind ahead of their individual lives, they eschew the biological urge for self-preservation for the greater good. Yet this sacrifice is not entirely altruistic, nor can we expect it to be.

These science fiction films imagine an alternate America, one that is ruled by a technocratic power structure that relies heavily on military force. In alien society, alien biology determines the organization of power. In human society, the military holds a monopoly of power, and social institutions like the government are hierarchical. Unfortunately, in all three films, this chain of command supersedes humanity's greater good, resulting in the need for a small minority of humans to take matters into their own hands, assuming the risk of personal injury and death, rebelling to win the war. This illustrates the failure of human structures of power that silence individual voices, rendering the power structure itself ineffective and impeding the survivability of the human race.

Humanity's pursuit of freedom in apocalyptic situations requires a more nuanced protocol than mere self-sacrifice. While the aliens are willing to sacrifice the individual out of necessity to save the whole species, human beings demonstrate a reciprocal willingness to sacrifice for each other, even if it does not directly result in the betterment of the species. As humans are willing to go against self-preservation of their own lives (a core tenet of biology) and die for the sake of freedom, I conclude that survival is not synonymous with freedom. It is not the end but the means; the choice to self-sacrifice outweighs the biological urge to survive. These films leave us with the lingering sense that soldiers do not save the world, people do. At the heart of it, the alien apocalypse is not canceled by the hero or heroine shouldering the burden of humanity's fate. All it takes is a brother avenging his brother's death (Raleigh), a daughter avenging her family (Mako), a surrogate father protecting his adoptive daughter (Pentecost), a father sacrificing his son who goes on a suicide mission to destroy the Breach and end the war (Hercules), a man wanting to protect the woman he might love but letting her choose to sacrifice her life anyway (Cage), a father wanting to save his daughter's life (Dan), a daughter who believed in her father even when he failed her (Muri), and a father trying to earn his son's forgiveness (James).

We are all simply fighting for the promise of a tomorrow, one that is obtained through our own choosing. Perhaps, that ability to fight is the greatest freedom of all. And true to its paradoxical form, the freedom of this tomorrow is beheld only in the gaze of a freedom that has won the war and lost the battle. As Howard F. Stein posits, the "American cultural ethos (effective organizations) and eidos (cognitive organization) of freedom is thoroughly enmeshed in a system of paradox such that freedom can neither be denied nor fulfilled, neither repudiated nor attained" (151). Freedom in the modern age seems to be a Sisyphean ordeal, an endless struggle receding into infinite tomorrows. Yet, the optimism that suffuses these films is undeniable. In true postmodernist fashion, freedom will inevitably be incomplete. Freedom is a state that will never be fully attained, only aspired to in the fight of becoming. Today is the eve of tomorrow. War is always coming. Just as there is no winning of the war without sacrifice, there is no freedom without its antithesis. The salvation of humanity is not the only goal, but the individual's sacrifice of their freedom serves a dual purpose: the survival of the species and the protection of the right of choice, which is tantamount to freedom. As the legislators of freedom, humans "must decide for [themselves]... seeking, beyond himself, an aim which is one of liberation... that man can realize himself as truly human" (Cornea 232).

Works Cited

Barnett, S. A. *Biology and Freedom: An Essay on the Implications of Human Ethology*. Cambridge University Press, 1988.

Cornea, Christine. *Science Fiction Cinema: Between Fantasy and Reality*. Edinburgh University Press, 2007.

Cubitt, Sean. "*Delicatessen*: Eco-Apocalypse in the New French Science Fiction Cinema". *Aliens R Us: The Other in Science Fiction Cinema*, Pluto Press, 2002, pp. 18-33.

del Toro, Guillermo, director. *Pacific Rim*. Warner Brothers, 2013.

Fingeroth, Danny. *Superman on the Couch: What Superheroes Really Tell Us about Ourselves and Our Society*. The Continuum International Publishing Group, 2004.

Han, Byung-Chul. *Psychopolitics: Neoliberalism and New Technologies of Power*. Translated by Erik Butler, Verso, 2017.

Kermode, Frank. *The Sense of an Ending: Studies in the Theory of Fiction with a New Epilogue*. Oxford University Press, 2000.

Liman, Doug, director. *Edge of Tomorrow*. Warner Brothers, 2014.

McKay, Chris, director. *The Tomorrow War*. Amazon Studios, 2021.

Pitetti, Connor. "Uses of the End of the World: Apocalypse and Postapocalypse as Narrative Modes." *Science Fiction Studies*, vol. 44, no. 3, Nov. 2017, pp. 437-454.

Sardar, Ziauddin. "Introduction". *Aliens R Us: The Other in Science Fiction Cinema*, Pluto Press, 2002, pp. 1-17.

Stein, Howard F. "Freedom and Interdependence: American Culture and the Adlerian Ideal." *Journal of Individual Psychology*, vol. 30, no. 2, 1 Nov. 1974, pp. 145-158.

Jasmine Tan Hui Jun has a Master of Arts in English Literature from Nanyang Technological University (Singapore). Her research interests are at the intersections between contemporary poetry and biology and also include science fiction, fantasy, popular culture, monster theory, mythology, and ecocriticism, as well as creative writing. She has presented papers at international literature and science conferences. Her poem "The Water Cycle" has been published in *To Let the Light In: An Anthology of Life and Death* (2021). She is currently working on a chapter investigating the act of reading and interpreting monstrous palimpsests as part of an edited collection on Stephen Sommers's *The Mummy* films.

The Freedom of "the Endland of the Convergence" or "the Long Soft Life" in DeLillo's *Zero K*

Stephen Hock

Just after the dawn of the twenty-first century, in an essay published in the online magazine *Salon* on October 23, 2001, Jeffrey MacIntyre argued for the relevance of Don DeLillo's work in an America upended by the 9/11 terrorist attacks. "From attacks on American money markets to bioterror in the heartland," MacIntyre noted, "DeLillo's work has long anticipated a world in which acts of terror would achieve unprecedented historic consequences." Appearing little more than a month after the 9/11 attacks, MacIntyre's essay suggested that, "In light of the events of Sept. 11, Don DeLillo's America may assist many readers in making sense of a newly uncertain world."

Whatever assistance DeLillo might have provided in making sense of the world, America's attention was quickly eclipsed by alternative frameworks for understanding the 9/11 attacks and their aftermath, most obviously in the rush to war propagated by the Geoge W. Bush administration. Bush himself offered a particularly tidy encapsulation of the situation facing America in an address to a joint session of Congress on September 20, 2001, when he declared, "Americans are asking, why do they hate us? They hate what we see right here in this chamber—a democratically elected government. Their leaders are self-appointed. They hate our freedoms—our freedom of religion, our freedom of speech, our freedom to vote and assemble and disagree with each other" ("Address").

The notion of "freedom" has, of course, been a touchstone of the American project since its beginnings. For Bush, "freedom" served as the rhetorical prism through which to frame an existential conflict between America and a range of enemies around the globe. More recent American presidents, would-be presidents, and would-be presidential kingmakers have extended this logic to pose "freedom" as the defining question governing not only America's foreign policy but also its domestic policy and politics. "Freedom," in fact, is the first word Joe Biden speaks in the video announcing his 2024 reelection campaign, in his opening statement, "Freedom. Personal freedom is fundamental to who we are as Americans." Later in the video, Biden argues, "The question we're facing is whether in the years ahead, we have more freedom or less freedom" (@JoeBiden). In mirror-image fashion, Donald Trump, in his announcement that he would seek the 2024 Republican nomination for president, claimed, "The radical left Democrats have embraced an extreme ideology of government domination and control. Our approach is the opposite, one based on freedom, values, individual responsibility, and just plain common sense" ("Former"). Similarly, Ron DeSantis, in announcing his candidacy for the 2024 Republican nomination, offered, "Now, these past few years have given me a new appreciation for the fragility of our freedoms" ("Live"). DeSantis's announcement occurred in a conversation on Twitter Spaces that involved, among others, Twitter owner Elon Musk, whom DeSantis praised later in the conversation as "a free speech advocate," in response to which Musk noted, "we're absolutely committed to freedom of speech.... Twitter was indeed expensive, but free speech is priceless" ("Live"). Freedom, then, in its various vicissitudes, has continued to serve as a central referent in American political discourse in the first quarter of the twenty-first century. If nothing else, "freedom" functions as a shibboleth marking one's identity as a member of a given political tribe, whichever tribe that may be and whatever particular permutation of freedom it claims to value, whether the freedom to obtain an abortion in the wake of the Supreme Court's *Dobbs* decision, the freedom to keep businesses and schools open during the COVID-19 pandemic, the freedom to post hate speech on social media, or any other variety of freedom that might appeal to a particular demographic slice of America.

Apropos of MacIntyre's claim for the continuing value of DeLillo's work in assisting "readers in making sense of a newly uncertain world," my purpose in the present essay is to suggest that DeLillo's work can likewise aid in understanding the uncertain word "freedom" in twenty-first-century America. In particular, this chapter will take as its subject DeLillo's 2016 novel *Zero K*, which offers a number of possible figures of freedom in twenty-first-century America. Most obviously, we might read *Zero K* as a parable for the neoliberal faith that it is possible, through the flow of capital, to buy freedom from any limits, even the limits imposed by mortality. This freedom found in the extension of (American) capital's encroachment over the globe is incarnated in the person of Ross Lockhart, the man who funds the cryonics project that occupies the center of the novel.

The novel's skeptical or ironic treatment of Ross Lockhart's quest to create a utopia where the power of capital can triumph over death, however, prompts readers to look elsewhere for figures offering viable paths to freedom. Indeed, *Zero K* offers several alternate ways of thinking through the quest for freedom. Readers might consider, for instance, the air of religiosity that accompanies the Monk, and the promise it seems to offer of freedom through apocalypse. Even more resonantly for those reading the novel after Russia's 2022 invasion of Ukraine, DeLillo gives us another figure of freedom in Stak, who dies in the 2014 fighting between Ukrainian forces and pro-Russian separatists in Konstantinovka.

Each of these possibilities, though, shares with Ross Lockhart's quest the belief that freedom lies in a flight of transcendence, the longing for which is encapsulated in a phrase that appears toward the end of the novel, "the endland of the Convergence" (266). By contrast, the story of Ross Lockhart's son Jeffrey, the narrator of *Zero K*, leads to a reading of the novel that emphasizes the freedom not of the transcendent but rather of the immanent, freedom within the quotidian, what Jeffrey refers to as "the long soft life" (268). More feasible but also more restrained—indeed, more feasible precisely because it is so restrained—the freedom of "the long soft life" serves as a rejection of the transcendent modes of freedom offered by "the endland of the Convergence" and the neoliberal and neofascist political analogs that the novel aligns the Convergence with. At the same time, *Zero K*'s framing of the immanent freedom of "the long soft life" also underscores the limits of that mode of freedom as it evokes what might be termed the caretaker liberalism characteristic of the twenty-first-century American polity.

Zero K opens with a declaration from Ross Lockhart, "*Everybody wants to own the end of the world*" (3). Ross's son Jeffrey's narration following this opening sentence provides context that suggests the novel's alignment of the late-capitalist faith that it is possible to *own* everything with the idea of freedom in the form of transcendence. Jeffrey explains, "This is what my father said, standing by the contoured windows in his New York office—private wealth management, dynasty trusts, emerging markets. We were sharing a rare point in time, contemplative, and the moment was made complete by his vintage sunglasses, bringing the night indoors" (3). This opening scene sets the stage for *Zero K*'s alignment of late capitalism, the global economic system incarnated in the person of Ross Lockhart, with transcendence, in the core sense of going beyond one's limits to achieve a state of superiority to and freedom from one's surroundings. We see this, for instance, in the fact that Ross is wearing "his vintage sunglasses, bringing the night indoors." Wearing sunglasses indoors at night functions as a telling detail that hints at Ross's disregard for the boundaries of space or time, a smaller version of the disregard for boundaries that, on a much larger scale, manifests itself in his investment in the Convergence, the project that aims to extend life beyond its natural boundaries by cryonically preserving bodies until some future time when disease and, ultimately, death itself can be engineered away.

Indeed, *Zero K*'s discussion of the Convergence repeatedly frames that project in terms of transcendence, especially when it comes to the novel's treatment of Jeffrey's stepmother, Ross's wife Artis Martineau, who undergoes the process of having her body frozen at the instant of her death in the hope of being reborn into a future free of disease and death. As Laura Barrett observes, Artis's "discontentment with the transience and imperfections of life compels her to seek transcendence" (113). Indeed, the term "transcendence" itself comes up in Jeffrey's reflections on Artis's faith in the Convergence: "the future she'd just described was another matter, a purer aura. This was transcendence, the promise of a lyric intensity outside the measure of normal experience" (47-48).

In this context of freedom through transcendence, it is important also to note the other aspect of Ross's character that the novel's opening sentences draw our attention to, namely, his status as an avatar of late capitalism, in the reference to his work in "private wealth management, dynasty trusts, emerging markets." Ross's wealth, insofar as it helps to fund the Convergence, is what allows him to attempt to break free of the boundaries of life and death, as the novel reminds us at various points, for instance, when the leading figures of the Convergence whom Jeffrey dubs the Stenmark twins pepper their speeches with statements like "Life everlasting belongs to those of breathtaking wealth" (76). *Zero K* thereby draws our attention to the fact that capital itself has, by the early twenty-first century, become transcendent, able to traverse freely any boundaries that we might imagine could limit it, even as it offers the possibility of transcending the ultimate boundary of mortality. One of the other invitations the Stenmark twins make to their investors, for example, is to "think beyond the godlike touch of fingertip billions" (76). We might also recall the reference late in the novel to Ross's "worldwide resources" as a more geographic sign of the power of capital to pass freely through any terrestrial political boundaries (255), reflecting the dominance of what Elisabeth R. Anker describes as neoliberalism's "postulate that governments should serve the market because the market alone produces freedom" (113).

These passages that suggest a reading of *Zero K* as a parable of capital's boundless faith in itself call to mind Fredric Jameson's well-known theorization of postmodernism as "the cultural logic of late capitalism," what Jameson describes as "the purest form of capital yet to have emerged, a prodigious expansion of capital into hitherto uncommodified areas. This purer capitalism of our own time," Jameson continues, "thus eliminates the enclaves of precapitalist organization it had hitherto tolerated and exploited in a tributary way" (36). In *Zero K*, death itself becomes one of those "enclaves of precapitalist organization" whose boundaries capital will no longer respect, as capital asserts itself as the transcendent force not just of our time, but also of the future of billionaire immortality that those like Ross imagine capital can bring into being. As Wendy Hui Kyong Chun observes, "In an odd extension of commodity fetishism, we now wish to be as free as our commodities: by freeing markets, we free ourselves" (10), even to the point, in *Zero K*, of believing we can free ourselves from death.

While Ross may share Artis's faith in the Convergence—he later chooses to undergo the cryonic process, despite his apparent good health, in order to be with her—Jeffrey does not. At one point, Jeffrey reflects on the procedure Artis is about to undergo by thinking, "She would die, chemically prompted, in a subzero vault, in a highly precise medical procedure guided by mass delusion, by superstition and arrogance and self-deception" (50). Given Jeffrey's role as the narrator of *Zero K*, his skepticism permeates the novel's treatment of the Convergence, ironizing and undercutting this particular neoliberal model of freedom. As Graley Herren writes, "Jeff serves as chief spokesman for DeLillo's own skepticism and at times downright denunciation of the utopian pipe dreams peddled at the Convergence" (214). To a large degree, Jeffrey's skepticism about the Convergence is built on the sense that the cryonic process will fail to resurrect those who undergo it. The phrasing of David Cowart's reading of this aspect of the novel is telling: "DeLillo depicts the Convergence as a kind of ultimate bait-and-switch: consumers are sold a pod or capsule that turns out to be just a coffin after all" (144). Cowart's reference to those seeking freedom from death through the Convergence as "consumers" reminds us that the failure of the Convergence's dream of immortality likewise indicts the failure of the neoliberal dream of markets bringing freedom.

One of the more concrete ways in which *Zero K* underscores the failure of the Convergence to deliver its promised version of transcendent freedom lies in the novel's repeated presentation of the Convergence facility as a space of strictly enforced boundaries, where access is limited and movement is controlled. When Jeffrey first arrives at the facility, located in a remote location in post-Soviet Central Asia, he is greeted by the sight of two armed guards who "stood behind a set of bollards designed to keep vehicles from entering the immediate area" (5), highlighting that whatever freedom the Convergence promises is premised on exclusion. As Anker notes,

"Neoliberalism guards both the flow of wealth and the bodies of the wealthy from confrontation with the people it exploits and excludes" (114). The fact that the Convergence's logic is fundamentally one of excluding the mass of the world's population from the freedom it promises comes up again when Jeffrey hears one of the Stenmark twins pose the rhetorical question, "What about those who die? The others. There will always be others. Why should some keep living while others die?" followed by the other twin's comment, "Half the world is redoing its kitchens, the other half is starving" (70). This image of global populations starving recurs during Jeffrey's stay at the facility when Ben-Ezra, another of the apparent leaders of the Convergence, speaks to Jeffrey "about the hundreds of millions of people into the future billions who are struggling to find something to eat not once or twice a day but all day every day" (126), even as he also suggests that, in order to understand the Convergence, Jeffrey will need "to shake free of the conventions that you've brought here with you" (123). This motif of the exclusion of the starving masses from the freedom offered by the Convergence highlights the failure of the neoliberal dream of markets bringing global freedom, on the most basic level of freedom from starvation.

Moreover, readers come to realize that, despite Jeffrey's position as one of the privileged few who is granted access to the Convergence, one of the underlying conditions of his time at the facility is that he lacks another basic freedom, namely, the freedom of movement. Just after Jeffrey's arrival at the facility, he notes that Ross "gave me a small flat disk appended to a wristband. He said it was similar to the ankle monitor that kept police agencies informed of a suspect's whereabouts, pending trial. I'd be allowed entry to certain areas on this level and the one above, nowhere else. I could not remove the wristband without alerting security" (10). Jeffrey's status at the facility becomes that of a suspect or a prisoner. Even later, when Jeffrey is given "admission to areas previously restricted" and enters a conveyance whose "effect was a free-floating sensation, nearly out-of-body" (90), the previously restricted area that Jeffrey finds himself in leaves him "feeling hemmed in, close to being trapped" (91). Later, observing three pods containing cryonically preserved bodies, Jeffrey reflects:

> I wondered if I was looking at the controlled future, men and women being subordinated, willingly or not, to some form of centralized command. Mannequined lives. Was this a facile idea? I thought about local matters, the disk on my wristband that tells them, in theory, where I am at all times. I thought about my room, small and tight but embodying an odd totalness. Other things here, the halls, the veers, the fabricated garden, the food units, the unidentifiable food, or when does utilitarian become totalitarian. (146-47)

At this apotheosis of the Convergence's attempt to harness the power of capital to extend not freedom but control, readers of *Zero K* see, in Jeffrey's closing meditation on the Convergence's "totalitarian" aspect, the ease with which the neoliberal can slide into the neofascist, a trajectory all too familiar to observers of American politics in the first quarter of the twenty-first century.

Jeffrey's first visit to the Convergence takes up the entirety of the first part of *Zero K*, which is titled "In the Time of Chelyabinsk," in reference to the meteor that exploded over Chelyabinsk, Russia, in 2013. Like the Convergence project, this reference likewise speaks to a longing for a certain perverse sort of transcendent freedom from earthly concerns, particularly as that longing is expressed by the Monk, another of the figures Jeffrey meets at the Convergence facility. The first time Jeffrey speaks with the Monk, he speculates that the Monk's role is to "reassure" the dying of "The continuation. The reawakening" (40). The Monk, however, indicates that he doesn't care about the Convergence's promise of rebirth into immortality. As he says, "I just talk about the end.... I want to die and be finished forever. Don't you want to die?" (40). The Monk goes on to explain that he "was a member of a post-evangelist group" that, in fact, prayed for death, in the form of "An object striking the earth" (41). The Monk's description of the cosmic collision that his group prayed for further emphasizes his drive toward the transcendent: "It would come from out there, the great expanse of the galaxies, the infinite reach that contains every particle of matter. All the mysteries" (41). In a sense, this prayer was realized, the Monk acknowledges, in the Chelyabinsk meteor, albeit in a form that utterly failed to bring the prayed-for transcendent freedom that the Monk locates in death through cosmic extinction (42). If, as Chun notes, "Freedom cannot be reduced to something innocuous. Freedom entails a decision for life or death" (293), then in praying for deliverance from earthly concerns through cosmic extinction, the Monk highlights the overall orientation of the Convergence not toward life but toward death. In this way, the presence of the Monk reinforces the reading that Nathan Ashman offers of *Zero K*: "As the opposition between immortality and death is indiscernibly blurred, it becomes demonstrably clear that the Convergence is not really offering immortality beyond death, but immortality *in death*" (309). The "totalitarian" project that is the Convergence takes on the mantle of a fascist death cult, paradoxically demanding the freedom to die in its own specified manner.

Following "In the Time of Chelyabinsk," *Zero K* presents a short interlude imagining the state of Artis's subjectivity in cryonic suspension, then moves into its second part, which is titled "In the Time of Konstantinovka." This transition marks a shift from figures of freedom that the novel associates with transcendence to figures of freedom associated with a grounding in the world of lived experience, and ultimately with immanence. Apropos of what Barrett identifies as "the seemingly contradictory impulses toward the ordinary and the transcendental in

DeLillo's work" (107), however, the break between freedom conceived of in terms of transcendence and freedom grounded in immanence is not entirely a clean one. This is particularly the case when it comes to the figure of Stak, Jeffrey's lover Emma Breslow's adopted son from Ukraine. The fact that the second part of *Zero K* is titled "In the Time of Konstantinovka" highlights Stak's importance. As we learn toward the end of the novel, Stak, after running away from his adoptive parents, is killed in Konstantinovka in 2014 while fighting in a battle between Ukrainian forces and pro-Russian separatists. This element of *Zero K* takes on a new resonance for debates about the value of "freedom" in American foreign policy—not to mention domestic politics—for readers following the 2022 invasion of Ukraine by Russia. For Stak, however, as for the millions of starving people excluded from the freedoms imagined by the Convergence, pressing concerns of life and death demand greater attention, even in the early stages of the conflict between Russia and Ukraine in 2014 that largely escaped American attention. Indeed, Stak's concern with the events in Ukraine seems to puzzle, or even slightly irritate, Emma, as she explains to Jeffrey the terms of Stak's relationship with her and with her estranged husband: "He talks with his father about recent events, she said. Doesn't have much to say to me. Putin, Putin, Putin. This is what he says" (187).

Despite this shift from the fantasies of immortality and apocalypse that fill "In the Time of Chelyabinsk" to the more grounded concerns about the threatened state of Ukrainian freedom of "In the Time of Konstantinovka," Stak's path in some respects still resembles the attempted flights to freedom in transcendence associated with the figures of the Convergence—not least because they all end in death. The novel first suggests the element of transcendence in Stak's quest for freedom in its description of the "enormous wall map of the Soviet Union" that hangs in Stak's room (187). As Jeffrey considers the map, he links it to two of the dreams of transcending the limits of the body or of the universe that the novel has already considered: "There was so much to see and feel and be ignorant of, so much to not know, and there was also Chelyabinsk, right here, where the meteor had struck, and the Convergence itself buried somewhere on the map in the old U.S.S.R." (188). Notably, Jeffrey wraps up his consideration of the map by observing that Emma "was no longer standing next to me but had wandered out of the room and back into local time and place" (188). Here, the map becomes more clearly set apart from the "local time and place"; instead, the map offers Stak a vision of transport out of his immediate circumstances. In this regard, Cowart's identification of Stak as "a son who, like Ross the father, journeys to the East to throw his life away" highlights the characters' shared attempts at flights out of the self in the quest for freedom, whether the freedom from death that Ross seeks or the freedom for Ukraine that Stak seeks to fight for (151). Even as Stak's vision of freedom is more grounded than Ross's or the Monk's, it still falls into the trap of transcendence, overlooking the freedom that Jeffrey comes to associate with the immanent.

This sense of the immanent that Jeffrey turns to in the latter part of *Zero K* offers a distinctly different model of freedom than the one he associates with "the endland of the Convergence" (266). Instead of the "endland" of freedom that Ross and Artis seek in cryonic preservation, or that the Monk prays for in cosmic death, or that Stak finds in blood-soaked Ukraine, Jeffrey reflects near the end of the novel that "The long soft life is what I feel I'm settling into" (268). Notably, this statement comes only a few pages after Jeffrey comments that, after his return from his final trip to the Convergence—where, by some astronomical coincidence, he witnesses Stak's death in Konstantinovka on the facility's video screens that repeatedly show disaster footage—he takes to walking in Emma's neighborhood, "expecting to see nothing, learn nothing, but feeling an immanence" (266).

Indeed, this second half of the novel is filled with moments that emphasize Jeffrey's experience of an immanent freedom grounded in his local time and place.

Jeffrey's experience of immanence culminates in *Zero K*'s final chapter, a simple scene of Jeffrey hearing a child crying out on a bus upon witnessing the phenomenon of Manhattanhenge, or, as Jeffrey describes it, "a natural phenomenon, here in Manhattan, once or twice a year, in which the sun's rays align with the local street grid" (273). Jeffrey is unfamiliar with the name of the phenomenon, but that does not stop his absorption in it: "I didn't know what this event was called," he reflects, "but I was seeing it now and so was the boy," emphasizing the lived reality of the phenomenon itself (273). Alla Ivanchikova identifies this experience as "a moment of transcendence" (77), but I read this experience as qualitatively different from the earlier attempts at transcendence in *Zero K* insofar as it is an experience grounded in Jeffrey's immediate time and place. That emphasis on the local and the immediate marks this as a different order of experience, one that is better understood within the context of *Zero K* not as transcendence but as immanence. In tracing such moments of immanence in earlier works by DeLillo, Cornel Bonca writes:

> "Immanence" indicates here a kind of ontological indwelling or presence—God for many, Being for Heidegger—which is hidden but inherent in the physical world, something which might, were it somehow verified, or even simply believed in, provide a center for consciousness's attention, a connectedness to the world, a ground for credible metanarratives, and a basis for reliable relationships with the world around the self which would sidestep a number of postmodern skepticisms, from Derrida's to Foucault's, Lyotard's, and Baudrillard's. (59)

While *Zero K* maintains a healthy skepticism of the narratives of freedom offered by "the endland of the Convergence," Bonca's reading of the moments of immanence in DeLillo's work as providing "a connectedness to the world" resonates with the ways in which the latter part of *Zero K* repeatedly emphasizes Jeffrey's sense of connection and relation to the immediately present world around him, what Ivanchikova describes as rejecting the promises of the Convergence "in favor of the life affirmed as it is—in all its fragility and finitude" (77).

Jeffrey's sense of freedom immanent in his immediate lived environment notably manifests itself in the experience of freedom of movement. So it is that Jeffrey reflects on "the palpable relief of being in unmetered space for a time, a scattered crowd safe in our very scatter, people free to look at each other, to notice, admire, envy, wonder at" (196). Such an experience stands in contrast to the restrictions on movement that are enforced at the Convergence facility. This contrast is only sharpened when Jeffrey returns to the Convergence for one final visit, to accompany Ross as he is put in cryonic suspension. For Jeffrey, the experience of being back at the Convergence prompts the following meditation:

> I was thinking about the free play of step-by-step and word-for-word that we experience up there, out there, walking and talking under the sky, swabbing on suntan lotion and conceiving children and watching ourselves age in the bathroom mirror, next to the toilet where we evacuate and the shower where we purify.
>
> Now here I am, in a habitat, a controlled environment where days and nights are interchangeable, where the inhabitants speak an occult language and where I am forced to wear a wristband that contains a disk that reports my whereabouts to those who watch and listen. (247)

As it happens, Jeffrey is not required to wear the wristband on this final visit, but the dichotomy remains: freedom in the movement and wonder of the quotidian immanent, found in relation to the people with whom one shares one's local time and space, on the one hand, versus the restrictions and control of a totalitarian fantasy of transcendence on the other.

Jeffrey's framing of this immanent freedom in terms of "people free to look at each other" and "the free play of step-by-step and word-for-word that we experience up there, out there, walking and talking under the sky" resonates with the work of a number of theorists of freedom who conceive of freedom in terms of relation with others in an open space of movement. Hannah Arendt, for instance, observes, "We first become aware of freedom or its opposite in our intercourse with others, not in the intercourse with ourselves. Before it became an attribute of thought or a quality of the will, freedom was understood to be the free man's status, which enabled him to move, to get away from home, to go out into the world and meet other people in deed and word" (148). In similar terms, Jean-Luc Nancy draws on Arendt when he writes:

> Freedom cannot be presented as the autonomy of a subjectivity in charge of itself and of its decisions, evolving freely and in perfect independence from every obstacle. What would such an independence mean, if not the impossibility in principle of entering into the slightest relation—and therefore of exercising the slightest freedom? The linking or interlacing of relations doubtless does not precede freedom, but is contemporaneous and coextensive with it, in the same way that being-in-common is contemporaneous with singular existence and coextensive with its own spatiality. (66)

Framing freedom in terms of an encounter with the world outside oneself, rather than in the independence of the self, Arendt and Nancy underscore the illusory quality of the freedom promised by "the endland of the Convergence."

Indeed, when Jeffrey makes his final trip to the Convergence, freedom enters his thoughts in terms of the isolation against which Arendt and Nancy oppose their conceptions of freedom, as he notes, "I wanted to be free of references and relationships" (232). This impulse to pull back from relationship with the world lurks within the Convergence, just as it does within the Monk's prayers for death from the stars. As Byung-Chul Han puts it:

> Fundamentally, freedom signifies a *relationship*. A real feeling of freedom occurs only in a fruitful relationship—when being with others brings happiness. But today's neoliberal regime leads to utter isolation; as such, it does not really free us at all. Accordingly, the question now is whether we need to redefine freedom—to reinvent it—in order to escape from the fatal dialectic that is changing freedom into coercion. (2-3)

Accordingly, Jeffrey finds that sense of immanent freedom in his relationships with the world around him, not least of all in his relationship with Emma, who, Jeffrey notes, "kept me free of total disaffection" (187). In his later description of Emma, "She took things as they came, not passively or uncaringly but in the spirit of an intervening space" (193), Jeffrey affirms the value of the immanent freedom he finds in "the long soft life."

While *Zero K* presents the immanent freedom of "the long soft life" as a decidedly preferable alternative to the transcendent freedom of "the endland of the Convergence," that does not mean that the novel enthusiastically endorses Jeffrey's preferred mode of freedom. It is, after all, a mode of freedom that is necessarily limited in its scope, one that even Jeffrey realizes is enabled by his relatively privileged position, not only as an American but also as the son of a wealthy man. Echoing his description of Emma as someone who "took things as they came," Jeffrey later tells Ross, "I like to drift into things," even as his narration goes on to note that such preference for drifting "gave me a free sense of being outside the established course of executive routine when in fact what I was out of was a job" (205). As an American living "the long soft life" in relative material comfort, Jeffrey may not be actively engaging in the neoliberal and neofascist programs that preoccupy "the endland of the Convergence," but neither is he actually doing much of anything else. In this regard, Jeffrey's freedom evokes that espoused by what we might call the caretaker liberalism that, in twenty-first-century America, seems all too content with nothing more than softening the edges of the neoliberal and neofascist programs, a larger-scale version of Emma's practice of "[taking] things as they came, not passively or uncaringly but in the spirit of an intervening space."

Of course, "nothing more than" also implies "nothing less than," and *Zero K* suggests there is value in such freedom, however limited its scope. As Barrett notes of Jeffrey, "By the novel's end, his chronic unemployment is interrupted by a position that sounds only mildly less bureaucratic than his former jobs, 'Compliance and Ethics Officer' at a Connecticut college, but this one bears a sense of responsibility and a sense of place" (122). Similarly, Jiena Sun argues that "Jeffrey might still suffer from his sense of universal vulnerability, yet his obsession with the quotidian at least gives him a solid foothold in a shifting society. By slowing down, or even pausing momentarily, Jeffrey manages to reflect on his past experience, have a better grasp of his present circumstances, and hopefully prepare himself for an unpredictable future" (188). That "unpredictable future" is, of course, precisely what *Zero K* suggests the transcendent freedoms of "the endland of the Convergence" cannot do anything to prepare us for. The novel's skepticism toward the billionaire fantasy of preserving life through cryonics reminds us of the analogous skepticism toward, for instance, Elon Musk's dreams of colonizing Mars to guard against the collapse of global civilization; as "senior advisor for science and exploration at the European Space Agency" Mark McCaughrean put it in response to Musk's ideas, "I'm less concerned about making humans a multi-planetary species than I am about making the Earth a sustainable multi-species planet" (qtd. in Devlin). The transcendence offered by "the endland of the Convergence," *Zero K* suggests, can never hope to achieve such an outcome, though the immanent and relational freedom of "the long soft life" just might.

Works Cited

"Address to a Joint Session of Congress and the American People." *National Archives*, 20 Sept. 2001. georgewbush-whitehouse.archives.gov/news/releases/2001/09/20010920-8.html.

Anker, Elisabeth R. *Ugly Freedoms*. Duke UP, 2022.

Arendt, Hannah. "What Is Freedom?" *Between Past and Future: Eight Exercises in Political Thought*, Viking, 1968, pp. 143-71.

Ashman, Nathan. "'Death Itself Shall Be Deathless': Transrationalism and Eternal Death in Don DeLillo's *Zero K*." *Critique: Studies in Contemporary Fiction*, vol. 60, no. 3, 2019, pp. 300-10.

Barrett, Laura. "'[R]adiance in Dailiness': The Uncanny Ordinary in Don DeLillo's *Zero K*." *Journal of Modern Literature*, vol. 42, no. 1, 2018, pp. 106-23.

Bonca, Cornel. "Being, Time, and Death in DeLillo's *The Body Artist*." *Pacific Coast Philology*, vol. 37, 2002, pp. 58-68.

Chun, Wendy Hui Kyong. *Control and Freedom: Power and Paranoia in the Age of Fiber Optics*. MIT Press, 2006.

Cowart, David. "Don DeLillo's *Zero K* and the Dream of Cryonic Election." *Don DeLillo*, edited by Katherine Da Cunha Lewin and Kiron Ward, Bloomsbury Academic, 2019, pp. 143-57.

DeLillo, Don. *Zero K*. Scribner, 2016.

Devlin, Hannah. "Life on Mars: Elon Musk Reveals Details of His Colonisation Vision." *Guardian*, 16 June 2017, theguardian.com/science/2017/jun/16/life-on-mars-elon-musk-reveals-details-of-his-colonisation-vision.

"Former President Trump's 2024 Campaign Announcement." *C-SPAN*, 15 Nov. 2022, www.c-span.org/video/?524197-1/president-trumps-2024-campaign-announcement.

Han, Byung-Chul. *Psychopolitics: Neoliberalism and New Technologies of Power*. Translated by Erik Butler, Verso, 2017.

Herren, Graley. *The Self-Reflexive Art of Don DeLillo*. Bloomsbury Academic, 2019.

Ivanchikova, Alla. "The Fantasy of Technoimmortality and the Psychoanalytic Infinite." *The Comparatist: Journal of the Southern Comparative Literature Association*, vol. 45, 2021, pp. 64-89.

Jameson, Fredric. *Postmodernism, or, The Cultural Logic of Late Capitalism*. Duke UP, 1991.

@JoeBiden. "Every generation has a moment where they have had to stand up for democracy. To stand up for their fundamental freedoms. I believe this is ours. That's why I'm running for reelection as President of the United States. Join us. Let's finish the job. JoeBiden.com." *Twitter*, 25 Apr. 2023, 6:00 a.m., twitter.com/JoeBiden/status/1650801827728986112.

"Live with Ron DeSantis." *Twitter Spaces*, 24 May 2023, twitter.com/i/spaces/1eaJbrAlZjjJX.

MacIntyre, Jeffrey. "Don DeLillo." *Salon*, 23 Oct. 2001, www.salon.com/2001/10/23/delillo_4/.

Nancy, Jean-Luc. *The Experience of Freedom*. Translated by Bridget McDonald, Stanford UP, 1993.

Sun, Jiena. "Ekphrasis and Ways of Seeing in DeLillo's *Zero K.*" *Critique: Studies in Contemporary Fiction*, vol. 63, no. 2, 2022, pp. 176-89.

Stephen Hock is an associate professor of English at Virginia Wesleyan University. He is the editor of *Trump Fiction: Essays on Donald Trump in Literature, Film, and Television* (Lexington Books, 2020) and the coeditor (with Jeremy Braddock) of *Directed by Allen Smithee* (University of Minnesota Press, 2001). His essays have appeared in a number of journals and edited collections.

Allegorical Tensions between "Freedom to" and "Freedom from" in Jonathan Franzen's *Freedom*

Peter Krause

"The next real literary 'rebels' in this country might well emerge as some weird bunch of anti-rebels, born oglers who dare somehow to back away from ironic watching, who have the childish gall actually to endorse and instantiate single-entendre principles. Who treat plain old untrendy human troubles and emotions in U.S. life with reverence and conviction. Who eschew self-consciousness and hip fatigue. These anti-rebels would be outdated, of course, before they even started. Dead on the page. Too sincere. Clearly repressed. Backward, quaint, naïve, anachronistic. Maybe that'll be the point. Maybe that's why they'll be the next real rebels. Real rebels, as far as I can see, risk disapproval. The old postmodern insurgents risked the gasp and squeal: shock, disgust, outrage, censorship, accusations of socialism, anarchism, nihilism. Today's risks are different. The New Rebels might be artists willing to risk the yawn, the rolled eyes, the cool smile, the nudged ribs, the parody of the gifted ironists, the 'Oh how banal.' To risk accusations of sentimentality."

—David Foster Wallace
"E Unibus Pluram: Television and U.S. Fiction" (1993)

Writing at the one year anniversary of the events of 9/11, Jonathan Franzen, in "Mr. Difficult: William Gaddis and the Problem of Hard-to-Read Books," asserts that readers should be dissatisfied with "chilly, mechanistic, and exhausting" (109) fiction and instead seek literature that allows for "a direct, personal relationship with art" (111).[1] In short, he critiques the sprawling "systems novels" of literary postmodernism, including his own early work (104). Franzen maintains that novels should be relatable, connective, and entertaining, not alienating. "The deepest purpose of reading and writing fiction is to sustain a sense of connectedness, to resist existential loneliness," he says (100). Readers, Franzen knows, seek novels in order to be confronted by both mirror and window, and they seek comfort and recognition in both. Moreover, he is adamant that fiction can be accessible and relatable while remaining aesthetically dazzling and stunningly smart.

Yet, why spend almost ten thousand words in the rarified real estate of *The New Yorker* advocating for simple, reader-friendly prose? Why fixate on a pivot in the tone and style of the American novel one year after American tragedy? In this chapter, I suggest that the events of 9/11 accelerated a pivot in arts and letters away from literary postmodernism and towards the new sincerity, a movement (which both Franzen and Wallace describe, but do not name) that emphasizes classical novelistic constructions, plots that subvert ideas to characters and not the other way around, and an un-self-conscious willingness to "endorse single-entendre principles" (Wallace 92).[2] The events of 9/11, says Julia Keller, hasten "the end of postmodernism and its chokehold on the late 20th-Century cultural imagination... its indulgent insistence that all meanings are contingent, all truth subjective." In the wake of catastrophe, readers and writers have less of an appetite for intentionally repellant prose that takes little seriously.[3] In advocating for literature that transcends the postmodern project, Franzen reminds readers that catastrophes like 9/11 can nullify old genres and necessitate new forms of expression. Safety, salvation, family: these ostensibly retrograde values—quaint, suburban, powerfully *arrière-garde*—can become, after calamity, robust sources of meaning and comfort.

In *Freedom* (2010), Franzen creates two allegorical characters, Walter and Richard, who exemplify the competing camps of literary postmodernism and the new sincerity. In dramatizing this tension at the turn of the millennium, Franzen depicts how seductive but ultimately unfulfilling the freedom to explode convention, indulge in gamesmanship, and revel in relativism is, and instead suggests that simplicity, vulnerability, and sincerity are better tools for healing after a crisis. This argument finds purchase in the principles of novel writing and in the larger critical conversation. Little has been written about allegory in Franzen's novels aside from Nathan Hensley's "Allegories of the Contemporary," in which Hensley astutely reads *The Corrections* (2001) as "the allegorical retelling of the waning American century" (288). Regarding allegorical characters, it should be noted that Franzen endows Walter and Richard with representative meaning without making them two-dimensional. As he notes in a 2010 interview, "When you don't have the ready-made cartoon characters at hand like I did with *The Corrections*... you have to invent the characters from scratch" ("The Art of Fiction"). As such, in *Freedom* such characters retain psychological depth while also representing major literary trends.

Fundamentally, the critique of American life at the heart of the new sincerity is ethical: after decades of dizzying capitalistic expansion, numerous cultural upheavals, and the widespread affectation among intelligentsia of a blasé, jaded cynicism, it remains clear that some issues *should* be taken seriously, and some truths *are* worth considering independent of the fact that they may be relative. Some ideals *are* worth vulnerability. On the one hand, Richard exemplifies the pre-9/11 freedom of the wry, cynical postmodernist to indulge in theory, experimentation, and play without the circumscription of traditional authorly obligations to verisimilitude and readability. On the other hand, quaint, principled do-gooder Walter (partially a stand-in for the biographical Franzen himself) typifies the post-9/11 freedom of the "post-pomo" author eager to jettison irony and artifice and, instead, write unabashedly realist, character-driven fiction. Richard exemplifies freedom to indulge in, as Wallace put it, infinite jest, while Walter embodies a freedom from excess and a retreat to classic, stable ideals.

Since the freedom advocated for in the new sincerity is actually a limitation on freedom, a narrowing of the range of possibilities that filters out that which is frivolous and indulgent and clarifies that which is essential and genuine, it exists primarily as an aesthetic movement, rather than a legal or political one. Even so, political theorist Isaiah Berlin's 1958 lecture "Two Concepts of Liberty" is a useful touchstone. "No doubt we cannot be absolutely free, and must give up some of our liberty to preserve the rest," asserts Berlin (7). In the context of *Freedom,* Walter and devotees of the new sincerity give up certain attitudes and behavior that they deem inessential to redouble their commitment to more spiritually-affirming, community-building virtues. Richard and the postmodernists indulge a less circumscribed version of freedom. "Liberty," writes Berlin, drawing on Bentham and Mill, "means freedom *from,* absence of interference beyond a certain frontier" (7). In this respect, we can say that Walter's attitude engages the liberty of the escapee, the defector, and—recall Wallace—the rebel. Richard may seem to be the reactionary firebrand in the novel, but, if we understand him to embody an ethos outmoded by the turn of the millennium, then Walter is actually the agitator who has shrugged off the previous order.

In Franzen's essays and in the allegorical subtext of *Freedom*, the author advocates for a reigning in of the kind of novel caught up in the gravitational pull of novels like Don DeLillo's *Underworld* (1997) and Thomas Pynchon's *Gravity's Rainbow* (1973)—a restoration of stories that are constructed with human scale in mind. A key purpose of such stories is to meet readerly demands, whether to entertain, alleviate loneliness, or simply help answer life's big questions. Indeed, in "Perchance to Dream: In an Age of Images, a Reason to Write Novels," Franzen critiques storytelling "that raises more questions than it answers" (53). Regarding the tendency of the postmodern novel towards completism and encyclopedism, Franzen notes: "Expecting a novel to bear the weight of our whole disturbed society—to help solve our contemporary problems—seems to me a particularly American delusion. To write sentences of such authenticity that refuge can be taken in them: isn't this enough? Isn't it a lot?" (49). In short, Franzen finds the permissive freedom of literary postmodernism exhausting and seeks instead to offer a respite from artifice and fabulation. Just because an author is free to indulge heavily in irony, reflexivity, and allusion does not mean they should. What will not only entertain readers, but also nourish them?

In the same way that *The Corrections* captures the zeitgeist of the I-95 corridor in the 90s, so too does *Freedom* capture the hallmarks of the Midwest and mid-Atlantic both pre- and post-9/11. The novel serves as a model for a new kind of fiction unafraid to do away with the frenetic, knowing busyness of the postmodern by staging the duel between the dominant qualities of literary postmodernism and their opposites. Franzen deeply knows human beings and human behavior. Sam Tanenhaus locates the rub of Franzen's project in the interplay of everyday preferences and prejudices in his characters rather than in overarching philosophies: "Franzen grasps that the central paradox of modern American liberalism inheres not in its doctrines but in the unstated presumptions that govern its daily habits." As such, Franzen depicts the end of the twentieth century and the beginning of the age of the War on Terror from inside the relatively normal American family, as opposed to outsourcing the viewpoint to an unbelievable or unrelatable source. As Jesús Blanco Hidalga notes, "Although ongoing political issues (e.g. globalization, neocon hegemony, the Iraq War) also occupy an important place in Franzen's subsequent novels, in them the novelist refrains from evoking acts of systemic rupture and concentrates instead on narratives of potential salvation within the realm of the family" (13). Franzen retains his "confidence in the mimetic properties of language and the stability of perspective" (Donovan 11). As a writer engaged in the new sincerity, Franzen knows that language is representative and that stories are always approximations of life, and that the relationship is imperfect. He's willing to tell us a good story and is unafraid that the necessary machinery of that story—structure, language, characters, etc.—will be visible to readers. He is *free* of self-consciousness, of the fear that he might be labeled *just* a novelist, and of the urge to jettison novelistic convention.

As I've suggested, to study characterization as a way of illuminating a novel is to depart from dense, impersonal worlds of ideas and data. "In traditional postmodern fiction," writes Stephen J. Burn, even when characters do appear to be psychologically robust and believable, they often "seem to have emerged more or less out of nowhere" (24). On the contrary, Franzen meticulously builds his characters and not only recounts but very often devotes whole chapters to depicting their backgrounds and development. Walter and Patty are introduced as "the young pioneers of Ramsey Hill," a neighborhood in St. Paul, Minnesota where the "collective task" is to "relearn certain life skills your parents had fled to the suburbs to unlearn" (4). Nostalgia, simplicity, and slowness reign. A quaint belief in people's actions and words to effect change persists. Characters in novels of the new sincerity often give the impression of having tried and failed to make sense of the world with critical theory and philosophy before realizing that community, compassion, and simplicity—ideals so bland that they can seem naiveté or childishness—are better remedies.

In establishing a compelling competitive binary between Richard and Walter, Franzen engages the philosophical debate having to do with what to value and why. In "Achieving Their Country: Richard Rorty and Jonathan Franzen," Áine Mahon offers an interpretation of Rorty's critique of contemporary American literature for being smug and cynical and shows how Franzen's *Freedom*, "deeply compassionate" and even "patriotically hopeful," is a strong counterexample to Rorty's schema (92). Mahon recounts Rorty's project as "an ongoing negotiation between American liberalism and postmodernism," which is, I submit, exactly what *Freedom* is about. Franzen encodes the very tensions that fascinate Rorty into his characters. Mahon's primary point of reference in Rorty's scholarship is his 1997 book *Achieving Our Country: Leftist Thought in Twentieth Century America*. Rorty, Mahon explains, diagnoses in postwar American fiction a binary between "a literature of 'knowingness' (or protective cynicism) and a literature of 'inspiration' (or utopian romance)" (91). The former fictions are bleak, impersonal, and sneer at any prospect of "political regeneration or moral improvement," while the latter are willing to engage unironically with "general principle[s]" like hope, patriotism, and truth (92). That *Freedom*, writes Mahon, "aspires to be at once sharply satirical and deeply compassionate troubles immediately any straightforward oppositions between the complex and the sentimental, the highbrow and the lowbrow, the privately and the publicly useful" (92). Franzen's novel not only refuses to inhabit one side of the binary, but it incorporates, both as part of its plot and its stylistic composition, the mission to dramatize the tension between poles of the kind described by Rorty.

Mahon's argument is especially useful in this analysis because she highlights how Franzen's novel is fundamentally about "contingency, the never-ending freedom to self-create" (94). A basic assumption of my argument is that *Freedom* is as much about personal and cultural change and re-creation as it is about anything else. At its core, the novel *is* a story about multiple life stories in which people gamble on different schools of thought to guide their behavior and then deal with the outcomes. While Mahon focuses on Patty and Joey as the novel's foremost self-creators, I understand Walter and Richard's antipodal self-fashioning to be far more narratively prominent and, frankly, interesting.4

Richard Katz and the Freedom to Play, Mock, and Take Little Seriously

When Patty—and readers—meet Richard, he embodies moody post-graduate ennui: sprawled on a couch in a tight black t-shirt reading Thomas Pynchon's novel *V.* (1963). If Franzen's major characters are written to typify turn-of-the-millennium trends in literature and American culture, then Richard is a stand-in for the disaffected, knowing devotee of postmodern theory: "one of those young men who look like they possess massive amounts of data about small-label rock bands or avant-garde literature or video technology; the very size of these data-sets affording a kind of psychic protection"—which is how Franzen describes his younger, Gaddis-obsessed self ("Mr. Difficult" 103). Richard, says Narcisi, is "completely free of the ethical angst that plagues Walter" because he chooses, with juvenile brashness, not to believe in anything (79). Richard affects an air of blasé, jaded disinterest in almost everything and everyone besides himself and his own musical ambitions and sexual conquests. In terms of his evaluation of culture, he typifies the precocious thinkers and artists described by Rorty who "try to get to the point where we no longer worship *anything,* where we treat *nothing* as quasi-divinity, where we treat *everything*—our language, our conscience, or community—as a product of time and chance" (Donovan 22).

Patty, whose childhood was suburban and banal and whose college friends are largely uncritical fellow athletes who appreciate being part of a team, becomes obsessed with Richard, whose hardscrabble Yonkers background, aloof cynicism, and allergy to team spirit are exotic to her. Whereas her interactions with Walter are defined by painfully earnest authenticity and sunny optimism, conversations with Richard are exercises in wordplay, allusion, and affected jadedness, often at her expense. Richard is hardly ever straightforward and his tone is rarely neutral. Like the reckless literature he is meant to embody, he speaks in double entendre and allusion. He needlessly complicates otherwise banal conversation with references to the work of Thomas Pynchon, "this chick Margaret Thatcher" (100), and the psychoanalytic theory of transactional analysis developed by twentieth century American psychiatrist Thomas Harris ("I'm not Okay. You're not Okay. Whatever") (106).[5] While Walter is also at times long-winded in his moralizing about environmental causes, he tends towards redundant over-explanation, which is juxtaposed with Richard's unwarranted and contextless allusions, which leave other characters—and presumably many readers—perplexed until they get the reference, or look it up.

Richard's first remark to Patty, "And what are you," is a question phrased and punctuated as a statement, cold and judgmental (67). Richard asks Patty whether she is considered tall for a female basketball player. When she replies, "I'm not considered tall," he counters with wry repartee: "And yet you are quite tall" (69). Patty fumbles for a witty reply and eventually ends up explaining awkwardly that broken fingers in basketball are rarer than popularly believed. This, for Richard, does not constitute compelling banter, a fact that Franzen brings to the fore. "This was not an interesting or plot-advancing thing to have said, she sensed it immediately, how Richard didn't actually give a shit about her playing basketball," he writes (70).[6] Later, when Patty is alone, she cries. In staging such scenes, Franzen highlights the self-absorbed and even cruel nature of those who indulge in word games for the sake of word games at others' expense, those who aim to outmaneuver and out-reference rather than connect and affirm. In conversations governed by Richard, it is far more important to be "interesting or plot-advancing" than to actually care what others say, or about how they feel.

In typical postmodern form, Richard is constantly self-conscious and thinks metafictitiously, often commenting outright on the de-naturalized narrativity of a moment. After Patty's friend and Richard's lover, Eliza, is revealed to be a manipulative fraud, Richard notes, "Only Walter saw the truth from day one. The truth about Eliza. That's not a bad title" (100). Richard is also unfailingly intertextual, allusive, and attentive to language. When meeting Patty for a second time, his only greeting is: "Patty who is not considered tall" (100). He often operates with the knowing, authorial attitude of someone aware of how to situate themself in a tableau and when to deliver the witty line, while those around him simply blunder forward through scenes impossible to predict, muttering the patently unpolished lines that constitute real-life dialogue. Hensley notes that Franzen's work often "advertises its own 'meaning,' calling attention to the recoding operation it has just performed" (290). In *Freedom*, Franzen has consciously moved away from writing blatantly self-conscious fiction, such that self-conscious performativity is recategorized as a character trait in service of allegory rather than a trait of narration. In other words, he tags Richard as an allegory for the philosophy embodied in his dialogue. The same can be said for Walter. As Michiko Kakutani, James Wood, and other reviewers and critics have rightly noted, Franzen is most masterful in his creation of characters and relationships. It is sensible that he would ground his project in *Freedom* in the makeup of his characters, rather than in the narration around them.

It is a truism of novel-writing that Franzen's characters only think and say the things they do because Franzen himself has had those thoughts, either organically as part of the composition of the novel or previously in the course of life. In order for the novel to "work" on the most basic level, readers suspend their disbelief that the author, who when composing *Freedom* was an established, award-winning professional writer and avid reader in his late forties, and the 22 year old Richard have read the same number and breadth of texts. Richard's internal collection of books read and referenced is not impossible, but reading him as a stand-in for literary postmodernism does make it easier to understand why he is able to cycle so deftly through allusions, references, and critiques. When Patty rightly scolds Richard for going through Eliza's personal things without her permission, he dismisses her remark by invoking French novelist Émile Zola's 1898 open letter to French President Felix Faure: "*J'accuse!*" (68). When Patty continues to balk, he switches to 1970s vernacular: "Cool your jets" (68). It is likely that to contemporary readers phrases like this sound forced and humorous—something approaching camp.[7]

In addition to constantly playing wry word games, Richard acknowledges the performativity implicit in everyday life and exercises his own cleverness by switching roles at will, while those around him (especially Walter) remain more or less authentically themselves. A few paragraphs later, Richard, Patty, and Eliza are sitting around in a dorm room while Eliza nervously strums a guitar. She announces that she is too nervous to play in front of Patty. Immediately, Richard plays the psychoanalyst: "Interesting. Why is that?" (69). Then, when Patty points out that her supportiveness makes Eliza anxious, Richard becomes the sarcastic tormentor: "That's very bad of you. … You need to will her to fail" (69). In Richard's behavior there is a certain amount of flirtation, showmanship, and youthful posturing, for sure. Yet, these traits in Richard amount to more than simply the characterization of the obnoxious, punk-rock cynic. Just as Walter is described as "pathologically considerate" of others, so too is Richard compulsively, habitually the embodiment of literary postmodernism's least flattering, most grating qualities as parsed by Franzen (102).

Walter Berglund and the Freedom from Insincerity and Artifice

When Richard and Patty depart in an unreliable van owned by a member of the Traumatics, Herrera, Patty's first impression is "it's not so fun to be on a road trip with a driver who considers you, and perhaps all women, a pain in the ass" (109). Is this so different from the contempt that Big Book literary postmodernists can be said to have for their readers, especially casual readers? While Richard is content to leave late and subsist on chewing tobacco and no bathroom breaks, Patty "didn't consider it excessive to ask" to stop periodically for food and to use the bathroom (109). Is this so different from readers who embark on the many-hours voyage of Gaddis' *J R* (1975) or Pynchon's *Gravity's Rainbow* and are made to feel silly when they cast about for the orienting basic building blocks of a parsable novel?

After getting as far as Chicago, Patty announces to Richard that she is going home and "go home she did," writes Franzen (116). Home, she has decided, is Walter: the nurturing, forgiving antithesis of all of the cooler-than-thou acrimony and resentment that Richard embodies. "Walter's cheeks were rosier than ever," she notes, as she fell off a Greyhound bus and "threw her arms around him" (117). While she once interpreted this rosy-cheeked appearance as fresh-faced and naive, she now sees it as sanguine: Walter himself is earnest, wholesome, and healthy, and, crucially, he is also these things *for her*. If, as Johannes Voelz does, we read the new sincerity as literary hospitality, then the comically inhospitable nature of literary postmodernism is on full display in Richard's exceeding unaccommodating treatment of Patty, which is juxtaposed with Walter's genuine care for her. There are, it turns out, far more substantial, nourishing experiences in consuming literature and media than to scoff at the ignorance of someone who is not "in" on the joke. Walter embodies such hospitality, which is at the heart of the new sincerity. Hidalga notes of Franzen's work, "Although ongoing political issues (e.g. globalization, neocon hegemony, the Iraq War) also occupy an important place in Franzen's subsequent novels, in them the novelist refrains from evoking acts of systemic rupture and concentrates instead on narratives of potential salvation within the realm of the family" (13). Since Franzen's oeuvre is defined by the Tolstoyan truth of the unhappy but interesting family, Walter's family life is far from idyllic, but he still symbolizes the well-meaning nucleus of sincerity and care.

Later on, Patty gloats that she has married "the nicest guy in Minnesota" (119). However, niceness is limited as a currency in Patty's family, which instead emphasizes political savviness (her mother is a New York state politician), sportiness, and enthusiastic drinking. Though tolerant of teetotaling, principled, and dorky Walter, Patty's parents and siblings balk at his selfless idealism and earnest desire to have "a rational conversation about [population] growth" and the sensibleness of moderate consumption and environmentalism at a rowdy dinner party (122). This juxtaposition highlights Walter's principled simplicity in the context of a larger New York-area intelligencia, who scoff at him. At first, Walter appears to Patty to be a sweet-hearted anachronism, a pitifully too-good-to-be-true boy who asks her questions, gives her gifts, and invites her to stage plays in a campus milieu in which the norm is to project general dissatisfaction and go to punk rock concerts (75). When Patty later sees his childhood bedroom for the first time, she remarks, "It was such a sweetly clean, old-fashioned room, and Walter was such a sweetly clean, old-fashioned person" (130). Walter turns out not to be naive, but simply quaint: an anachronistic, principled teetotaler who abhors his frenemy Richard Katz's snide, knowing cynicism for the sake of snide, knowing cynicism. Walter is, in Patty's memory, almost a flat Norman Rockwell-esque caricature: he has a "friendly midwestern smile" (70), is "genuinely nice" (74), and practically radiates sincerity. He is blithely cultural in an intensely countercultural situation.

At first, Patty does not take Walter seriously because he seems naive and vapid. She is polite with him and marvels at his seemingly superhuman ability to be, at all times, cordial, mature, self-effacing, and painfully polite. He is responsible in situations that encourage recklessness. He is thoughtful even with those who slight him. Further exemplifying the turn away from literary self-consciousness, Franzen's Walter exhibits an aversion to unnecessary wordplay, which wry frenemy Richard likes to point out: "Admittedly not a perfect analogy" (144), "All right, so it's a dumb analogy" (145), "Already a problem with that analogy, of course" (382). To Richard, language is theater: an opportunistic playground in which to distort, obscure, and abuse meaning. To Walter, language is unifying: a means to connect, be honest, and do good. This is not to say that Franzen or Walter are unsophisticated literalists. On the contrary, Franzen uses irony, self-consciousness, and experimentation sparingly. Put another way, we might note Christopher Donovan's observation that, in contemporary, post-postmodern fiction, "the narrative audience, the narrative ironist, is willing to embrace relativism so long as the story is accessibly told, credible within its circle of logic; so long as the story remains a story, unreconstructed" (10).

In *Freedom,* Richard's mocking detachment leads him to be an out of touch has-been, bewildered by post-9/11 life and even in his fifties dressing "like a late seventies twenty-year old," while Walter capitalizes on his earnestness and focuses on areas where he *can* effect change (535). In middle age, it becomes clear that Walter is comfortable with himself, while Richard continues to engage in contortion and posturing.

Conclusion

Walter, in NYC for a meeting, is accompanied by Lalitha, his attractive assistant whom Richard suspects Walter used to lure him into meeting in the first place (207-08). While in the years following their college graduation Richard was always the reckless Lothario and Walter the hapless prude, the dynamic has changed. Richard notes this immediately: "As Walter rose from the table to embrace Katz, the girl's eyes remained fixed on Walter; and this was indeed a weird twist for the universe to have taken. Never before had Katz seen Walter in studly mode, turning a pretty head" (208). The change has occurred, of course, because Walter, always willing to have principles and act on them, has in middle age dedicated himself, with increasing success, to environmentalist and conservationist causes. Richard, on the other hand, has constantly lacked any convictions beyond self-gratification. Thus, the gamble at the heart of *Freedom* is clear: in the long-run in American life, good-naturedness and an earnest willingness to care about an ideal higher than the self outlasts and outperforms a selfish, snide preoccupation with artifice and indulgence, and an unwillingness to be vulnerable enough to care. Narcisi points out that Richard has such disdain for normativity that he does not fit in with either Walter and Patty's domestic do-goodery or his bandmate's constant counter-cultural debauchery (84). Franzen makes it clear: Richard is a performative, anachronistic outsider not to be envied.

While literary postmodernism may appear to offer enormous freedom to express, contort, comment, and otherwise represent, as well as freedom from rules and convention, it is ultimately unfulfilling. Conversely, Walter persists as a beacon of optimistic, occasionally naive, do-goodery whose quaint earnestness Franzen provides not as nostalgia or escapism but rather as a worldview urgently necessary for the twenty-first century. When James Wood describes Franzen's *The Corrections*, a proto-new sincerity text, as "an essentially dark book that stays in the memory as warm and comic," he describes the balancing act of movement that must depict the troubles of twenty-first century life while also renewing the tone and style through which they are expressed. Franzen himself notes that part of the inspiration of the title has to do with his desire to make "a correction towards more traditional and humane motives for a novel" ("Interview"). Framed in these terms, the new sincerity is a corrective and literary postmodernism is an aberration, unsustainable and temporary.

Though Franzen was intrigued by the brainy panache of the postmodernists, and seduced by the apparent academic consensus about their urgent importance, he notes that, with the exception of DeLillo's novels, he didn't actually *like* the fiction they wrote. While he appreciated the *idea* of the sardonic, all-critiquing, thousand-page Systems novel—indeed, he was working on his own "ridiculous, overplotted monster" (*Paris Review* 68)—and craved the "academic and hipster respect" that such novels garnered, he preferred the reading experience of classically constructed, character-driven fiction ("Mr. Difficult" 103). "Bellow and Beatie, not to mention Dickens and Conrad and Brontë and Dostoyevsky and Christina Stead, were the writers I actually, unhiply enjoyed reading," says Franzen (103). These authors fill their novels with robust, vividly-drawn, relatable characters and emplot them in formally traditional realist stories that take place at the recognizable intersection of the personal and the social.[8] Postmodern literature "wasn't supposed to be about sympathetic characters," notes Franzen. "Characters, properly speaking, weren't even supposed to exist. Characters were feeble, suspect constructs, like the author himself, like the human soul. Nevertheless, to my shame, I seemed to need them" (103). Indeed, Franzen not only "needs" characters, but goes to great lengths to build them, and, through them, to allegorize key aspects of twenty-first century American life.

Notes

1. Franzen's pivot to address 9/11 is most evident in the juxtaposition between "My Father's Brain," a personal history about his father Earl Franzen's experience with Alzheimer's disease, published one day before the attacks in the September 10, 2001, issue of *The New Yorker* and Franzen's contribution to "Tuesday, and After: *New Yorker* Writers Respond to 9/11," a collection of short essays published one week later on September 16, 2001.

2. According to the *Oxford English Dictionary*, "sincerity" means "the character, quality, or state of being sincere." Sincerity, the definition continues, also means "freedom from falsification, adulteration, or alloy" and "freedom from dissimulation or duplicity."

3. See also Sunyoung Ahn's "New Sincerity, New Worldliness: The Post-9/11 Fiction of Don DeLillo and David Foster Wallace," Mitchell Aboulafia's "Voices and Selves: Beyond the Modern-Postmodern Divide," and Matthew Balliro's *The New Sincerity in American Literature* (2018).

4. I applaud Mahon's keen emphasis on Patty, especially since, admittedly, more has been written about Walter and Richard than Patty, but I disagree that Patty and Joey are the "most psychologically complex of *Freedom*'s characters" (96). Yes, fully a third (the second and fourth sections of the novel's five parts) of the novel is a framed narrative entitled, "Mistakes Were Made: Autobiography of Patty Berglund (Composed at her Therapist's Suggestion)," but Walter and Richard are depicted with just as much psychological complexity. Indeed, Patty's autobiography is often *about them*, rather than herself. I read Patty as a character who exists largely in the orbit of Walter and Richard, and someone who is often an audience to their drama.

5. See *I'm Ok—You're Ok* (1967) by Thomas A. Harris.

6. This sentence, which seems to warrant a "[sic]" due to the odd syntax and punctuation, is transcribed correctly.

7. For more on the interplay between the new sincerity and camp, see Jon Pareles's 2005 *New York Times* article "Sincerity Swathed in Camp."

8. Of all of the canonical Realist authors mentioned by Franzen, McEwan, and Delillo in essays, interviews, and fiction, perhaps the most compelling is Leo Tolstoy, whose novels are mentioned in both *Freedom* and *Saturday*. For more Franzen and Tolstoy, see "Life, Liberty, Happiness, and Jonathan Franzen's *Freedom*" by Camilla Nelson and "Going to Bed with Tolstoy: Jonathan Franzen and the Moral Consequences of Reading (And Writing)" by Charles Pastoor. Reviews that parallel Franzen and Tolstoy include "It's Not Tolstoy, But It Does Belong to High Literature" by Wood and "Peace and War" by Tanenhaus.

Works Cited

Burn, Stephen J. *Jonathan Franzen at the End of Postmodernism.* Continuum, 2008.

Donovan, Christopher. *Postmodern Counternarratives: Irony and Audience in the Novels of Paul Auster, Don DeLillo, Charles Johnson, and Tim O'Brien.* Routledge, 2005.

Franzen, Jonathan. *Freedom*. FSG, 2010.

———. "The Art of Fiction No. 207." Interview by Stephen J. Burn. *The Paris Review*, no. 195, Winter 2010.

———. "Interview: Jonathan Franzen." Interview by Donald Antrim. *Bomb*, 1 Oct. 2001, bombmagazine.org/articles/2001/10/01/jonathan-franzen/.

———. "Mr. Difficult: William Gaddis and the Problem of Hard-to-Read Books." *The New Yorker*, 30 Sept. 2002.

———. "Perchance to Dream: In the Age of Images, a Reason to Write Novels." *Harper's*, April 1996, pp. 35-54.

Hensley, Nathan K. "Allegories of the Contemporary." *The Contemporary Novel: Imagining the Twenty-First Century*, a special issue of *NOVEL: A Forum on Fiction*, vol. 45, no. 2, Summer 2012, pp. 276-300.

Hidalga, Jesús Blanco. *Jonathan Franzen and the Romance of Community*. Bloomsbury, 2017.

Mahon, Áine. "Achieving Their Country: Richard Rorty and Jonathan Franzen." *Philosophy and Literature*, vol. 38, April 2014, pp. 90-109.

Narcisi, Lara. "'At least This Is an Actual Place': The Places and Displacements of *Freedom*." *Journal of the Midwest Modern Language Association*, vol. 48, no. 1, Spring 2015, pp. 67-95.

"Sincerity." *OED Online*, Oxford University Press, March 2023, www.oed.com/view/Entry/180056.

Tanenhaus, Sam. "Peace and War." *The New York Times*, 19 Aug. 2010.

Voelz, Johannes. "The New Sincerity as Literary Hospitality." *Security and Hospitality in Literature and Culture: Modern and Contemporary Perspectives*, edited by Jeffrey Clapp and Emily Ridge, Routledge, 2016, pp. 209–226.

Wallace, David Foster. "E Unibus Pluram: Television and U.S. Fiction." *Review of Contemporary Fiction*, vol. 13, no. 2, Summer 1993, pp. 151-194.

Peter Krause, Ph.D., is Assistant Director and Career Advisor in the Center for Professional Development at Dartmouth College, where he specializes in working with students who are studying the humanities. Peter received his Ph.D. from Fordham University. His most recent work,

"'The Card Games Ended After the Towers Fell'—The Post-9/11 Transatlantic Novel: From Postmodernism to the New Sincerity," can be found on ProQuest. Peter's published work can also be found in the *Journal of Comparative Literature and Aesthetics*, *World Literature Today*, *Script & Print*, *Veritas*, *The Missing Slate*, and *Medieval & Renaissance Drama in England*. He has delivered talks about contemporary literature, the literature of war, and professional issues related to the humanities in the U.S., Canada, France, Australia, and Portugal. As of this writing, Peter lives in the Hanover, New Hampshire, area with his wife, Julia, son, Maxime, and dog, Obi.

"The Time for Expeditions was Over":
Infectious Collaborations, Multispecies Justice, and Troubled Freedoms in Jeff VanderMeer's *Southern Reach Trilogy*

Ashasmiti Das

> "You just go on telling how the mammoth fell on Boob and how Cain fell on Abel and how the bomb fell on Nagasaki and how the burning jelly fell on the villagers and how the missiles will fall on the Evil Empire, and all the other steps in the Ascent of Man."
>
> —Ursula K. Le Guin
> "The Carrier Bag Theory
> of Fiction" (1986)

> "Plants can destabilize, exceed, or bypass our limited human faculties and our efforts at world-making rather than necessarily upgrading or augmenting these efforts."
>
> — Natania Meeker
> & Antonia Szabari
> *Radical Botany* (2019)

Vegetal Adventures: A Gathering of Freedoms

The conquering hero, the pioneer, or the intrepid explorer needs an object of triumph, something that functions as a discrete object of inquiry, or as a surface for the inscription of meaning and as a resource for relentless instrumentalization and exploitation. He, for he is invariably male and white, has through careful application lifted himself from the state of brute nature. He is the figure of freedom and progress and is entrusted with the stewardship of the world. He levels the towering, omniscient gaze of Enlightenment Reasoning and reduces landscapes to placid, immobilized background/empty space/*terra nullius* without histories, peoples, and/or multispecies ecologies. Terraforming, or the organization of lively, vibrant, messy lifeworlds into landscapes that are controlled and ordered in the pursuit of profit, has had devastating and uneven consequences. Fears about the resurgence of "nature" and the categories and identities forced into synonymy with it resurrect the purificatory logic of binaries and disclose the anthropocentric conceptualization of freedom in terms that are oppositional to nature.

Tracking, threading, and weaving through Ursula Le Guin's thoughts on the form of our cultural narratives ("The Carrier Bag Theory of Fiction" 1989), I turn towards Jeff VanderMeer's *Southern Reach Trilogy* (2014) as an alter-storytelling and worlding practice that strays from the imperatives of narratives about the individual hero and his tale of action or quest to kill the monster and return with a bounty. It is an unfitting, ongoing, disruptive tale of adventure in which, as Donna Haraway details in *Staying with the Trouble* (2016), plants, people, animals, and soil do not figure as mere "props, ground, plot space, or prey"; they are not simply there "to be in the way, to be overcome, to be the road, the conduit" (39). Instead, the vegetal rears its tendrilous head, and the landscape surges and swerves, regurgitating grotesque aberrations, commingled bodies, strange hybrids, and complex spatiotemporal organizations beyond human comprehension, will, intention, and design. The vegetal colonizes and displaces the human as the only important actor in more-than-human worlds, unravels the definitive mappings of species boundaries, and demonstrates the enmeshment of landscapes and bodies.

Conditions for the notion of "universal human freedom" are derived from and dependent upon long histories of imperialism, settler colonialism, contract labor, and slavery. Freedom embedded in anthropocentric logic is tethered to the idea of bounded individualism, sovereignty, and development, and more likely than not, in economic development. The adventure tale affirms these concentric narratives of progress, heroism, freedom, dignity, and the quest for knowledge and transcendent truth. Generally, what is at stake and what is continuously restored in such tales are suppositions about the liberal human subject, notions of purity and boundaries, and correlates like "truth," "facts," "disembodied vision," and "objectivity," through which the concept of empirical reality is concretized. But the question is what happens to this ideal and universal concept of freedom when our inherited starting points and confident epistemologies are no longer tenable? What constellations of thought circulate around and refigure freedom when the entanglements of ethics-knowing-being can no longer be overlooked?

In *Another Freedom* (2010), Svetlana Boym recuperates the ludic play at the heart of freedom by addressing it as "co-creation," a worldly entanglement that requires response and response-ability towards indeterminate and unpredictable others. Freedom in this sense is an adventure involving an encounter with "the incalculable that forces us to change life's calculus" and disrupts the self-evident truths of Western metaphysics (6). Instead of the heroic, combative tale of weapons, tools, and words, the *Southern Reach Trilogy* (2014) offers messy tales of encounters, contaminations, symbiotic relations, and becoming-with.

These tales trouble the contours of freedom as well as those of bodies, subjectivities, and relations. I argue that the monstrous vegetal within the trilogy disperses and scatters freedom beyond notions of estrangement, individual agency, and sovereignty. In time and space out of joint, freedom is an emergent gathering only possible under conditions of infections, contaminations, and border crossings.

The vegetal irrupts into visibility only in "monstrous" figurations that exploit the Darwinian apprehensions of common organic descent and the extant weird homologies between plant and human life. The devaluation of vegetal life in the Great Chain of Being as non-sentient, insensate, unintelligent, and sessile is contiguous with the banishment of other non-human forms of life from the exclusionary logic structuring anthropocentric thought. Vegetal exuberance and unruliness often refuse to be contained by or adhere to anthropocentric optics and ethics and Enlightenment ways of classifying the world.[1] Plants do not confirm or conform to human desires, ethics, and conceptualities. Furthermore, they resist apprehension as merely passive and inert materiality, or receptacle and resource for human manipulation and instrumentalization. The figure of the monstrous, category-defying plant condenses and encodes this strange fear and anxiety launched by the peculiarities of vegetal life in general.

In the Wake of the Monstrous Vegetal

Vegetal life is lively and complex: it moves, proliferates uncontrollably with no apparent purpose, engages in complex chemo-signaling, refuses incorporation into human conceptualities and frameworks of desire, interiority, intent and purpose, orientation, and demonstrates an openness to the external environment. It signals thick interimplications and strange intimacies, kinship, entanglement, and a "radical collectivity" (Houle

111) that cannot be subsumed into the cultural imaginary of liberal humanism and its tenets of autonomy and sovereignty. Through their temporalities, complex morphologies, and underground spatiality, they embody alterbiologies, or radically different ways of being in the world. Plants thus perceived as immutably weird are not afforded the same acknowledgment, subjecthood, and affinity that we are only now beginning to acknowledge with respect to animals. Indeed, plants and their varied capacities for movement and their propensities for collaborative living and communication are often disregarded in favor of their instrumentalization for human purposes. Given the anthropocentric biases governing our perception and understanding of plant life, literature has more or less unassumingly adopted identical frames for depicting vegetality as a placid and inscrutable landscape or backdrop and/or as poetic metaphors, symbols, and correlatives for human feelings, memories, and thoughts.

This radical weirdness and alterity of vegetal life has been speculatively engaged with in a plethora of weird fiction and speculative fiction, both new and old. Vegetal and fungal bodies (though not collapsible categories, as there are significant differences in the modalities of their living) are non-individuated, decentralized bodies, displaying forms of hybridity and permeability that deconstruct the normative, liberal humanist notions of self, bounded individualism, and embodiment. Liberated from the limitations of realist fiction and its reliance on notions of human exceptionalism and mastery, speculative fiction has often articulated the anxieties surrounding speciestic discourses and anthropocentric thought with its depictions of monstrous cross-species transformations and corporeal entanglements. Consequently, apart from a myriad of lively, nonhuman animals, organic and inorganic beings, monstrous plants have also been a persistent presence in speculative fiction.

Particularly, weird fiction as a genre, mode, or aesthetic has articulated the anxieties surrounding speciestic discourses and human sovereignty with its depictions of cross-species transformations and corporeal entanglements. The qualifying criteria of the weird[2] seems to be a deep preoccupation with exploring that which inhabits the limits of human identification and knowledge as well as with exposing the gaps and inadequacies of our conceptual frameworks.[3] Consequently, apart from a myriad of nonhuman animals and organic and inorganic beings, plants have also been a persistent presence in imaginings of the weird since the early twentieth century. Earlier writers of the weird engaging in transformative encounters with vegetal life include Algernon Blackwood ("The Willow" 1907), Luigi Ugolini ("The Vegetable Man" 1917), Clark Ashton Smith ("The Seed from Sepulchre" 1933), Roger Wulfres ("The Air-Plant Men" 1930), John Wyndham (*The Day of the Triffids* 1951), Donald Wandrei ("Strange Harvest" 1953), and Kathe Koja ("The Neglected Garden" 1991), to name a few.

Discussion of the Literature

Scholars of the burgeoning field of plant studies point out the impasse that vegetality portends to human attempts at imagining, comprehending, and interpreting vegetal life and plant-human interactions. While this gap is generative of human thought and practice and associated with a "speculative excess" (Meeker and Szabari 3), it also indicates a failure to read and experience vegetality outside of the structuring rules of desire, language, mortality, interiority, and intent.[4] Meeker and Szabari (*Radical Botany: Plants and Speculative Fiction* 2020) are not alone in pointing out the generative possibilities of the encounter with the vegetal monstrous. Plants, they posit, "compel us to imagine an ingeniously animated and animating matter that we are never able to observe in all its operations" (2). Plant life cycles and queer temporalities in particular recall to human minds the vegetal beginnings and potential vegetal endings of the planet, all the while hinting at the fearful ontological proximity between "human" and plants. Therefore, the vegetal monstrous in fiction can bring to relief the "plant-ness" that composes us and resist its instrumentalization or conversion into etherized objects of knowledge. Meeker and Szabari do not correlate vegetative imaginary and fictions pertaining to the vegetal monstrous to evolutionary anxieties alone. They track the vegetal in the pre-romantic, materialist fascination with plant life across the nineteenth, twentieth, and twenty-first centuries.

This stands in obvious contrast to T. S. Miller's ("Lives of the Monster Plants: The Revenge of the Vegetable in the Age of Animal Studies" 2012) slightly simplistic reading of plant horror as symptomatic of anxieties surrounding Darwinian theories of evolution, enmeshment, and shared stories of descent. In *Plant Horror: Approaches to the Monstrous Vegetal in Fiction and Film* (2016), Dawn Keetley advances her argument about fictions and films dealing with figurations of the vegetal monstrous by connecting their destabilizing force to their acknowledgment of the constitutive and so-far forgotten vegetal in the human. She aligns herself with Michael Marder (*Plant Thinking: A Philosophy of Vegetal Life* 2013) and observes that plants, through their ways of being, strike at and unravel the foundations of human subjectivity and metaphysics.[5] The radical otherness and incomprehensibility of vegetal matter foreclose and preempt possibilities of feeling affinity and enacting kinships with plants or even acknowledging that plant life could have its own distinct subjectivity. A vegetal consideration and vegetal thinking stand to transform anthropocentric optics and ethics and offer new ways of theorizing embodiment, intimacy, and kinship. But its more propulsive force seems to be its ability to enable a reconceptualization of life as matter, processual and dynamic, and existing across the divides of living and non-living, organic and inorganic, growth and decay, life and death. The implications of thinking so are terrific: standard discourses of life, species, and identity become untenable in this enfolding of bodies within other bodies and materials. The persistence of the vegetal in the human accentuates and draws attention to our shared histories, co-evolutions, and dependencies while forwarding alternative theories of body ecologies, of bodies as open-ended, dynamic, situated, and historical systems.[6]

Freedom and Boundary-Crossings: Thinking through Porosities and Vegetal Body-Ecologies in *Annihilation, Authority* and *Acceptance*

Jeff VanderMeer's *Southern Reach Trilogy* productively engages with the ramifications, challenges, and adaptations required for living through the porosities and blurred boundaries between life and nonlife, self and other, human and nonhuman, organic and inorganic in the Anthropocene. The trilogy stages a series of vegetal and fungal encounters and transformations through which the body opens up, is of, and is in the environment. The novels contend with the ingestions, inhalations, and epidermal perforations that enable sympoietic, generative, and/or uncomfortable, hurtful, and unwanted relatings, transits, and exchanges between strangers. VanderMeer treads around the contours of his monsters and their monstrous intimacies to work out the consequences of thinking material agency. The texts reinscribe a number of Posthumanist themes and concerns that I shall be dealing with in this chapter, shortly: bodies as fluid and emergent through encounters, an agential account of matter, a doing away with anthropocentric notions of human exceptionalism, and an emergent ethics of entanglement and enmeshment with human and nonhuman others.

At the start of the first book of the trilogy, *Annihilation*, we are introduced to Area X as a mysterious wilderness that staggers human efforts at deciphering, interpreting, and decoding through its sheer opacity and material recalcitrance. The attempts to create a homogeneous, master narrative of origins for Area X persists throughout the trilogy in various forms. In *Annihilation*, the narrative still mobilizes the nature/culture divide to propel a myth of a prelapsarian, pristine wilderness that originated as an environmental catastrophe triggered by a military experiment. Area X appears as a "pristine," undifferentiated wilderness, an undulating landscape instead of a network/mesh of relations, entanglements, intra-actions, and distinct ecologies, an obvious instance of plant-blindness that sabotages the expedition from the start. Area X monstrates by coming into undeniable prominence with its indeterminate morphology and plasticity, relentless mutations, and the incorporation of its surroundings. With their deindividuated appearance as networks, labyrinthine underground mycorrhizal connections, complex spatiotemporal organizations, and the simultaneous inhabitation of the dual zones of earth and air (Houle 106), the vegetal monstrous fractures our conventional perception of reality.

Area X grows and materializes the "intra-actions" (as Karen Barad would say), the transits, and sympoetic exchanges taking place between and across bodies. "What strange matter mixes and mingles?" the Biologist asks (*Annihilation* 192). Area X mixes genetic matter on a cellular level and carries out processes of biomimicry and camouflage. It transforms the materiality it encounters in unpredictable and unregulated ways and spews out organisms that exceed their material and conceptual limits. The vegetal exuberance and relentless diversity of these organisms eschew the containing logic of species boundaries and biological classifications that generally preclude recognition and acknowledgment of relationalities and entanglements.

The exact nature of Area X is never defined and it is only known through its effects and material consequences. Nonetheless, Allen Whitby, a Southern Reach employee, offers a provisional definition of Area X in terms that are contiguous with the vegetal mode of existence: as a "machine or creature or some combination of both that can manipulate molecules, that can store energy where it will, that can hide the bulk of its intent and machinations from us" (*Acceptance* 310-11). Area X's approximation of the tentacular, invasive, purposeless growth of the botanical tendril also functions in the unyielding gaze and regard in (and of) Area X. Despite its resolute and implacable rootedness, the vegetality of Area X moves and grows in unprecedented ways, failing to adhere to anthropocentric regimes of classification and order. This recalls Michael Marder's elaboration on the kinds of movements that vegetal matter engages with, particularly through changing its state through growth, proliferation, and decay (20). Within the trilogy, vegetation colonizes, consumes, and transforms humans, and this infiltration has nothing to do with intent, agency, or intelligence defined in anthropocentric terms. Its growth knows no limit, end, moderation, and purpose and is recognizably monstrous.

The vegetal permeates, pervades, and punctures through innocuous ways, leading to the disintegration of those qualities believed to be essentially human. As the human dissolves into the milieu and becomes the milieu itself, it is no longer possible to deny our embedded and embodied reality. Given our inextricable entanglements and exchanges with the material world, it is not surprising that VanderMeer uses the processes of touch, inhalation, and ingestion to suggest the endless ways in which bodies commune, communicate, and interact. The Biologist's contamination through inhalation of the fungal spores is only one of such trans-species entanglements. Underlying Control's apocalyptic vision of Area X moving and absorbing "building, roads, lakes, valleys, airport. Everything" (*Authority* 308) is the fear of the vegetal subsumption, as Keetley reminds us, "not [of] what's in its path, exactly, since it has no path, but what lies in its field, which is everywhere" (15). Area X is moving in imperceptible ways: changing its state, invading, and decaying. Furthermore, Area X seems to be consistent with the modular structure of vegetal life where essential functions are not organized around discrete organs but distributed throughout. It thus refuses to ratify our questions and concerns regarding both teleology and functionality, principles through which Western metaphysics dissects the question of Being.

Proliferating across the sprawling, involuted, hybrid, and lively network that constitutes (and is of) Area X are monstrous, metamorphic, and undifferentiated bodies in varying stages of composition, decomposition, and recomposition. These are Haraway's "Chthonic ones" that inhabit "all sorts of temporalities and materialities…[and] are not safe… [but] writhe and luxuriate in manifold forms in all the airs, waters, and places of earth" (*Staying with the Trouble* 2). This motley group of organisms demonstrates continuity and inseparability from vegetal matter on morphological and/or genetic levels and includes organisms with monstrous morphic possibilities such as the mangy, commingled hog-slug-vegetal hybrid, the glinting and glittering plant-mirror creature (that infects Saul Evans), the plant-fungal symbiotic assemblage constituting the infectious sprawl in the Tower walls, etc.

Vegetal Freedoms: Troubling History, Causality, Agency in *Annihilation, Authority,* and *Acceptance*

Area X materializes the complex spatial-temporal dimension of the monstrous vegetal by carrying out inexplicable distortions of time and space. Although the trilogy does not engage with these themes extensively, it sporadically drops hints regarding such unusual spatial and temporal conceptions. The existence of Proto-Area X (christened thus by the Biologist), the last will and testament of the Biologist, and its recorded history spanning thirty years, the startling information that Gloria, the former Southern Reach Director, has lived in Area X for three years when out there in the "real" world only a couple of months have passed, as well as the accelerated rates of decay noted by several expedition members, all seem to imply that time operates a little differently in Area X. Area X disperses and scatters homogeneous, abstract time, i.e. time as singular and determinate—linear, progressive time associated with colonialism and capitalism. It offers a counter to Eurocentric progress narratives and works against the regulatory schema of a universal clock time by attending to a multiplicity of corporeal temporalities.

However, at the end of the day, human perception and vision as experienced by the expedition members, continue to be hauntingly limited by the questions of "whoever or whatever had created that pristine bubble" (*Authority* 37). In fact, the hypnotic conditioning that all the members of the expedition go through as part of their training as well as the paradigmatic inhibitions of their profession result in a series of occlusions. It ensures that the normative accounts of individual bodies and sovereign selves contained within the boundary of the skin prosper at the cost of an ethics of entanglement.

Ghost Bird, after having read the testimonies of the Biologist, Control, and Grace, is convinced that the idea of causality not only misunderstands and misconstrues but is also inadequate for understanding Area X: "idea of causality, of purpose as that word might be recognizable to the Southern Reach. But what if you discover that the price of purpose is to render invisible so many things?" (*Acceptance* 157). Ghost Bird's revelations stand in stark contrast to Control, who still seeks to cast Area X in a tale of revenge which is perhaps a more humanly comprehensible, intelligible, and certainly less upsetting story. Compared to his fears of Area X and its goals of destroying mankind, Ghost Bird redirects her attention to the entanglements, intra-actions, and contaminations that it makes possible by suggesting that: "organisms can have a purpose and yet also make patterns that have little to do with that purpose" (189). The narrative never definitively settles the questions of agency and intent and seems to scuttle that distinction altogether by delivering a number of origin stories that are partial, inconclusive, and situated.

Though formally Saul Evans's narrative frames the conclusion, chronologically it is the "first" (if there can be only one) account of contact and infection. Upon witnessing a shimmering, glinting thing among the vegetal bodies on his lawn, his interest is piqued, and he reaches out to touch it. The confidence of his actions gives away his security in the idea of his own containment, something which receives a rude awakening:

> *Whatever it was*, it was delicate beyond measure, yet perversely *reminded him* of the four-ton lens far above his head… But *whatever it was*, it swirled and glinted and eluded his rough grasp, and he began to feel faint… He felt a sliver enter his thumb. There was no pain, only a pressure and then numbness… Nothing now glittered on the ground in front of him. No light at the base of the plant. No pain in his thumb. (*Acceptance* 24-25; emphasis added)

This moment of infection is defined through a confused succession of associations and a mushrooming of sensations related to epidermal porosities and perforations. The lighthouse keeper is unable to place the shimmer or the glint within taxonomic categories. Neither are we allowed to learn if his transformation has begun, if part of the infection is being unable to detect its process. It may well be that the infection is enabled by their intra-action and dynamic relationality. As his senses are scrambled, he is unable to categorically define his experience as "real." Although there is no obvious link between the glint and the glass from the lighthouse beacon, he is reminded of it, as something of the diffractive interference and non-local nature of the lighthouse beacon's lens suggests/symbolizes/embodies the nonlocal, entangled, enmeshed nature of all life within Area X.

Indeed, the Biologist's own contamination and large-scale symbiogenesis with Area X reveals how agency is enacted only in and through dynamic relations and intra-actions. She is the landscape even as she moves through it and clearly comprehends that matters of biological classifications and taxonomic divisions impede certain kinds of relations. With her transformation, she abandons the arrogance of unknotting and resolving the problem of grasping Area X in its totality and observes that her own attempts were "incomplete, inexact, inaccurate, useless" as Area X is always "changing, becoming different than before" due to its porosities, and as a result of entangled intra-actions (192).

It is to his credit that VanderMeer does not resurrect biology as static, deterministic, and eternal but as changeable and adaptive.[7] He imagines vegetality as material, non-anthropomorphic, and vibrant without a transcendent principle of will, desire, intent, spirit, or personality. Within the bounds of this trilogy, he accelerates and intensifies the adaptive learning of vegetal matter that remains imperceptible to the anthropocentric gaze. Even though plants (and even fungi for that matter) learn from and adapt to the environment they are exposed to, this is routinely obscured through the imaginary of a static, fixed, and unchanging nature. But plants do acquire behavioral characteristics that can eventually become an evolutionary trait of the species through the process of genetic assimilation, as is evident in the trilogy.

At the end of *Acceptance*, the last book of the trilogy, Ghost Bird provides us with what can be considered the final version of the story of Area X's origin. As far as origin stories go, neither of the narratives we have so far claim to have arrived at a comprehensive understanding of Area X. Like a snake eating its own tail, the origin story eradicates the need for one; instead of attributing intelligence, cause, and agency to an event or actor, the narrative conducts a series of displacements through a network of enabling and disabling relations:

THE TIME FOR EXPEDITIONS...

> She *saw* or *felt*, deep within, the cataclysm like a rain of comets that had annihilated an entire biosphere remote from Earth. Witnessed how one made organism had fragmented and dispersed, each minute part undertaking a long and perilous passage through spaces between, black and formless, punctuated by sudden light as they come to rest, scattered and lost—emerging only to be buried, inert, in the glass of a lighthouse lens. And how, when brought out of dormancy, the wire tripped, how it had, best as it could, regenerated, begun to perform a vast and preordained function, one compromised by time and context, by the terrible truth that the species that had given Area X its purpose was gone. (286-87)

Clearly, the passage indicates an extra-terrestrial event, a catastrophe that destroyed an alien biosphere and somehow ended up being embedded in the lighthouse lens. The rapid shifts between active and passive voice do nothing to dispel the confusion about Area X and where it came from. What catalyzed the destruction of the biosphere? Who or what fragmented the "made" organism referred to in the passage? Does "made" insinuate a divine or an extraterrestrial presence, and if the term is applicable to all life in the sense that we are all made through our continuous exposure to the environment, what weight does the word hold? Was there some design, purpose, or intention around the fact that it comes to rest where the lighthouse keeper will finally touch it? The narrative does not have answers to any of these questions.

What is clear is its insistence on the dynamic relationality through which a kind of chain reaction is initiated. Probably the most telling statement is the revelation that "the species that had given Area X its purpose was gone" and in light of this, the identified "vast and preordained function" is rendered meaningless. Therefore, there is no cause behind the development of Area

X, no direction or intent behind its proliferation and development: i.e., nothing that can be rendered in accordance with humanist models of agency and actors.

Freedom and the Sensorium: Making Monstrous Knowledge in Area X

Through its imagining of human encounters with the monstrous vegetal, the *Southern Reach Trilogy* offers new scientific imaginaries. To read knowledge-making as embodied, fleshly, sensuous work, I shall use Haraway's concept of "situated knowledge" and Karen Barad's "intra-action." It is not only the human observer, subject, or experimenter who sees, knows, and intervenes, but there is what Barad calls "intra-touching." Any properties discerned are only emergent features resulting from the entanglement of subject and object. Therefore, any attempt to see the monster cannot be complete or exhaustive, as these entanglements are unfinished and relentless. To this end, I argue that the monster never stops showing and calls for a response of vulnerability and care.

Recalling her encounter with a strange species of starfish, the Biologist offers an invective against the demands of scientific rationality and disembodied vision. This passage comes in the wake of her recognition that any attempt to fix Area X in knowledge was futile, impossible, and almost ludicrous, given the fact that "[her] instruments are useless, [her] methodology broken, [her] motivations selfish" (192). Paying attention is no longer perceived as an epistemic act but rather as a process of attending to the ongoing divergent, wayward, heterogeneous world-making projects carried out by Area X and in which she is implicated. The Biologist's reflection on this experience provides some insight into the monster's disruption of the known regimes of truth and ways of organizing the world:

the longer I stared at it, the less comprehensible the creature became... There was something about my mood and its dark glow that *eclipsed sense*, that made me see this creature, *which had been assigned a place in the taxonomy-catalogued, studied, and described—irreducible to any of that.* (175; emphasis added)

There are and can only be partial ways of organizing the world, and these involve the breakdown of the traditional distinction between subject-object. The object is conceived as participating in its own production of knowledge instead of as a discrete, transcendent subject of study. The Biologist slowly develops acts of noticing and attunement that rely on her exposure and vulnerability to the world she is embedded in, a kind of knowledge practice that shares accountability for the myriad ways in which beings make and unmake each other: "I saw each drop fall as a perfect, faceted liquid diamond... The wind was like something alive; it entered every pore of me" (74). I call such knowledge-making "monstrous," as embodied and partial forms of knowing do not fix the monster in its knowledge. Instead, it revels in the excess of the monster that can only be felt. Situated knowledge emerging from direct material engagement with the world is fluid and metamorphous.

The Biologist is forced to reckon with the remains or residues of her encounter with the monstrous Crawler. She eventually concludes that her instruments, the very scales of her perception and comprehension, were inadequate and could not arrest and extricate the monster from its ongoing configurations. The expedition team is tasked with rendering Area X comprehensible and intelligible within human frameworks of meaning and perception. The leveling anthropocentric gaze of the scientific expedition characterizes Area X as a stage for unfathomable and sinister vegetal entanglements. This is a sinister echo of colonial endeavors to control new lands through epistemological and mapping exercises.

The Biologist meditates upon this at the start of the quest and wonders whether "the map had been the first form of misdirection, for what was a map but a way of emphasizing some things and making other things invisible?" (*Annihilation* 6). Indeed, intentionality is integral to the quest for determining and fixing Area X in knowledge. The members of the commission are not named but are identified by their professions (the Psychologist, the Anthropologist, the Surveyor, and the Biologist), indicating the anthropocentric segmentation of thought at the heart of scientific inquiry. It discloses the extractivist logic compelling the scientific efforts to attribute an intent, will, and purpose to the incessant vegetative growth and proliferation of Area X. Deliberating on its ontological status, Ghost Bird finally relinquishes definitives and determinisms, admitting that "Area X was all around them; Area X was contained in no one place or figure" (283).

The trilogy underscores the sentient and agential properties of vegetal matter, particularly in the presentation of Area X as a material entity that "knows what to do with molecules and membranes, can peer through things, can surveil, and then withdraw" (81). Originally, the Biologist experiences Area X as a pristine, natural, untroubled, pure, unpenetrated wilderness, but she is soon forced to reckon with how the "stuff of matter generates, composes, transforms, and decomposes" (Alaimo 25).[8] Stacy Alaimo's redrawing of the material into the conversation about bodies, a reconsideration of the body as embedded in and exposed continuously to the environment, is germane to this discussion. Her concept of "trans-corporeality" situates the body back into its thick network of relations with toxic and non-toxic substances and other human and nonhuman organisms (20). The previously bounded, unified, abiological, and discursively constructed subject dissolves into a multiplicity of relations, poly-temporal sympoetic connections, and entanglements, with contamination becoming the order of the day.

The encounters with the monstrous-vegetal in the trilogy contaminate, transgresses, and enact generative and/or destructive connections and entanglements that need to be constantly negotiated for survival and collaboration. Despite their initial predilections, both the Biologist and Control unlearn to read Area X within the reductive dynamic of reclamation of nature by culture or a return to a state of nature before culture. The Biologist, in particular, comes to understand the language of contamination through encounters and remarks: "human beings had so transformed the world... even Area X had not been able to completely reduce those signs and symbols" (*Acceptance* 241). The Biologist realizes that Area X possesses an intelligence that is "far different from our own" with entirely incomprehensible modes of operation (*Annihilation* 126).

Area X intra-acts with, reads, and transforms everything it comes into contact with. Furthermore, Area X surveys and assesses the devices and technologies dispatched and employed by Southern Reach and renders them obsolete and non-functional. This explains the hesitation behind equipping the expedition members with modern technology given Southern Reach's apprehension about Area X's resistance to, transformations of, and manipulations of technology. In the beginning, all the members of the expedition, including the Biologist, exhibit an attachment to and reliance on anthropocentric notions and values of modes and attitudes of knowing, objects of knowledge, values, devices, and measures. Taking for granted the epistemological distance between subject/object, affects/facts, knowledge/world, they are quick to dismiss sightings of trans-species assemblages like the living, breathing Tower, the Crawler, and a bevy of animals with eerily human eyes. The Biologist, like the rest of her team, believes that the objective truth would reveal itself under the gaze of the microscope, that she only needed to document its behavior and affix its place in the taxonomy of things. But the Biologist finds her gathered tools and knowledge inadequate for dealing with the thriving, monstrous Crawler. She is left grappling with metaphors of "refraction" rather than reflection to suggest the ungraspability and un-fixability of its being. Studying a sample of the Crawler's skin under the microscope, she notes:

> At first I didn't know what I was looking at because it was just so unexpected. It was brain tissue—and not just any brain tissue. The cells were remarkably human, with some irregularities. (72)

But the realization that the sample of tissues that had the appearance of human brain tissue had actually been drawn from the exterior unsettles and unmoors her from the epistemology that she had put so much stock in. Despite evidence to the contrary, the Biologist is still guided by the liberal humanist notions of individuality, species identity, and objective neutrality. This leads her to conclude that "neither the Crawler nor Tower was intelligent, in the sense of possessing free will" (92). It is only later when she is not limited by her faculty of vision alone or the trappings of scientific objectivity that she comes to a firmer understanding of the complexities at work: "Perhaps it is a creature living in perfect symbiosis with a host of other creatures. Perhaps it is 'merely' a machine. But in either instance, if it has intelligence, that intelligence is far different from our own" (191).

This shift in perspective occurs after she becomes an unwary participant in a sympoetic assemblage through the inhalation of the spores she encounters in the walls of the Tower. The Biologist's hypnotic conditioning evaporates when she encounters the vegetal-insect-fungi symbiosis in the Tower/Tunnel. The illusion of being inside a structure of stone and coquina gives way to the realization of being enmeshed, entangled, and implicated within a living, breathing, organic being. Initially, the Biologist wonders if the words on the wall are a form of communication and if the words were simply building material without any referential component. The flowering, symbiotic script turns the representational feature of human language on its head, converting it into flesh. These words initiate some kind of "fertilization" via its spores (61). However, no real clarification is provided as to what made the spores explode. The text dithers between suggesting that it "chose that moment to burst open" (which hints at choice, decision, agency) or that the nodule was simply "triggered by a disturbance in the flow of air" when the Biologist leaned in to read the words (44). VanderMeer's decision to avoid this explication is a further move away from narratives of linear causality and of agency as a property to possess.

In *Meeting the Universe Halfway* (2007), Barad offers her own account of the indeterminacy associated with embodied encounters. Phenomena, she writes, "are the ontological inseparability/ entanglement of intra-acting agencies" (139). Instead of a distant subject and a false sense of objectivity, Barad offers a way of reading that disrupts linear and fixed casualties associated with ways of knowing and perception. The spores entering the Biologist produce a mysterious shining that transforms her subjectivity, affects, and perceptions. This openness of bodies to being impacted and affected, usually considered improper to the scientific attitude, exposes her to the infectious proximity of the vegetal monstrous within the texts. The skin functions as an intelligent, meaning-making surface, re-negotiating terms and forms of embodiment. It is where subjectivity and objectivity converge, as the Biologist is transformed by the very thing she is trying to encounter, make knowledge of, and study. It is no longer possible to see either the subject or the object divorced from their relatings, and they become part of an ongoing "intra-activity."

The Biologist registers this dissolution of boundaries, realizing that, "I did not feel as if I were a person but simply a receiving station for a series of overwhelming transmissions" (172). We are thus invited to a reading where both subject and object participate and contribute to valid and effective knowledge. Proximity, touch, and tactility frustrate any attempt at detachment or any attempt at objectivity. The parameters of rational and objective knowledge based on vision can no longer be applied, as the measuring instruments used to collect and record data of Area X return altered. What it measures does not fit into the conceptual maps we have. The observing body that is part of the encounter itself becomes an affordance or an instrument to affectively read what cannot be objectively known. Haptic and affective forms of communication attend to what passes across, within, and between bodies, and these can only be felt but not easily articulated. Instead of total epistemic control, such forms of knowing accept the unknowability of the monster. Therefore, the text articulates a form of feeling as partial knowing instead of total epistemic control of the visual.

Conclusion

In "Photosynthetic Mattering: Rooting in the Planthroposcene" (2016), plant-anthropologist Natasha Myers picks on our anthropocentric plant-blindness to suggest a new, aspirational episteme for collaborative survival in the Anthropocene.[9] This calls for transformation in our forms of representation and epistemologies to better support voluble and voluminous ontologies. VanderMeer's monstrous vegetal defies taxonomic rules and the maps of heroic conquest stories that take the human as their diagnostic and reference point. Instead, they rely on alternate forms of storytelling that can imagine a transversal subjectivity in light of the displacement of traditional demarcations between vegetal/human, organic/inorganic, born/manufactured, and flesh/ metal.

The *Southern Reach Trilogy* does not bandy in celebratory stories of progress and clean, satisfying endings. Turning our back towards the linear narrative of progress, messianic salvation, techno-fixes, and/or despair is to trouble inherited narratives of genealogical and biogenetic kin, security of bodily boundaries, and human exceptionalism. It means attending to the messy, dirty, infectious entanglements of which we are part; there is no getting ahead but only the possibility of collaborative survival through viral encounters. As Ghost Bird points out, there has always only been relentless contingency: "There was nothing to warn anyone about. The world went, even as it fell apart, changed irrevocably, became something strange and different" (*Acceptance* 328).

Notes

1. Thomas Huxley, in his essay "On the Border Territory between the Animal and Vegetable Kingdoms" (1876), called these interstices "no man's land" (177) that were inhabited by category-defying species which threw Linnaean ontological distinctions into crisis. Other fugitive plants, animals, and fungal species existed in the interstices of these kingdoms. These included higher insectivorous and carnivorous plants that exhibited faculties generally attributed to animal life, like powers of predation and even will.

2. The tradition of the weird is integral to Jeff VanderMeer's work and his attention to vegetal and fungal contaminations and entanglements. In his introduction to *The New Weird* (2008), he points out the continued influence of "old weird," "science fiction," "steampunk," "surrealism," "horror," and the "fantastic" on the genre popularly defined as the "new weird" and with which he is closely associated. The weird in its new and old formulations exposes the permeabilities of the human body by depicting it through processes of flux, metamorphosis, composition, and decomposition.

3. This epistemological impasse or withdrawal of an object from human understanding and knowledge has been closely investigated by proponents of speculative realism and object

oriented ontology like Ian Bogost, Graham Harman, Quentin Meillassoux, and Steven Shaviro. Accordingly, this gap between the "reality" of an object and human perceptions of it renders reality itself weird. Michael Marder draws heavily on this ontological turn in his book *Plant-Thinking: A Philosophy of Vegetal Life* (2013) to explain the inaccessibility and unavailability of the vegetal to human attempts at interpretation.

4. Plant biologist Stefan Mancuso and Alessandro Viola (*Brilliant Green: The Surprising History and Science of Plant Intelligence* 2015) read vegetal sensory and adaptive behaviors through paradigms of neurobiology. They arrive at an understanding of vegetal intelligence as distributed and organized around multiple data processing centers (18). But they are still committed to moving plants closer to humans rather than otherwise, thus reinstating consciousness and intelligence as the referential starting points and fundamental qualities of life.

5. Marder, like Keetley, insists upon the sheer inaccessibility of plant life, its obdurate and unyielding materiality, and a persistent withdrawal from attempts at understanding and comprehension. This strand of thought persists in other works like *Thinking with Animals* (2005), where Lorraine Daston and Greg Mittman remark: "Our failure to recognize ourselves in plants leads to an epistemological impasse" (16). This echoes Randy Laist's (*Plants and Literature: Essays in Critical Plant Studies* 2013) appraisal of the problematics of imagining plant life and the difficulties of thinking of vegetality as even animate. It finds its most confident formulation in Meeker and Szabari's *Radical Botany: Plants and Speculative Fiction* (2019), which supports the view that the withdrawal and unavailability of vegetal life to human knowledge launches the need for speculatively engaging with and apprehending vegetal matter.

6. This continuity and inseparability of vegetal matter from "human" histories has found different articulations in recent years. Natasha Myers ("Photosynthetic Mattering: Rooting into the Planthroposcene" 2016) looks at vegetality as complex, world-building, biogeochemical forces that changed the composition of the atmosphere billions of years ago, creating conditions for the survival of aerobic organisms in a process appropriately titled

"Oxygen Catastrophe." Similarly, in "Animal, Vegetal, Mineral: Ethics as Extension or Becoming?" (2011), Karen Houle points out that we are built from the carbon of plants (92) before pondering upon the more complex ways through which plant-ness constitutes us. Michael Marder and Anaïs Tondeur's *The Chernobyl Herbarium: Fragments of an Exploded Consciousness* (2016) uses a series of photograms and text fragments to meditate upon the shared vulnerabilities of plant life and human beings to their environment.

7. In "Bodies and Biology" (1999), Lynda Birke starts a discussion of the biological body as changing continuously and responding to the environment. She references the shedding of skin, the renewability of cells, and bone metabolism or remodeling to illustrate her arguments. For that matter, Haraway ("Situated Knowledge" 1988) too participates in the queering of traditionally perceived nature and biology and does not only work out the implications of hetero-biology but also deliberates on the impossibility of objectivity and neutrality.

8. Alaimo is responding to the bracketing of the social, cultural, psychical, and biological aspects of the body by the purely discursive turn in literary theory and criticism. An emphasis on representations and discourse without attending to the lived realities and corporeal practices ignores the ethical, political, and epistemological entanglements of life. This new materialist turn surfaces in the recent works of Claire Colebrooke, Rosi Braidotti, and Elizabeth Grosz, who modify their definition of life beyond the organic as that which exceeds material and conceptual limits through its force, dynamism, inventiveness, and creativity. Indeed, the question of ontology and ethics is explored extensively by both Karen Barad and Donna Haraway.

9. Her call for a special "planthroposcene" and/or "plant mattering" heralds a recent turn to acknowledging the plethora of animal, vegetal, and mineral entities that pervade and commune within and with the human. In their introduction to *Arts of Living on a Damaged Planet* (2017), Anna Tsing et al. similarly ponder upon extending livability in the Anthropocene by turning to generative and productive symbiotic makings and knottings. Similarly, in a special issue of the *GLQ* titled "Queer Inhumanisms" (2019), Dana Luciano and Mel Y. Chen address the

concerns of the Anthropocene while shifting away from the teleological and oppositional frameworks embedded within and informing terms like posthumanist and anti-humanist. They associate this moment of precarity and planetary crisis in the Anthropocene with the queer desire of the body (human or not) to persist through unexpected alliances and entanglements, maintaining that although queer reproductions of weird entanglements are not the product of our time, they are definitely necessitated by it.

Works Cited

Alaimo, Stacy. *Bodily Natures: Science, Environment, and the Material Self.* Indiana University Press, 2010.

Barad, Karen. *Meeting the Universe Halfway: Quantum Physics and the Entanglement of Matter and Meaning.* Duke University Press, 2007.

Boym, Svetlana. *Another Freedom: The Alternative History of an Idea.* University of Chicago Press, 2010.

Chen, Mel Y. *Animacies: Biopolitics, Racial Mattering, and Queer Affect.* Duke University Press, 2012.

Haraway, Donna. "Situated Knowledges: The Science Question in Feminism and the Privilege of Partial Perspective." *Simians, Cyborgs, and Women: The Reinvention of Nature*, Routledge, 1991, pp. 183-202.

———. *Staying with the Trouble: Making Kin in the Chthulucene.* Duke University Press, 2016.

Houle, Karen, and Canadian Society for Continental Philosophy. "Animal, Vegetable, Mineral: Ethics as Extension or Becoming?" *Symposium*, vol. 19, no. 2, 2015, pp. 37-56, doi: 10.5840/symposium201519221.

Keetley, Dawn, and Angela Tenga, editors. *Plant Horror: Approaches to the Monstrous Vegetal in Fiction and Film.* Palgrave Macmillan, 2016.

Laist, Randy, editor. *Plants and Literature: Essays in Critical Plant Studies.* Rodopi, 2013.

Le Guin, Ursula K. "The Carrier Bag Theory of Fiction." *Dancing at the Edge of the World: Thoughts on Words, Women, Places*, Grove Press, 1989, pp. 165-70.

Luciano, Dana, and Mel Y. Chen. "Queer Inhumanisms." *GLQ: A Journal of Lesbian and Gay Studies*, vol. 25, no. 1, Jan. 2019, pp. 113-17, doi: 10.1215/10642684-7275600.

Marder, Michael. *Plant-Thinking: A Philosophy of Vegetal Life.* Columbia University Press, 2013.

Marder, Michael P., and Anaïs Tondeur. *The Chernobyl Herbarium: Fragments of an Exploded Consciousness.* Open Humanities Press, 2016.

Meeker, Natania, and Antónia Szabari. *Radical Botany: Plants and Speculative Fiction.* Fordham University Press, 2020.

Miller, T. S. "Lives of the Monster Plants: The Revenge of the Vegetable in the Age of Animal Studies." *Journal of the Fantastic in the Arts*, vol. 23, no. 3 (86), 2012, pp. 460-79.

Myers, Natasha. "Photosynthetic Mattering: Rooting into the Planthroposcene." *Moving Plants*, edited by Line Marie Thorsen, Rønnebæksholm, pp. 123-30.

Sperling, Alison. "Second Skins: A Body Ecology of Sickness in the Southern Reach Trilogy." *Paradoxa*, vol. 28, Dec. 2016, pp. 231-55.

———. "Queer Ingestions: Weird and Sporous Bodies in Jeff VanderMeer's Fiction." *Plants in Science Fiction: Speculative Vegetation*, edited by Katherine E. Bishop, et al., University of Wales Press, 2020, pp. 194-213.

Tsing, Anna Lowenhaupt, editor. *Arts of Living on a Damaged Planet.* University of Minnesota Press, 2017.

VanderMeer, Jeff. *Annihilation.* Farrar, Straus and Giroux, 2014.

———. *Authority.* Farrar, Straus and Giroux, 2014.

———. *Acceptance.* Farrar, Straus and Giroux, 2014.

Ashasmiti Das is a Ph.D. student in the Department of English at University of Hyderabad, India. Her thesis examines the dissolution of the notion of the "self" and the idea of the "human" in contemporary works of speculative fiction. Her work attempts to address the posthuman reframing of concepts such as ethics, care, kinship, and relationality in more-than-human worlds of entangled and shared living. Her research encompasses the various modalities of the "monstrous" (vegetal, technological and geological) while attending to them as beings that are both material and meaningful and as actively participating in the production of their own knowledge.

SECTION 2
What Threatens Freedom?

"You Gave Up the World":
Freedom and Responsibility in Jenny Offill's *Weather* and Lydia Millett's *A Children's Bible*

Claire P. Curtis

> "For human beings to be able to act freely, the future must be open."
>
> —Byung-Chul Han

Understanding something as a challenge to freedom depends on your understanding of freedom itself. Is freedom doing what you wish, free from external coercion? If so, then challenges to freedom will take the form of coercions understood as laws, norms, power, even expectations from others. If, however, you think about freedom as acting in accordance with a set of rules that you have chosen for yourself, then challenges to that freedom will take the form of obstacles to your choosing, or conditions under which your capacity to choose well are challenged. Because we choose among and with others, the second understanding of freedom connects us to those others, while the first understanding potentially pits us against them, since any of those people might become a source of coercion. But both of these competing views of freedom raise questions about how the external conditions of our lives impact our being free.

The epigraph above describes one condition that is necessary for freedom: the open future. What does open mean in this context? Han argues that the predictive powers of data analytics have closed off possibilities for our lives, by essentially presenting to us what the future *will be*. This chapter argues that our fear about climate change forecloses particular futures in a similar way; the fact of climate change produces anxiety that seems to freeze many in apathy, doubt, and dread, thereby undermining our capacity to be free. If we assume that nothing can be done, then we cease to be freely acting people. Furthermore, in doing so we threaten the possibility of free action for younger generations.

One duty of parents is to raise their children to facilitate their future self-direction, to enable them to take responsibility for their lives. It is a responsibility to raise young people to become aware of their own need to be responsible. Responsibility is thus more than responsibility to oneself. Responsibility is embedded in communal interactions and shared sets of expectations for the future. Marx notes in The Communist Manifesto (1848) that under communism we will live under conditions in "which the free development of each is the condition for the free development of all" (ch. 2). Both liberal and radical understandings of freedom assert that individual freedom is connected to the freedom of others. Referencing Marx's theory of freedom, Han notes that "being free means nothing other than *self-realization with others*" (18). This realization is itself dependent on the idea of a "working community" (18). Being free requires knowledge of, care for, and commitment to others.[1]

Han argues that the contemporary, neoliberal subject is unable to be free in this way. Capitalism has changed the relationship we have with others and with our larger community, such that instead of engaging with others in the well-being of the community we are merely "onlookers and consumers" living in a "spectator democracy" (30). Han's concern in *Psychopolitics* (2017) is not climate change, but his argument about neoliberalism's challenges to freedom are certainly relevant for thinking about living under conditions of uncertainty and change. The novels discussed here describe versions of Han's spectators, who seem unable to wrap their heads around their responsibilities to their own children and to others.

Fictional accounts can both help readers diagnose the situations under which they live and suggest different ways of living. The two novels discussed here offer both diagnosis and a challenge to live differently.[2] Jenny Offill's *Weather* (2020) and Lydia Millett's *A Children's Bible* (2020) are both set in the potential present, dominated by the recognition of climate change and uncertainty about the future. These novels are examples of a newer trend of realist climate fiction. The value of realist climate fiction is that it neither relies on the heroics of a survival story nor is speculating about a far-flung future. Instead, these are novels of unhappy people living under all too familiar conditions of ennui, apathy, anxiety, dread, and boredom. *Weather* focuses on a woman working as a librarian who feels responsible for her marriage, her son, and her brother's mental health, and who becomes increasingly panicked about the prospect of a changing climate. The novel reads as a somewhat disjointed set of snapshots of the mental processes of someone who is caught like the proverbial deer in the headlights. *A Children's Bible*, in contrast, bypasses the simultaneously apathetic and uselessly panicked adults and focuses on a set of young people thrown together for a summer at a country house rented by their parents for an impromptu college reunion. What begins as a novel of teenagers entertaining themselves absent their phones (the only rule the parents seem to have established) shifts focus sharply after a catastrophic hurricane strikes.

Weather focuses on the anxiety of a mother and *A Children's Bible* on the frustrations of a teenager. Both novels consider what it means to be prepared for the future by considering the idea of refuge where one can maintain a life fully recognizable as free. The adult protagonist of *Weather* feels powerless and essentially unfree. The teenaged narrator of *A Children's Bible* feels similarly at a loss, and yet she acts, being responsible, for her younger brother and her parents. In neither novel are the protagonists thinking of themselves as doing what they wish, although in both cases one could argue that neither necessarily knows what they want. Both novels illustrate the obstacles in the way of feeling free to imagine, and perhaps begin to enact, a different future. Together, the novels show us that the possibility for a future where we can act as free people is dependent on being able to imagine that future. Obstacles to that imagination include the belief that there is no future and the stifling wishful thinking of a wholly safe place. The protagonists of these novels must move beyond these obstacles if they are to act freely, to take responsibility for the next generation.

1. What kind of future is there?

Halfway through *A Children's Bible*, after the hurricane, the young people have taken shelter in a different house when they are joined by "trail angels" from the Appalachian Trail, also seeking shelter. Eve, the teenaged protagonist and narrator, watches her younger brother and others taking impromptu lessons from the angels in biology, poetry, and history. She describes the scene: "Children who sat there learning from their teachers, full of trust. Secure in the knowledge that an orderly future stretched ahead of them" (136). This is Eve's imagining of Han's open future: trust in adults who have the children's best interests at heart, and who can share a world of knowledge. Of course, by this time in the novel, this idea of an orderly future facilitated by caring adults is revealed to be mere fantasy.

Eve acknowledges that her parents (and their generation) have failed to protect the idea of the future.

Early in the novel, observing her parents, she notes, "the future flew past in a flash of grim. The clock was ticking, and I didn't like that clock" (13). This initial "flash of grim" has, at first, more to do with the repulsion felt by a young person toward her older parents than with specific worries about climate change. Eve is one of a cohort of offspring brought together in a summer house. Their parents went to college together, but the offspring have never met. These parents establish few rules for the children, but they do confiscate their electronics. This stricture has the consequence of throwing the young people together in opposition to their parents. The children establish a "PARENT FREE ZONE" (6) and play a game in which they refuse to acknowledge any particular parent as theirs.[3] The parents—"those garbage-like figures that tottered around the great house were a vision of what lay in store—hell no" (13)—are not a model for how to live but a source of shame, "a cautionary tale" (13). These children see their parents as useless, aimless, gross, indifferent, "slugs" (15).

What starts as a familiar adolescent rejection of the parents and their bodies and life choices shifts into a more specific recognition of the larger ways in which these parents have failed their children, individually and collectively. In the long aftermath of the devastating hurricane, Eve considers the trash in her parents' car, an "almost fond" memory of discarded snack bags and drinks. She notes to herself that she would never pick up this trash, instead seeing that as a parent's job.

> Once we had let them do everything for us—assumed they would. Then came the day we didn't want them to.
> Still later we found out that they hadn't done everything at all. They'd left out the important part.
> And it was known as: the future. (171)

Eve begins with the familiar shift from childhood to a kind of quasi-adulthood where the young person rejects parental help as a process of growing up. But she notes here that coming to make one's own decisions depends on adults ensuring a world into which the young can grow. The parents in *A Children's Bible* have not merely failed in their parental duties during this summer, where supervision is slim and curiosity about or love for their offspring is absent. These parents have failed to uphold any kind of duty towards the future in which their children will live. There is a brief mention (28) of sending children to a summer camp with survival skills—an idea echoed in *Weather*, where Ben and Lizzie consider sending their son Eli to camp (137)—but even these actions do nothing to change the conditions of the world. They are limited to a kind of consumerist prepperism. The parents in these novels have been marinated in the message Han has highlighted: that change is either impossible or available through purchases.

Eve indicts her parents for not confronting what she sees as the end of the world. And she sees it as her responsibility to share with her younger brother what is to come. Even as she is convinced that there is no future, Eve keeps moving forward. By contrast, Lizzie, the protagonist of *Weather,* also worries about the possibility of there being no real future, but in a way that traps her in place. "Young person worry: what if nothing I do matters? Old person worry: What if everything I do does?" (21-22). In being worried about everything, she is incapable of doing anything. She sees futures that the parents in *A Children's Bible* do not. But this mental doomscrolling is not a spur to action. "[Y]ou're never going back to that website where you put in the year Eli was born and then watched the numbers go up, up, up. No. Never" (89). Lizzie's internal mental scroll is only one step less urgent than her brother's simultaneous fall off the deep end into obsessive cycling through worst case scenarios concerning his newborn daughter.

Lizzie begins working as an assistant to her former graduate school advisor, Sylvia, who lectures on the threats of climate change. In this work, Lizzie takes over from Sylvia the task of responding to people's questions about the lectures. One recurring question from audience members and letter writers is about the elusive "safe place." "They take notes during Sylvia's talk, but in the end they still have one nagging question: what will be the safest place? No one they'd consulted with would give them a straight answer" (52-53). These supposedly safe places are sought out merely as potential purchases. There is no thought of working with one's community to build resilience. Lizzie imagines buying such a place, a doomstead, a house in a place close to water, outside of the city, but her imaginative bubble is burst by Sylvia. "'Do you really think you can protect them? In 2047?' Sylvia asks. I look at her. Because until this moment, I did, I did somehow think this. She orders another drink. 'Then become rich, very, very rich,' she says in a tight voice" (127).

Sylvia is both rejecting the idea of such a safe place as actually safe and noting that such an illusion can only be maintained with extreme wealth. This is the wealth possessed by the parents of the other teens that the protagonists of *A Children's Bible* run into on their beach adventure. These parents have purchased compounds outfitted as "a survival home for chaos times" (29). The parents of these yacht kids are performing the freedom of doing as one wishes, and their offspring see the parents as "their insurance policy" (32), as part of a transactional deal for which they pay premiums in good grades and a "perfect record" (33). The yacht teens' parents have not changed the world, and yet they are certainly still responsible, the deserving targets of the anger of the younger generation. Those who seek a safe place are denying the open future, by imagining only a single, narrow path through a larger world of danger, to which they refuse to give any attention and for which they take no responsibility.

It is not simply the seemingly closed-off future that the characters fear. It is the challenge, for the adults, to accept responsibility for the situation. The adults of *A Children's Bible* never accept responsibility for their part in maintaining the world as it is. The offspring do accept responsibility: for themselves, their younger siblings, their safety, and their future. If it is only in accepting responsibility that one can begin to be free, then the possibilities of freedom in these novels are clear.

2. Taking Responsibility

Lizzie is at least both aware and concerned about the future; she sees the ways in which possible futures are blinking out. One can almost imagine, if the characters in these two novels could speak to one another, that Lizzie would welcome the blame that that Eve and her friends lay upon their parents.

> "Do you blame *us*?" asked a mother. Pathetic-sounding.
> "We blame you for everything," Jen said evenly.
> "Who else is there to blame?" added Rafe.
> (Millet 193)

The protagonist of *Weather* obsesses over the future possibilities that the parents of *A Children's Bible* never seem to entertain. The words "Everything is going to be OK!" (201), which Eve's dad cheerfully asserts to his children after everything has fallen apart, have certainly never crossed her lips. If *A Children's Bible* depicts the adults who have decided that someone else is surely going to deal with the future, and who do nothing, then *Weather* describes the choking anxiety and dread of someone who can hardly imagine action. Lizzie imagines potential futures but has almost no capacity, willingness, or ability (which is it?) to consider what she might concretely do.

Lizzie, unlike the parents in *A Children's Bible*, is in a world of responsibilities that she readily accepts. And her response to her brother over his spiraling fear about parenting might provide a way of thinking about our own inaction today.

> "I'm going to do it wrong," my brother tells me. "I can feel all the wrong thoughts coming. What if I mess it up?" he wants to know. He is smoking now, one cigarette after another after another. "You will be forgiven," I tell him. (77-78)

Lizzie's blanket assertion of forgiveness for her brother Henry may be an act of grace. But it raises questions. Lizzie thinks more about climate change and is certainly not as thoughtless as the parents of *A Children's Bible*. But her thought processes, her own spiraling, and her yet undirected panic seem as useless as the drug- and alcohol-fueled ignorance of Millet's parents. Lizzie feels guilt, but she is incapable of acting. She is filled with anxiety and thoughts of action that never materialize. "I keep wondering how we might channel all of this dread into action" (137). And yet she has this thought about action while at a meeting at a church where, in response to other people's calls for action, she considers, "why do I feel so embarrassed?" (137). Lizzie feels responsible, but she does not feel free. She is still caught in the expectations of a world where she should be merely a spectator.

Offill herself offers a response by including a weblink on the page after the end of the novel. It provides, as Sylvia has done in her climate newsletters, the "obligatory note of hope" (203). The webpage notes, "there's a way in for everyone. Aren't you tired of all of this fear and dread?" (*Obligatory*). *Weather* might be read as a novel aiming to convince the reader that one should feel ready for something other than dread. If nothing else, our frustration with Lizzie might spur us to action.

Hope, which is essential for any possibility of free action, is absent among the parents in *A Children's Bible*.[4] The young people there are direct and unsparing in their assessment of their parents.

> "You were just stupid," said Sukey. "And lazy."...

> "You gave up the world," said David.
> "You let them turn it all to shit," said Low.
> (193)

The parents quickly note that they did not have the power to bring about change: "that's what they all said" is the offspring's quick reply (194). These teenagers recognize that their supposedly loving parents have simply abdicated all responsibility, not simply for their children but for the world in which they live. These parents are the "onlookers" of neoliberal society. They found what they thought was a degree of freedom in performing their consumptive roles. One way of understanding this is in the total mental collapse and eventual, inexplicable, disappearance of the parents (who seem to just walk away one night, not to be seen again) in *A Children's Bible*, who are revealed to be puppets of a system whose collapse left them without the capacity to live.

> "Listen. We know we let you down," said a mother. "But what could we have *done*, really?"
> "Fight," said Rafe. "Did you ever fight?"
> "Or did you just do exactly what you wanted?" said Jen. "Always?" (194)

Fighting for a different world is unthinkable to these parents. And while their lives are free from the obstacles of poverty or class or race, these parents are not free in any meaningful sense. They are tied to a system, one in which getting the deposit back on a rental house irreparably damaged in a storm is more important than seeking momentary safety for their children from rising waters and storm damage.

Neither is Lizzie free, although she seems better able to recognize the ways in which she is unfree, tethered both to her brother and his failing mental health, but more importantly tethered to a world where she imagines she can find a hideaway for her family. She imagines potentially carrying Eli to safety while simultaneously dismissing this fear: "You are not going to have to walk thirty-four miles with your child on your back. *But if I did*" (159).

Lizzie seems to be talking to herself here. And it is hard to reject completely her contention that she will not potentially be walking with her child on her back. Others clearly do. Lizzie's lack of freedom is her flip-flopping between thinking the worst and then dismissing the worst as ridiculous. "Lizzie's become a crazy doomer" (89), her husband notes, but he is the one who brings the possibility of action to the end of the novel. "He did the math, all the math, and now there's a quote from Epictetus above his desk. *You are not some disinterested bystander/Exert yourself*" (195).

Perhaps an exhortation more for the reader than for the characters, at least in the ending of this novel, this Stoic passage is an assertion of freedom. As Han notes in *Psychopolitics*, the neoliberal order wants people to think of themselves as disinterested bystanders, and more than this, to feel free in doing so. To be a spectator of the world, unconcerned about its outcome, is not a call to freedom. In both novels, the adult characters see themselves as powerless in the face of a changing climate. They express feeling out of control, of being unable to act. They do not consider themselves to be free enough to act for a different future. But this lack of freedom is less about the freedom they do not feel and more about the freedom that they do not perceive.

Being free means accepting that we do not know what the future might bring. Dread about the future is an assertion about what you think the future will be. It is not the changing climate that will make us unfree. It is our unwillingness to imagine that we could do something differently, and our refusal to own up to the responsibility that we have for others.

If freedom means being in control, and being in control means being able to plan for a future that you can imagine, then climate change portends a future that we do, on the one hand, have the control now to mitigate and that, on the other hand, is coming to be despite our individual actions. These novels remind us both that hope is a necessary precondition of freedom and that our responsibilities for the future extend beyond our own lives.

Notes

1. On this theory, unfreedom can be seen as being unable to accept responsibility. So the young child is unfree because the child is not making rules for herself. The robot is unfree because it is programmed. These are the straightforward and hence easy cases. But this theory of freedom has also been used to designate entire peoples as being childlike and unable to be free. The problematic consequence of linking freedom to responsibility is that to strip someone of the perceived capacity for responsibility is to designate that person as unfree. In "On Liberty" (1859), John Stuart Mill famously links children (those in their "nonage") to "barbarians," who also need a system of coercive rules to be able to reach a state of freedom (19). Societies might have roughly agreed upon limits to childhood, but for the rejection of responsibility for whole peoples there is no clear limit.

2. There are other climate novels that offer more prescriptive approaches. Kim Stanley Robinson's *Ministry for the Future* (2020) is the most comprehensive.

3. On this point, the novel is acknowledging Han's argument. Absent this rule about phones, the actions of the novel, the community of teens just figuring things out, would not happen.

4. In an interview with Amy Brady, Sheree Renee Harris, the editor of the Grist climate fiction collection *Afterglow* (2023), indicates that in their call for submissions they specifically sought stories that were more "celebratory." She notes, "*Afterglow* infuses a much-needed thread of radical hope and resilience to the growing genre of climate fiction."

Works Cited

Brady, Amy. "Interview with Sheree Renee Harris." *Burning Worlds Newsletter*, February 2023.

Han, Byung-Chul. *Psychopolitics: Neoliberalism and the New Technologies of Power*. Translated by Erik Butler, Verso, 2017.

Marx, Karl. *Communist Manifesto*. Project Gutenburg, 2 Mar. 2022, gutenberg.org/cache/epub/61/pg61-images.html

Mill, John Stuart. *On Liberty*. Project Gutenburg, 10 Jan. 2011, gutenberg.org/files/34901/34901-h/34901-h.htm

Millet, Lydia. *A Children's Bible*. W.W. Norton, 2020.

—————. *Obligatory Note of Hope*. obligatorynoteofhope.com. Accessed May 2023.

Offill, Jenny. *Weather*. Borzoi, Knopf, 2020.

Claire P. Curtis is Professor of Political Science at the College of Charleston. She is the author of *Postapocalyptic Fiction and the Social Contract: "We'll Not Go Home Again"* (Lexington, 2010) and the co-editor of the special issue of *Utopian Studies* dedicated to Octavia Butler (19.3, 2008). She has published articles on Ursula Le Guin, Octavia Butler, and contemporary Y.A. postapocalyptic fiction. Currently, she is writing a book on Martha Nussbaum's capabilities approach and contemporary post-apocalyptic fiction. As a political philosopher, she uses fiction as the experimental space of living together to analyze theories of justice. She teaches courses in the history of political thought, utopia/dystopia, and the contemporary intersections of gender, theory and law. She lives in Charleston, South Carolina.

"Sometimes That's All It Takes to Save a World, You See":
Reading Freedom and the Anthropocene in N. K. Jemisin's Writings

Katrina Newsom

Freedom and the Anthropocene

In *Freedom in the Anthropocene* (2015), Alexander M. Stoner and Andony Melathopoulos tell us that "humanity is not self-consciously choosing to control [earth's geological and ecological] transformation. In modern capitalist society humans are not free to control their control of nature, nor can they control their lack of control" (108).[1] They note this to challenge ideas of freedom in modern society that coincide with the notion of "responsible human activity," as distinguished from the belief that humans' fates are predetermined (which makes the proposition of individuals taking personal responsibility for the environmental crisis understandable)(12). However, for them, the idea of freedom does not negate that "the pattern of progress throughout the nineteenth and twentieth centuries has not been one of society freely determining itself" (13). In fact, they argue that "[t]he arrival of the Anthropocene coincides conspicuously with a sense that the twentieth century was characterized not by freedom, but the wholesale return of structural constraints that restrict self-conscious social transformation" and that this is what brought "a profound sense of helplessness" (20). Through an analysis of freedom in Georg Lukács's critique of reification, Theodor W. Adorno's negative dialectic, and Moishe Postone's revisitation of traditional Marxism, they explain that the Anthropocene must be understood as more than "a new geological epoch in which the activity of human societies has become the determinant force in the changing structure of the Earth's planetary systems" (19). Instead, they implicate it as a naturalizing mechanism of "capitalism in history," explaining that they see it this way "in part because it remains incapable of elucidating the connection between the failure of revolution and the subsequent rise of the state-centric capitalism" (69). The result has been that the process of the degradation of the earth's planetary system continues to be a mystery. Referring to the paradox of the mystery as "environmental-society problematic," they assert that an awareness of environmental crisis does not lead to transformations in society (22), but rather that "the Anthropocene is characterized by a growing gap between society's awareness of ecological degradation and our ability to change the underlying social structure that gives rise to this degradation" (qtd. in Stoner, "Sociobiophysicality" 103). In short, the "failure of contemporary environmentalism," then, is that it does not recognize its implications in the very structures that are preventing the revolutionary environmental moment.

To this end, Stoner and Melathopoulos explain that "environmentalism remains identical with society while appearing opposed to it" (65) and that "[t]he Anthropocene, then, is history from the standpoint of the identity thinking of contemporary environmentalism—a history characterized by unfreedom; hence, its drivers as well as the possibility of freedom and agency remain exogenous to society" (102). In this context, we are confronted with preset coordinates of freedom that Slavoj Žižek describes in his essay "The Leninist Freedom" as a condition of formal freedom in liberal democracies. According to Žižek, formal freedom has the appearance of freedom, given that it seems to offer opportunities for choice. Yet, the true nature of formal freedom, he says, offers nothing more than preset coordinates by which people are permitted to choose, even if they rationalize the choice as one of their own choosing. The formal freedom of Stoner and Melathopoulos's "environmental-society problematic" shows how the concept of the Anthropocene, as a theorizing method for possible points of departures for environmental sustainability, remains tethered to the very systems that generated the need for such departures. Likewise, the liberal responsible subject shows up right at the moment that environmentalism challenges liberalism as a viable space to address the problem. To wrestle freedom away from this paradigm, Stoner and Melathopoulos postulate that considerations of freedom within the Anthropocene should include an analysis of "the connection between economic growth and environmental degradation and how environmental degradation is necessarily connected to social domination under capitalism" (102).

With this conjecture in mind, I turn my attention to N. K. Jemisin's ecological science fictional writings, where she investigates environmentalism within the context of social domination and exploitation. In the *Broken Earth* series— *The Fifth Season* (2015), *The Obelisk Gate* (2016), and *The Stone Sky* (2017), along with the novelette *Emergency Skin* (2019)— Jemisin demonstrates a unique understanding of the correlation between social domination and environmental crisis and its connection to the foreclosed coordinates of freedom in ecocidal societies. She uses her fiction, more specifically the *Broken Earth* trilogy, to investigate the pairing of social domination and environmental crisis within the context of historical practices of subjugation and their correlation to humans' treatment of the earth. In her novelette *Emergency Skin*, she expands her inquiry to include an imagining of a world devoid of the dominant social orders that rule through practices of subjugation and to conceptualize a world where radical freedom prevails and a healthy planet exists. Through her fiction, Jemisin draws a connection between systems of social domination and exploitation and the predetermined and foreclosed coordinates of freedom within ecocidal societies to argue that revolutionary opportunities and environmental healing involve recognizing the social orders of domination and choosing coordinates of freedom outside of them.

Subjugation and Environmentalism in N. K. Jemisin's Fiction

N. K. Jemisin sets the story of the *Broken Earth* trilogy on an apocalyptic earth to explore the correlation between social domination and environmental crises. Jemisin imagines the social order in the trilogy as "generally democratic and capitalist," except in times of disasters, when it breaks up into small authoritarian communities ("A Not So Distant Future"). The trilogy begins right at the moment when the season of a climate catastrophe starts and when the social order is taking shape according to the mandates of survival. The irony, however, is that the focus of the preset-foreclosed coordinates of freedom is not centered on the social order as it transitions into authoritarian models, as would be expected. Rather, through a narration of remembering, it zeroes in on the domination of social orders that arise amid pre-apocalyptic-level environmental catastrophes. It is in those pre-apocalyptic times that Jemisin explores the foreclosure of freedom within the social orders.

The social orders are described through the narration of the stone eater, Hoa, a mystical creature who has lived thousands of years on the planet, looks like a stone statue when on the earth's surface, and travels through the earth's crust and rocks with lightning speed (even if it takes him an eternity to walk up a flight of stairs). His narration takes the form of remembering, by which he details the social orders within hundreds of years of the current season and those of the social order at the time when he was a tuner created in a human image for the service of Syl Anagist, a city on the earth that existed many millennia ago, when the landmass comprised three continents, and that sets events in motion for the eventuality of the seasons. Hoa shares his story with Essun, the protagonist and hero of the trilogy, whose experiences on the Stillness are used to explore how the seasons ended.

In the first novel of the trilogy, *The Fifth Season*, Hoa describes the social order of the Sanze Empire, which emerged toward the end of a climate catastrophe referred to as the Madness. For over a thousand years, the Sanze Empire ruled over the people of the Stillness, a name given to the "vast, unbroken" continental landmass that developed after centuries of apocalyptic environmental catastrophes (2). In the social order of the Sanze Empire, the orogene—a race of people who have a sessapinae organ at the stem of their brain that gifts most of them, on one level or another, with the ability to detect, quell, and/or create seismic activity using kinetic energy and some the added receptivity "to the presence of predators, to others' emotions, to distant extremes of heat or cold, and to the movements of celestial objects"—are systematically subjugated and oppressed (343). Their abilities are used to generate wealth and to maintain power for the empire. Yet, at the same time, their power is not used to explore how to end the seasons. Rather, it is used to maintain tactics of survival for the continuation of their subjugation and the hegemony of the Sanze Empire's social order. As such, perceptions of their power are used in fables and myths to cast them as the monster or the villain that must be conquered. Their power makes them the source of fear and, if they are born among small communities, they are hunted and killed. Referred to systematically by the racial slur rogga, they are kept in a constant state of fear and subjugation.

In the third novel of the trilogy, *The Stone Sky,* Hoa shares with Essun memories of the social order that existed at the time he was created. Much like the Sanze Empire, the Sylanagistine Empire started with a group of people in one geographical location who branched out to colonize people in other locations. As Hoa explains, "Syl Anagist started out as part of Kakhiarar, then all of it, then all of Maecar, too. All become Syl Anagist" (208). Hoa recounts how the Thniess, one of the groups on the Cilir land, became the focal point of Syl Anagist's practices of subjugation and domination. He recalls that Syl Anagist, who referred to the Thniess as Niess, first conquered their land, causing the Niess to disperse among other lands and peoples. Next, the Sylanagistine developed a social system that included fables and studies that othered the Niess. Their fear and hatred of the Neiss were based on the Niess's relationship to magic. Unlike the leaders of Syl Anagist, who hoarded and coveted magic, the Niess did not believe that magic should be owned. They used it without practical intent, creating, instead, plutonic engines just for the sake of art. The Niess plutonic engines, however, were more advanced in harnessing power than anything that the Sylanagistine built. Similar to the treatment of the orogenes on the Stillness, the Thniess became the subjugate of the Sylanagistine Smpire. Hoa recalls:

> Perhaps it began with whispers that Niess irises gave them poor eyesight and perverse inclinations, and that the split Niess tongues could not speak truth. That sort of sneering happens, cultural bullying, but things got worse. It became easy for scholars to build reputations and careers around the notion that Niess sessapinae were fundamentally different, somehow—more sensitive, more active, less controlled, less civilized—and that this was the source of their magical peculiarity. This was what made them not the same kind of human as

everyone else. Eventually: not *as* human as everyone else. Finally: not human at all. (210)

This passage details the discursive practices entailed in subjugating a people. The Sylanagistine used not only culture but education as a way to strip the Niess of their humanity. However, Hoa asserts that they created him and the other tuners out of fear that the basis for their practices and culture were inaccurate. He recounts, "And only now, when we have been made over in the image of their own fear, are they satisfied. They tell themselves that in us, they've captured the quintessence and power of who the Niess really were, and they congratulate themselves on having made their old enemies useful at last" (211).

In addition to recalling the educational and cultural practices of subjugation used against the Niess, Hoa recounts how he learned that many of the Niess were kept alive and placed in a briar patch, a place where they were fused with vines to generate, regenerate, and harness their magic (echoing a similar practice of condemning orogenes in the Stillness to the living-dead status of node maintainers who were used to quell seismic activity). Hoa recalls seeing them "sprawl[ed] motionless amid the thicket of vines (lying atop the vines, twisted among them, wrapped up in them, speared by them where the vines grow through flesh)" (262). Although Hoa sees in the painlessness of the process an act of "kindness" toward the Niess, the entirety of the magic generation process for Syl Anagist's two hundred and fifty-six cities relies on subjugation. It requires complete domination of the Niess, given that "the sinklines take all the magic of life from them save the bare trickle needed to keep them alive. Keeping them alive keeps them generating more" (262). After recounting what he witnessed at the briar patch, Hoa recalls how he and the other tuners decided to prevent the opening of the Obelisk Gate and the Geoarcanity that was created to give humans unmitigated access to Father Earth's magic. However, Father Earth had other plans. He tried to use the concentrated power of the

Geoarcanity to stop the humans and to destroy life on the planet. Hoa reacted by redirecting the power toward the moon, which caused the moon to be pushed out of the earth's orbit.

What is significant about Hoa's recollection of the Sanze and Sylanagistine empires is that, in both cases, practices of subjugation directly correlate with the creation or perpetuation of climate catastrophes. This is evident in the ways that the social orders of domination in both Sanze and Syl Anagist cause the people within these empires to overlook the subjugation of Father Earth. As such, they continue in the practices that perpetuate the hurt they initially caused. In *The Fifth Season*, Hoa remembers the legend of Father Earth. He states:

> According to the legend, Father Earth did not originally hate life. In fact, as the lorists tell it, once upon a time Earth did everything he could to facilitate strange emergence of life on his surface. He crafted even, predictable seasons; kept changes of wind and wave and temperature slow enough that every living being could adapt, evolve; summoned waters that purified themselves, skies that always cleared after a storm. He did not create life-that was happenstance—but he was pleased and fascinated by it, and proud to nurture such strange wild beauty upon this surface. (379)

In this passage, Father Earth nurtures life on the planet. He ensures that it is habitable by providing "predictable seasons" and ecological systems that allow life on the planet to adapt. He is intentional in his efforts to expand and maintain the biosphere so that life flourishes, and he delights in the process.

Hoa continues to recount the legend that details how, despite Father Earth's care, humans sought to dominate him. The result is that they not only destroy the things

Father Earth provides them, but they also violate what is sacred to him:

> Then people began to do horrible things to Father Earth. They poisoned waters beyond even his ability to cleanse, and killed much of the other life that lived on his surface. They drilled through the crust of his skin, past the blood of his mantle, to get at the sweet marrow of his bones. And at the height of human hubris and might, it was the orogenes who did something that even Earth could not forgive: They destroyed his only child. (379-380)

According to the passage, the humans violated Father Earth by penetrating his body in order to extract from him things he did not freely give and by destroying that which was most sacred to him. Father Earth is described using imagery that is generally used in reference to biological organisms: blood, flesh, marrow, and bone. The passage also describes the earth's relation to the humans as other than familial. Humans are a species that happened to grow on the planet, and Father Earth decided to take responsibility for them. However, according to the passage, he has a child, and we learn in the second and third book of the trilogy that his child is the moon. His vengeance centers on the role that human social orders have played in perpetuating ecocidal practices across millennia and in separating him from the moon. The solution for the broken environment cannot be obtained because the problem is rooted in the ways the empires are ruled. When we consider Stoner and Melathopoulos's environmental-society paradox to understand this moment in *The Fifth Season*, what Jemisin seems to point out is a "gap between society's awareness of ecological degradation and [the] ability to change the underlying social structure that gives rise to this degradation" (qtd. in Stoner, "Sociobiophysicality" 103).

To ensure that this point does not go above the head of the reader, Jemisin writes a scene in the second book, *The*

Obelisk Gate, in which Alabaster, a ten-ring orogene, responds to Essun's skepticism regarding the Earth's sentience by speculating that "[t]hat's probably how they thought… The ones who decided to dig a hole to the word's core" (166). In other words, they did not consider the earth to be alive. Thus, the plot comes to revolve around Essun's quest to use her orogenic powers to undo the wrong. She, like Father Earth, has been severed from her child. By the end of the story, she is able to locate her daughter. She realizes in the process of locating her that Father Earth is alive and that the only way to keep her own child safe is to bring the moon back into earth's orbit. By doing so, not only does she give Father Earth back its child, but she is able to end the Seasons.

What It Takes to Save the World

Similar to the *Broken Earth* trilogy, the novelette, *Emergency Skin* also explores the question of human impact on the earth within the context of social orders of domination and expands it to theorize what it means to move beyond the restrictions of freedom (or the preset coordinates of choice) to find a space where radical freedom is possible. Earth, in this story, unlike in the trilogy, has been healed for some time by the people left to survive on it after the mass exodus of the white male elites who fled at the height of the environmental and social crises that plague the earth and its inhabitants, referred to as the Great Leaving. Awarded the Hugo Award for Best Novelette in 2020, *Emergency Skin* is recognized for the way it not only blatantly takes to task white supremacy, sexism, and classism, but explores them as social domination mechanisms that are the root causes of climate catastrophe.

Emergency Skin tells a story about an explorer from an exoplanetary colony where a large portion of its inhabitants are enslaved by being denied skin. The explorer volunteers to go on an expedition to Earth to gather information in hopes of being rewarded with skin. He is warned by the Founder clan, a ruling class of the colony and the descendants of the white male elites, that earth is a wasteland that houses only the structural remnants of a prior advanced civilization. However, when the explorer arrives on earth, he finds that it has healed and that its inhabitants are flourishing.

Thus, the social order of domination of the Founder clan that advances ideologies of exploitation and manufactured scarcity appears quite absurd. After leaving the earth, the Founder clans set up colonies on different exoplanetary locations. Most of them do not survive, causing their inhabitants to return to earth. However, the ones that remain are of the most extremist order, and their social systems are quite exploitative. For example, the Founder clan of the exoplanet represented in the "dynamic-matrix consensus intelligence," an implant in the explorer's brain that expresses "rationale and ideas," laud the beauty and value of white skin. Also, they do not recognize women as female unless they are pleasurers. They view people based on usefulness in relation to profit and access to sustenance and extravagance on merit. They create a system of scarcity based on skin. Most of the inhabitants on the exoplanet are engineered to have composites skin. The Founder clan rationalize this by asserting that that type of skin is "necessary to ensure the survival for workers building [their] habitats." It protects the workers from "solar flares or biohazard," and it "reduces labor costs lost to bathroom breaks, meals, personal hygiene, medical care, interpersonal communication, and masturbation" (17). The composite skin serves to generate the ideal capitalist labor force, one that is amenable to the maximum extraction of labor and whose disembodiment makes them a class of people that are physically incapable of enjoying the fruits of their labor.

As a way for the Founder clan to appear as if they are offering opportunities to advance based on merit, they establish a system that encourages volunteers, like the explorer, to return to earth to assess the state of the planet in order to earn human skin. They tell the explorer that "the guiding principle of our society" is that "[r]ights belong only to those who earn them." They promise him that once he completes his mission, he will earn rights and be "deserving of life, health, beauty, sex, privacy, bodily autonomy—every possible luxury" (22). Needless to say, the Founder clan are aware that the planet is healed and has returned to preindustrial conditions. They are also aware that the social system on earth has advanced in ways that have eliminated homelessness, hunger, and forms of exclusions such as the nation-state and borders. They tell the explorer:

> What these people believe isn't feasible. They want everything for *everyone*, and look at where it's gotten them! Half of them aren't even men. Almost none are fair of skin. They're burdened by the dysfunctional and deficient at every turn. A few must be intelligent, we suppose, or they wouldn't have managed what they've done with the planet, but for those bright few, what's been the reward? (22)

The irony is that, as the explorer begins to engage with the people near his landing spot, he learns that the true mission is to retrieve HeLA7713 cell cultures (Henrietta Lacks cells), which the Founder clan uses to "remain young and strong for centuries" (22). He is also told by some of the inhabitants that the clan sends explorers to earth frequently to acquire the cell culture and that the inhabitants provide the explorers with instructions on how to produce it so that there is no need for the clan to send others. However, the clan sends explorers because it supports the foundational myth of their social order that purports that they are a superior race of people who come from "great men who spent the last decade on the planet's life amassing the resources and technology necessary to save the best of mankind" (4). It is this myth that they utilize to delimit the explorer's choices. The explorer learns from another explorer who never returned to the exoplanet that the Founder clan lie because they do not intend to give the explorer skin. "[A]ll the ruling classes want are the HeLa cells. Why would they waste any on giving skins to glorified errand boys?" he asks the explorer (31). Thus, what becomes glaringly obvious, even to the ruling elite of the exoplanet, is that they were the ailments of earth. After the Great Leaving, the people on earth came together as a collective, restructured their social order, and developed technological advancement to ensure that everyone could have access to food, shelter, and education and that everyone worked to heal the earth. The Founder clan's practices of permitting rights and freedom to just a few were the causes of the environmental and social crises.

After having obtained information that unveils the Founder clan's lies and the limits for his freedom, the explorer decides to look upon the inhabitants of earth as beautiful and deploy his emergency skin. The skin he has is not white or beautiful according to the clan. It does not give him the "noble brow, the classical patrician features, the lean musculature" or "blond hair" (3). However, he decides to accept the skin and to "build transmutation hacks" so that the slaves on the exoplanet can have access to skin as well, even if the skin they can access is not white. The explorer finds help in the former explorer who agrees to aid him in disrupting the social order of the exoplanet and who encourages him by stating, "Some of them will decide that they also want to be beautiful and free, like you. Some will fight for this, if they must. Sometimes that's all it takes to save a world, you see. A new vision" (33-34). To ensure that this revolutionary moment is not missed by the reader, Jemisin has the explorer's comrade saying to him as he is deactivating the "dynamic-matrix intelligence" module in the explorer's brain: "Can't start a revolution with the enemy shouting in your head, after all" (34).

What Jemisin makes clear in her stories is the correlation between systems of social domination and exploitation on one hand and, on the other, the predetermined and foreclosed coordinates of freedom within ecocidal societies. She demonstrates this in the *Broken Earth* trilogy by writing a story that explores patterns of subjugation across many millennia as a way to draw a connection between those patterns and the ways the earth is treated. Once earth is recognized as sentient, the causes of the environmental crisis become unveiled. By using the strategy of telling the story from the point of view of the subjugated, she makes history both human and alive, as Anthony Bogues describes in his talk on the "Practices of Freedom." He argues the necessity of the subjugated subject's presence in human history. Through this presence, we are able to see the continued manifestation of those subjugations in present history. Using this approach, Jemisin imagines that real change is permissible. In her novelette *Emergency Skin*, she imagines real change that improves the environment and society outside the dominant social order and juxtaposes it to the hegemony of those implicated in the crisis that plagued the earth. This story shows the hegemony's practice of manufacturing crisis to maintain its social order. Jemisin seems to suggest that revolution and environmental healing involve recognizing the social orders of domination and choosing coordinates of freedom outside of them.

Note

1. The Anthropocene was first introduced in 2000 in the *International Geosphere-Biosphere Programme Newsletter* by scientists Paul Crutzen and Eugene Stoermer, who defined it as a geological epoch that traces the human impact on earth's ecological and geological systems from the advent of the Industrial Revolution in the eighteenth century to the present (484).

Works Cited

Bogues, Anthony. "Practices of Freedom." *YouTube,* uploaded by Brown University, 17 December 2013, *youtu.be/bFpzzMyhHWI?si =ToINF7Df4NCh1s8M*

Crutzen, Paul J., and Eugene F. Stoermer "The 'Anthropocene.'" *The Future of Nature: Documents of Global Change,* edited by Libby Robin, Sverker Sörlin, and Paul Warde, Yale UP, 2013, pp. 479-490, doi: 10.12987/9780300188479-041.

Jemisin, N. K. "A Not So Distant Future in N.K. Jemisin's *Broken Earth* Trilogy." Interview with Steve Paulson. *To The Best of Our Knowledge,* 23 December 2017, *ttbook.org/interview/not-so-distant-future-nk-jemisins-broken-earth-trilogy.*

———. *Emergency Skin.* Amazon Original Stories, 2019.

———. *The Fifth Season.* Orbit Hachetter, 2015.

———. *The Obelisk* Gate. Orbit Hachetter, 2016.

———. *The Stone Sky.* Orbit Hachetter, 2017.

Stoner, Alexander M. "Sociobiophysicality and the Necessity of Critical Theory: Moving Beyond Prevailing Conceptions of Environmental Sociology in the USA." *Critical Sociology,* vol. 40, no. 4, 2014, pp. 621-42.

Stoner, Alexander M., and Andony Melathopoulos. *Freedom in the Anthropocene: Twentieth-Century Helplessness in the Face of Climate Change.* Palgrave Macmillan, 2015.

Žižek, Slavoj. "The Leninist Freedom." *Marxist Internet Archive, marxists.org/reference/subject/philosophy/works/ot/zizek.htm.*

Katrina Newsom received her doctorate degree in English from Wayne State University in 2018 and is currently an assistant professor of English at Tennessee State University. Her research interests include African American literature, ethnic literatures, late twentieth and early twenty-first century American literature, work and labor studies, race, and, more recently, environmental studies. Presently, she is working on an article titled, "The Refuge of Responsibility and the Politics of Recognition in Ralph Ellison's *Invisible Man*" as well as a larger project that examines work and personal responsibility in twenty-first century American literature and culture. She currently lives in Nashville, Tennessee.

The Shadow of the Pit:
Freedom, Family, and Neoliberalism in Meghan Lamb's *Failure to Thrive*

Jay Fraser

In recent decades, there has been new information brought to the wider population of the United States about what it means to be hopeless. While it is inarguable that there have always been segments of the population in any country who have had intimate familiarity with hopelessness, the socio-economic circumstances spreading across the wealthier nations of the world—particularly across the Anglosphere—in the wake of the neoliberal experiments of the 1970s have introduced vast numbers of people to the idea of a rudderless life. As Joel Nelson puts it, people no longer have a "clear sense of a better future" (1). For many, the freedom to choose a future of their own appears to have been stolen away, and that theft has not been bloodless.

In many cases, this decline has been an expansion of existing inequalities rather than the wholesale introduction of new ones, and that is particularly true throughout the American coal-belt. This chapter will briefly analyze this expansion of misery throughout the region, which has long been a site of hardship and class struggle, before engaging with Meghan Lamb's novel *Failure to Thrive* (2021), a post-industrial work set in precisely these declining locales in Pennsylvania that evidences these experiences from a number of perspectives. First, however, it is necessary to establish general understandings of the socio-economic circumstances in which Lamb's narrative is set, as well as our definitions.

Over the last half-century, a shift has taken place in the major economies of the world away from production towards financial management. Wages have undergone extended depressions in a variety of industries as companies have sought to follow the maxim that "what is efficient," according to neoclassical economic calculations is, inevitably, "best" (Nelson 5). Although the origins of this shift pre-date him, in the United States this shift into what is now often called the neoliberal economy is generally associated with Ronald Reagan, whose presidential tenure coincided with the demolition of American unions in multiple sectors, aimed to push financial deregulation in as many fields as possible, and oversaw the beginning of a collapse in worker wages "in earnest" (Harvey 25), as outsourcing of labour allowed for greater financial returns on investment, devaluing the more expensive American worker. Put simply, it is fairly easy to use Reagan's administration as a starting point for examining the collapse of the American future.

Appalachian industry, based in large part on the mining and processing of coal, has suffered from these same processes of neoliberalization. In the last decade, after a continuous decline, the Appalachian coal industry reached record lows in both production and volume of employment, rendering entire towns and cities which had grown around these industries hollowed out (Schwartzman 343). This lack of employment prospects in the traditional industries of the area has predictably resulted in a general state of economic decline in precisely the areas least prepared to handle it—those which were already subject to deprivation in a variety of fields, from education to the now notorious "food deserts" which render even nutrition a challenge for many (Stump 210). Appalachia, a region already stereotyped as being largely poor, has grown poorer, and even those who may have once had a means of aspiration towards the higher income brackets by virtue of their work have seen those opportunities stripped away systematically by successive governments since the Republican boom that began with Reagan.

Problems such as this are never simply the causes of linear effects. Rather, the problem spirals; once it has begun, it forms a feedback loop, intensifying itself. Most notably, the phenomenon of "brain drain" has come to the region; poverty levels above the national average combined with the perception that job opportunities simply no longer exist have resulted in the most educated young people making the decision to leave Appalachia entirely. By some estimations, having a college degree quadruples the likelihood for a native Appalachian to seek work and a future elsewhere (Vazzana and Rudi-Polloshka 225). Consequently, it is precisely those individuals—the most highly qualified of the next generation—that should theoretically provide the basis for a richer future, but who are compelled to exit the environment entirely. The neoliberal project sets into motion a self-fulfilling prophecy for places such as Appalachia: blue-collar industry closed, and those most suited to pursue the modern industries of tech and information driven away. The past has been put to sleep, in large part, and the future has been similarly smothered. This lack of options—born from systematic political choices—compounded by the aftereffects of collective hopelessness, has created an Appalachia where everyone is seemingly without choice or control in their own lives. This is the environment in which Lamb's characters find themselves, adrift and directionless in places that continually degrade without any possibility of help from the outside and without the resources to fully help themselves. These are the socio-economic circumstances of *Failure to Thrive*.

What, then, of freedom? Of course, these circumstances are not ideal, but surely Appalachian towns are not denied the same freedoms as people in more financially prosperous states. On the surface, this may seem to be the case, however, the reality faced by Lamb's characters, as well as by their real-world analogues, reveals the way that socio-economic conditions imperil the existence of authentic human freedom. Freedom is a tendentious subject. What some call freedom is not what others might call it. Contrary to popular American mythologies of freedom which posit it as largely a matter of character, the reality is that most Americans harbor a heavy opposition to the notion of freedom. As Yale political scientist James C. Scott writes, despite a "self-image as a nation of rugged individualists," the American people are "among the most normalized [...] in the world" (127). It cannot, therefore, be taken for granted that freedom is a self-evident concept, justified or defined by the Constitution or by popular notions of American identity put forward by any particular political party or leader. Instead, a more careful definition is necessary before its existence can be confirmed or denied.

For the purposes of this chapter, the concept of freedom here refers to a Marxist interpretation. Rather than simply the permission from the state to do things, for Marx freedom is the possibility of both internal and external conditions to allow for an individual to engage in the "development of all abilities," personal and otherwise (Marx 242). Put simply, this leads to a common-sense conclusion: it is not enough to be told that you may do something in order to be free; rather, the practical possibility of doing it must also exist. Thus, our conception of freedom: to be free, one must be both theoretically permitted and practically able to act in accordance with their own, self-directed desires.

This conception cannot be credited solely to Marx alone. Indeed, a number of thinkers have adopted similar conceptions in their own work. Perhaps the most pertinent for our purposes is the anthropologist David Graeber, from whom another term shall be borrowed: "spiritual violence" (40). This is a multifaceted term, but the particular aspect of spiritual violence with which neoliberal Appalachia is most concerned is that of being denied meaningful action. To borrow again from Graeber's work, "a human being unable to have a meaningful influence on the world ceases to exist" on a certain level. Drawing on the work of German psychologist Karl Groos, Graeber emphasizes the importance of meaningful action for human beings (83-84). Ultimately, human beings situate themselves in the world through a variety of means, but the ability to act and have those actions cause effects is one with an inherently positive impact on human psychology. To have all possibility of meaningful action taken away is to cause serious damage on those denied that agency. The consequences of using such definitions of freedom are fairly plain to see: if freedom demands the ability for someone to act in accordance with their own desires and to be able to meaningfully impact their own circumstances—that is, the immediate world around them—then those living in impoverished communities with insufficient infrastructure cannot be said to be meaningfully free, even beyond the generalized Marxist frameworks of typical capitalist exploitation. Appalachia is not unique in its experience of this repressive context, but it is certainly exemplary.

Further, this analysis only considers the raw economic circumstances that are of particular relevance to the region, emphasised by the historically dominant modes of labor. That there is a particular viciousness to the neoliberal project in Appalachia comes with a hefty dose of irony. The region has generally been characterized in the public eye as being one of "inherent conservativeness," a claim which—while obtuse—has also been roughly true on the whole (Stump 6). Though it would be unfair to cast the entirety of Appalachia, a vast geographic expanse with as diverse a population as anywhere in the United States, as politically homogenous, it is nevertheless true that there has been a marked increase in the "extent to which conservative forces have successfully capitalized" on the decline in the material conditions of the region to increase the power of conservative cultural talking points, further inclining these states to the same political direction that is so responsible for the ruinous circumstances in the first place (Stump 150). That this cultural shift to the right harms precisely those people least able to leave for more pleasant conditions—the poor, the young, those with physical and mental impairments, and members of the LGBT community—is also hardly accidental, as the economic field marches in lockstep with the contemporary cultural fixations of the American conservative movement.[1]

It is this context that undergirds Meghan Lamb's 2021 novel *Failure to Thrive*, which takes on a tripartite structure in its approach to contemporary Appalachia. While no specific date is given, nor a specific location other than the state of Pennsylvania, many of the features that exemplify the lack of infrastructural support and economic prosperity parade throughout the novel in a manner that echoes throughout a variety of similar states: "this road," we are told, "is the start of a long line that only leads further away into nothing" (15). Lamb describes an endless rural road that drags inhabitants from run down place to run down place, each one replete with boarded up windows and closed work sites.

Failure to Thrive is organized very loosely around the frame narrative of an underground fire which has raged for years—and will continue to rage for many more—and it is worth examining the psychological implications of this fire before engaging directly with character and theme. The fire, we are told, manifests at first as a "low drone" that "whispers" its presence before the fire is "exhale[d]" from some great unknown earthen lung, incinerating everything in its path (153). The exact extent of this fire is not specified and, for all the imagination allows, it may rage beneath the feet of every single character of the novel in its subterranean home. This fire, a "shadow text" in Lamb's own words, serves to link location to location and reduce the fidelity of discretion; though each section may feel separate, they are in fact connected beneath the feet by a force that is destructive and consuming—a force which, nonetheless, envisions itself as welcoming and benevolent ("Interview"). It does, after all, claim to be "family" in a menacing resonance with various characters (*Failure* 108).

The metaphorical implications of this flame are not hard to grasp. For Freud, the taming of fire was the turning point at which humanity symbolically rejected the domination of animal instinct and became fully human in the contemporary sense; control over the flame represented the reward for the suppression of instinct (189). Losing this control, therefore, suggests a loss in that ability to control oneself beyond the base functions of life, a submission to the biological and a renunciation of the same ability to choose that indicates a loss of freedom. In this sense, then, the fire that rages beneath Pennsylvania is a welling up of growing resentment, of a subterranean anger that emerges from a culture that has been disconnected from its own future. That this flame is destructive and insidious only compounds this image, echoing the social and cultural destruction that coincides with the economic decline of Appalachia under conservative and neoliberal political decisions.

Lamb's choice of frame narrative is piquant, as the three subsections of the novel investigate various forms of this insidious cultural decline. The first, and the one which takes up the majority of the novel and of the analysis given here, revolves around a small family. The mother, Emily, and father, David, have a child named Olivia who has some form of unspecified neurodivergence, for which both parents are unprepared but to which each reacts in radically different ways. Emily, a near-archetypal motherly figure, embraces her daughter and seeks to learn as much as possible to best help Olivia—learning some sign language, working on new methods of communication to navigate around Olivia's non-verbal nature, and giving her a connection to their extended family beyond the nuclear unit. David, by comparison, is unable to handle these challenges. His response to Olivia's specific condition is to distance himself, an issue that worsens as Olivia ages with only minor moments of connection. "Emily and Olivia begin to feel like his other family" as his inability to adjust his expectations of nuclear perfection generate increased resentment between him and the women in his life (68). Ultimately this resentment grows until he leaves and returns to his parents, severing the nuclear unit entirely.

Presenting the family as a failed nuclear unit, Lamb is able to draw upon an ironic sentiment: the collapse of Appalachia drives the disintegration of the same family unit promoted by the conservative sentiment that caused the collapse. Recurrence is a theme that Lamb uses frequently, her paragraphs littered with parallel syntax and motifs that come up every few pages, as she taps into the cyclical lives of people who are locked into routines they never chose. The lack of sufficient infrastructure to help with Olivia's care drives a rift between Emily and David, as Emily sees the state of a nearby care facility and refuses to submit Olivia into its custody. With no support, no functional help to reach for, the family fractures irreparably. David's insistence that "maybe it's not the best […] but it's what they have to work with" functions as a cynical sentiment that is true of the community in general, far beyond the specificity of his own domestic circumstance (90).

Healthcare issues such as those experienced by Emily and David are common across Appalachia, as neoliberal economic policy has prevented the provision of adequate healthcare across the United States, and it is only natural, therefore, that poorer areas of the US would suffer more considerably from a reliance on for-profit care. In a study conducted in 2018, accessibility proved the biggest barrier to healthcare among persons with disabilities in Appalachia. When the services and infrastructure simply do not exist, the inability to pay for it becomes almost irrelevant (Kurowski-Burt and Haddox 99). That it is the child who suffers most from this arrangement is also a powerful statement. Conservative politics relies consistently on the rhetorical centering of the child, the symbol of heteronormative reproduction and the symbol of the continuation of the society seeking to be conserved, whereas Lamb demonstrates the negative effects that conservative policies have on an actual child. It is almost cliché to point out that, to the majority of the American political classes, children are more valuable as symbols of social reproduction than as real people. Once David leaves, Emily's illness overtakes her, and she passes away. Unable to comprehend this fully, Olivia loses whatever was left of her free choice: she becomes a slave to routine, completing one half of her daily tasks while those her mother would complete simply go undone. Her schedule consumes her life. Upon his return to the home, David finds Olivia's skin blistered by her own self-soothing behaviours and the body of Emily decomposing in another room. Olivia is the one who has been left to suffer the collapse of that patriarchal family unit. Only at this moment of complete rupture do "trained professionals" appear to "work on" Olivia—on, not with (Lamb, *Failure* 106).

This abandonment creates a profound contradiction within the family. "[T]here is a word for David's world," we are told—"it is Family" (89). That this claim can be made, and that David can behave as though he believes it to be true while simultaneously abandoning his family, reveals the internal failure of that family structure. For him, family may well be everything, but what family is becomes fluid and subject to other priorities. Importance can be transferred from his family with Emily to his own siblings and parents and then back as the course of his own desire shifts. His belief and faith, then, is entirely superficial. That the fire borrows these words—"the fire says, I know, we are a family"—in the course of its eternal burning only reinforces the ever-changing nature of David's belief and the fragility of his patriarchal position (108). After all, how can his masculinity be rooted in his position as the father when such a position can be simply traded away upon becoming inconvenient?

The ability to develop a flexible relationship with gender expectations—embodying or denying them as one chooses—represents another avenue of freedom that is largely removed from the totemic image of Republican Appalachia. Though inaccurate, the hegemonic depiction of the region as being essentially a zone of unquestionable patriarchal normativity is one carefully promoted by the American right wing—of both major parties. Indeed, even more radical presentations of political activity that question these conservative narratives are often framed within them, with female activists often proposing action in the name of a "mothering instinct" rather than from "conscious political choice" in the way that we might more commonly expect (Stump 158). Workerist notions of masculinity, however, prevent similar involvement from a larger proportion of men in the region, as the cultural image of the man and father as provider relies upon jobs that no longer exist, leaving the men yearning for the same fallen past to which the Republicans promise to return. The Trump campaign promise to "Make America Great Again" crystallizes a form of palingenetic ultranationalism that paralyses the possibility of a more radical masculinity (158-59).

The conservative rhetoric of nostalgic escapism is far from theoretical for Emily and David. Put at its most simple, Emily finds her discontent with the region and its inability to provide for her family becoming stronger, until she begins rejecting its institutions precisely by virtue of her love for Olivia. The only way she can find to escape this desire for change is to die. For David, by contrast, all that it takes to escape is to go back. When he returns from his trip home, all he finds is a corpse and a suffering child. Ultimately, the desire to play make-believe with history can only result in pain, and the only way forward is, bitterly but unsurprisingly, forward.

Framing masculinity in this way—as a culturally promoted political roadblock to freedom of choice in Appalachia—appears in the third of the novel's three parts as well. In this part, we meet Jack, a man who worked processing wood until a car crash robbed him of coordination and independence. Here, the relationship between capitalist labour practices is made explicit and our Marxist conception of freedom fits well. To power the metaphor, Jack's life pre-injury is a masterclass in reification. His identity, his manhood, and his confidence are bound to his role as a physical labourer, and in situations in which the worker is defined entirely by his role in the cycle of production, a body undergoes a process of "self-objectification" whereby the removal of the capacity for work results in the removal of the sense of identity (Lukács 92). It is no wonder, then, that after recovering from the worst of his injuries, the symptom that plagues Jack the longest is his amnesia and cerebral fog.

This crisis becomes self-evident as Jack questions everything about himself post-injury, asking himself, "Where is he?" (Lamb, *Failure* 184) and even experiencing a crisis of his heteronormative identity, losing his temper when his friend Gio remarks that he "didn't think [he] went for guys like that" (200). Ultimately, without a way to safely define himself within the structures of masculinity as a result of his injury—his inability to work stripping him of identity, in line with the American workerist ideology—he follows the same path as David does. He returns to the past and seeks a sense of self there. Very rapidly, he returns home to recover under his parent's care. While there, the only joy he can find is in the pleasures of childhood: of a "luminous", "gap-toothed" child riding a big wheel (217). While Jack's regression is considerably more sympathetic than David's, it is nonetheless an example of the infantilization of Appalachian masculine identity in a neoliberal world. Stripped of work, Jack feels no choice but to be a child, as he can no longer be a man. The ideology of conservative masculinity will allow nothing less.

The second of *Failure to Thrive*'s three parts mediates between Emily's story and Jack's. Like part three, part two relies on the echoes of a labour long gone. Unlike part three, however, and much more like part one, it follows the feminine expectation to be a caregiver—to manage. The narrative of part two follows Helen, who has trained as a nurse's aide some decades prior but who is now working as a dedicated caregiver to her father, who suffers from a combination of ailments and old age. Helen, too, finds herself trapped within the role of the caregiver, unable to escape, and just as Emily and Olivia found themselves entrapped in a routine so powerful that it survived past Emily's death, so too has Helen's role as carer become so routine that she enacts it long after she is no longer being paid for it. Caring for her father, she repeats various mantras to herself, remarking that it was what she remembered from her time as a nursing aid, "though that was almost thirty years ago" (120). Prefacing Jack's experience of becoming reified as a worker, Helen here is cast into the role of the eternal caregiver, something common in the "female-dominated service" industries that make up an increasing quantity of Appalachian labour as male extractive industry diminishes (Latimer and Oberhauser 285). However, contrary to Jack's desire to have his masculinity affirmed by the return to work, Helen finds herself deeply unsatisfied by her entrapment in the role of familial nurse. Unlike Emily, Helen does contemplate the possibility of escape to an unknown "elsewhere," but this is a vague aspiration (Lamb, *Failure* 139). For as long as her father lives, serving as a masculine figure entirely dependent on her for comfort and care, she is bound to the crumbling Appalachian geography that they both represent: him, enfeebled but unable to enact his own will through age and illness, her, captured in the progress of his needs and finding hers absorbed into the vortex of the caregiving female archetype.

A final image of the Appalachian contemporary finds root in part two, that of the drug user. Helen's father finds himself dependent on a variety of pills to treat his numerous ailments, and the parallel of the ongoing American opioid crisis is made obvious. They watch the news as it is announced that *"Local Doctor's Pill Mill Kills Five,"* before contrasting images of the local population are set against each other. "I hope this piece of garbage rots," says one woman, whose rage is immediately adjoined by her statement that "we need these pills to get by [...] without him, we're all gonna have an awful nothing-life" (125). The situation regarding drug usage is precarious and difficult to address with subtlety, yet Lamb's narrative skillfully provides the metaphorical veil required to at once criticize that industry which generates a problem—a crisis which most severely impacts "poor, rural regions" such as depicted in the novel—while presenting those who suffer from a lack of adequate healthcare infrastructure with appropriate sympathy (Flanigan 79). The only judgement here is systemic; the same system that cannot provide adequate care for Olivia also fails to provide adequate care to Helen's father, while allowing a vast increase in those who lose yet more of their freedom to drugs, without which they cannot bear to survive but from which the already-wealthy profit. There is no "clear sense of a better future," we are reminded yet again (Nelson 1).

Returning again to the fire beneath Pennsylvania, it is worth re-examining this flame from another angle. After all, while the destructive aspects of the fire are undeniable, there is also a long history of flame as both a symbol of cleansing and rebirth. The idea of "formative fire" is one that is put most plainly by Gaston Bachelard, whose work reminds us that fire too is born, breathes, grows, and acts as a source of warmth and protection to humanity, in a "projection of life" (56). A threat at first, it may be the case that destruction is what is needed for a new future for Olivia, for Helen, for Jack, and for all those trapped within the recurring cycle of political resentment cultivated for power that is used only to exploit and stir up further discontent.

Ultimately, *Failure to Thrive* assembles a powerful critique of the American state, particularly with regards to its treatment of the Appalachian region, leaving it crumbling, with failing infrastructure, failing resources, and rampant social inequality, yet all the while cultivating a festering conservative ideological bent that promises only a recurrence of that same suffering under the pretence of resurrecting a beautiful past. Lamb's presentation of characters who are fundamentally stripped of the ability to make meaningful decisions and control the direction of their own lives is synecdoche with Marx's claim that freedom is, in itself, unobtainable without these choices. "Personal freedom," we are told, exists only for "the ruling class, and only insofar as they [are] individuals of this class" (86). This denial of meaningful choice is the spiritual violence of which Graeber speaks—or at least, one powerful manifestation of it that emerges in various guises throughout the neoliberal state apparatus.

As Olivia is subject to the limited powers of the family system, she is locked into routines she cannot escape and, eventually, is committed to a care facility. She has no choice in the matter, and the conditions of both of nuclear familiar and the alienating American medical system ensures it. Helen, too, is trapped as the caregiver in a patriarchal relationship from which she cannot escape, surrounded on all sides by victims of that same medical system from which she has been alienated and an ongoing opioid crisis worsened by the state's demonization of the suffering. Jake, again, is alienated from his work by chance or misfortune, and so wedded to this work by the Fordist neoliberal culture that he can no longer entertain a sense of self without it. One cannot be free as a state of being, rather, one's freedom is a contingency, possible "only within the community," a community that has been structurally denuded by active political choice (86). This shattered landscape of hopelessness reveals itself through portraits of neurodivergence, an aging population, physical impairment, and the struggles to escape the expectations of gender. Lamb presents us with only one possibility for a different future: the creative power of the fire beneath that renders everything above to ash.

Note

1. Perhaps contrary to stereotypes, certain regions of Appalachia are far from the heterosexual, cisgendered bastions of conservative expectation. In one report published by the Williams Institute using data from CDC surveys, Appalachian states reported similar percentages of transgender individuals to other, more famously liberal states such as Vermont. Of particular note is their estimation of transgender youth numbers, in which West Virginia appeared to lead the survey (Herman, et al.). Although far from concrete numbers, such indications are enough to banish the idea of a cis-hetero monolith along the mountains.

Works Cited

Bachelard, Gaston. *The Psychoanalysis of Fire.* Translated by Alan C. M. Ross, Routledge, 1964.

Flanigan, Jessica. *Pharmaceutical Freedom: Why Patients Have a Right to Self-Medicate.* Oxford University Press, 2017.

Freud, Sigmund. *Standard Edition of the Complete Psychological Works of Sigmund Freud XXII.* Translated by James Strachey, Hogarth Press, 1964.

Graeber, David. *Bullshit Jobs: A Theory.* Simon & Schuster, 2018.

Harvey, David. *A Brief History of Neoliberalism.* Oxford University Press, 2007.

Herman, Jody L., Andrew R. Flores, Taylor N. T. Brown, Bianca D. M. Wilson, and Kerith J. Conron. *Age of Individuals who Identify as Transgender in the United States.* Williams Institute, January 2017, williamsinstitute.law.ucla.edu/wp-content/uploads/Age-Trans-Individuals-Jan-2017.pdf.

Kurowski-Burt, Amy, and John Christopher Haddox. "Barriers to Healthcare Participation in Persons with Disabilities in Appalachia: A Qualitative Pilot Study." *HERD: Health*

Environments Research and Design Journal, vol. 11, no. 4, 2018, pp. 95-107.

Lamb, Meghan. *Failure to Thrive.* Apocalypse Party, 2021.

———. "Interview with Meghan Lamb, Author of Failure to Thrive." Interview by Courtney Harler, *The Masters Review,* 9 November 2021, mastersreview.com/interview-with-meghan-lamb-author-of-failure-to-thrive/.

Latimer, Melissa, and Ann M. Oberhauser. "Exploring Gender and Economic Development in Appalachia." *Journal of Appalachian Studies,* vol. 10, no. 3, 2004, pp. 269-91.

Lukács, Georg. *History and Class Consciousness: Studies in Marxist Dialectics.* Translated by Rodney Livingstone, MIT Press, 1971.

Marx, Karl, and Friedrich Engels. *The German Ideology.* Prometheus Books, 1998.

Nelson, Joel I. *Post-Industrial Capitalism: Exploring Economic Inequality in America.* SAGE Publications, 1995.

Schwartzman, Gabe. "Power and the Future of Appalachia." *Southeastern Geographer,* vol. 61, no. 4, 2021, pp. 343-56.

Scott, James C. *Two Cheers for Anarchism.* Princeton University Press, 2012.

Stump, Nicholas F. *Remaking Appalachia: Ecosocialism, Ecofeminism, and Law.* West Virginia University Press, 2021.

Vazzana, Caryn M., and Jeta Rudi-Polloshka. "Appalachia Has Got Talent, But Why Does It Flow Away? A Study on the Determinants of Brain Drain from Rural USA." *Economic Development Quarterly,* vol. 33, no. 3, 2019, pp. 159-249.

Jay Fraser is a writer from Lincolnshire in the United Kingdom, near the North Sea. He is currently a doctoral candidate at the University of Lincoln studying representations of psychological aberrancy in the Gothic. Much of his influence comes from radical anarchist political writings, post-structuralist philosophy, and the beautiful harshness of the ocean and the thorns of nature. His writing has previously appeared in *Bodies, Power, and Noise in Industrial Music*, published by Palgrave MacMillan; the journal *Strukturiss;* poetry magazines *the tide rises, Fever Dream Journal,* and *Versification; Wickerpedia*, an anthology of essays on *The Wicker Man*, and in anarchist publication *Organise!* You can find him on Twitter/X @JayFraser1, or occasionally in fields picking rowan berries.

Can You Be Free If You're Not Real?:
Emily St. John Mandel on Freedom and the Simulation Hypothesis

John C. Merfeld,
Tom Richards,
and Noah Stengl

> "Is this the real life?"
>
> —Queen
> "Bohemian Rhapsody" (1975)

> "Shining on the inside. Maybe."
>
> — The Mountain Goats
> "Incandescent Ruins" (2022)

Introduction

At the turn of the century, *The Matrix* (1999) enthralled audiences with a mind-bending proposition: What if the reality we perceive is a simulation, a sort of hyper-detailed video game developed by tyrannical artificial intelligence to distract its human captives? Furthermore, if our perceived reality is a simulation, would we want to know? Testifying to the cultural fascination with this proposition, the billion-dollar film franchise went on to release three sequels, "redpilling" swiftly entered the zeitgeist, and the "brain-in-a-vat" version of simulated reality endures to this day as a sci-fi staple.

A few years after *The Matrix*, though to considerably less public acclaim, the "simulation hypothesis" was given serious philosophical teeth. In a now-famous paper, Nick Bostrom argued if we assume computing power continues to advance, a processor of "planetary mass" will eventually have the capacity to replicate the sub-neuronal activity of billions of brains. In this "posthuman" era, "a single such computer could simulate the entire mental history of humankind," running what Bostrom refers to as "ancestor-simulations," and "a posthuman civilization may eventually build an astronomical number of such computers" (247-48). In this case, he argues, one of three scenarios must be true: either 1) technologically-advanced civilizations go extinct before becoming posthuman, 2) posthumans are uninterested in running ancestor-simulations, or 3) we are likely living in a simulation (251-55). Provided the first two options are false, the third option comes down to simple probability. If there are an "astronomical number" of computers, each generating a plausible simulacrum of reality, then the likelihood our world is "base reality," or *unsimulated* reality, is practically zero. "Unless we are now living in a simulation," Bostrom writes, "our descendents will almost certainly never run an ancestor-simulation" (255). Or, inverting the logic, unless computing power ceases to advance, we are almost certainly living in a future civilization's ancestor-simulation.

Twenty years after Botsrom's first iteration of the simulation hypothesis, what may have seemed like an academic gloss on Hollywood fantasy has only become more credible. Prominent personalities from Elon Musk to Neil deGrasse Tyson seriously entertain that we may live in a simulation, and with advancements in computing power and the arrival of generative artificial intelligence, some now believe the "simulation point," or the dawning of Bostrom's "posthuman era," lies but a century or less in the future (Virk 107-09). Yet, while commentators have pondered the ethical and theological implications of the simulation hypothesis, relatively little has been said about the relationship between the simulation hypothesis and freedom. What would freedom mean in a simulated reality? Irrespective of the veracity of the simulation hypothesis, what can this discourse tell us about freedom in the twenty-first century and beyond?

These are questions taken up by Emily St. John Mandel in her novel *Sea of Tranquility* (2022). The simulation hypothesis functions within the narrative as an explanation for time travel: characters are able to travel through time without disastrous butterfly effects because they are altering not base reality but a simulated reality that can "repair" itself.[1] When a particularly intense "anomaly" resists repair, and moments from different centuries bleed into one another, the characters begin to suspect their world is not what it seems. Beyond this plot device, Mandel peppers *Sea of Tranquility* with allusions to a sneaking sense of unreality. Colonialism, pandemics, mass consumerism, ruptures in one's life, psychedelics, memory, the sensation of being lost in thought, and, most humorously, the layout and décor of hotel rooms all give the impression that our perceived reality is artificial or simulated, a shallow veneer atop a deeper, "more real" world. It is a more mundane and thus more disquieting study of unreality than high-flying sci-fi like *The Matrix*, and it challenges readers to confront the implications of the simulation hypothesis and other simulation-like phenomena in their own lives.

While space does not permit us to address each of the simulation-esque elements included in the novel, we take up several of them to think through the foregoing questions about freedom. We begin by providing a brief overview of the novel that accounts for the kind of freedom Mandel attributes to each of the main characters, and how this is troubled by the simulation hypothesis. Then, we consider how Mandel's interpretation of the simulation hypothesis may be analogized to twenty-first-century dilemmas and the threats they pose to freedom. Finally, we liken the underlying assumptions of the simulation hypothesis to the "ugly freedom" of colonialism and plumb the novel for a resistance strategy, or a means of freeing ourselves from the simulation.

Freedom and Simulation in *Sea of Tranquility*

Sea of Tranquility is divided into sections that focus on four different characters across different time periods, from 1912 to 2401. Section by section, Mandel presents the personal narratives and inner thoughts of Edwin, Vincent, Olive, and Gaspery, each of whom strikes out on their own in one way or another. As such, the reader experiences the world of the novel from the perspective of one character at a time.

However, these disparate characters and time periods are united by encountering a mysterious spacetime anomaly central to the novel. It is described as a kind of ontological bleeding, in which one place or time is intruded upon by the sights and sounds of another. Near the beginning of the twenty-fifth century, this anomaly would become the center of an investigation by an agent of the bureaucratic Time Institute (Gaspery), but, prior to that, it is witnessed by a man in 1912 (Edwin), a girl in 1994 (Vincent), and a woman in the late twenty-second century (Olive).

Contemporary discussions of freedom (at least in Europe and the United States) tend to focus on individuals and what they can and cannot do, own, say, and believe. Many classical liberals, neorepublicans, libertarians, and anarchists would characterize freedom as the degree of control an individual has over their own life, with most disputes arising over how far the boundaries of one's "own life" extend. Debate around mask mandates and vaccine requirements are only the most recent example of this logic. At first glance, Mandel's choice to structure the plot around each character's thoughts, decisions, and actions evokes this formulation of freedom as individual control. None of the characters become overly dependent on others, and most have an uncommon amount of resources, access, and opportunities to do as they choose. Yet, the novel also explores how this apparent freedom can be jeopardized by external events and systems beyond the individual's control, with the ultimate and most extreme example being the spacetime anomaly that destabilizes the very fabric of reality in which each character purports to act freely. As a result of this exploration, a tempered version of freedom-as-control emerges.

The first character the reader encounters, Edwin St. John St. Andrew, is the epitome of privilege. Born in England just before the turn of the twentieth century, as the British Empire ascended to its historical apex, Edwin is the third son of a future earl. He is a beneficiary of an institution of structured inequality that offers him more resources and opportunities than the vast majority of Britons, and yet he is unsatisfied. At the outset, Edwin is frustrated by the rigid constraints of the aristocracy, being somewhat bitter that his brother, not he, is in line to inherit the family title and estate. He is also upset with his own role in a ruthless imperial institution, epitomized by his mother's fixation on her youth in British India. When his disgust for the subjugation of native inhabitants under the British Raj (and colonialism, more generally) bubbles to the surface during a dinner party, Edwin embarrasses himself and his family, and is thereafter exiled from England. Sent on remittance, he eventually lands at the far-western edge of the Commonwealth in Victoria, British Columbia.[2]

Edwin exercises considerable control over his life, even after his banishment from British society. In Canada, he spends his days painting, playing chess, drinking, and even making a brief foray into farming. Money is of no concern and his real occupation is, as he wistfully puts it, "just contemplating [his] next move" (Mandel, *Sea* 24). Yet, this control is rendered precarious as Edwin walks through the forest in a remote outpost on Vancouver Island. Finding himself under a broad maple tree, he is suddenly plunged "into a flash of darkness.... He has an impression of being in some vast interior, something like a train station or cathedral, and there are notes of violin music, there are other people around him, and then an incomprehensible sound" (29). In the order of the narrative, Edwin is the first character to experience the anomaly. For all his privilege, he will spend the rest of his life questioning his sanity.

The next character to encounter the anomaly is a thirteen-year-old girl named Vincent Smith, who walks under that same (albeit older) maple tree on Vancouver Island in 1994. While the reader spends relatively little time with Vincent in *Sea of Tranquility*—for the most part, she is a memory in the mind of her friend, Mirella—she is central to Mandel's previous book, *The Glass Hotel* (2020). Of the four characters presented here, she most explicitly considers freedom as control.

Around the time of the anomaly, Vincent's mother dies, and she is forced to make a way for herself in the world. Her mother was a formative figure in her life, being a "woman who'd imagined writing poetry in the wilderness but somehow found herself sunk in the mundane difficulties of raising a child and running a household in the wilderness instead. There's the idea of wilderness, and then there's the unglamorous labor of it" (Mandel, *Glass* 61). Remembering her mother, Vincent meditates on one of the limits to personal freedom: when one makes a choice and opens one door, one closes the door on many other possibilities. With this in mind, Vincent enters an arrangement with the much older Jonathan Alkadis—she becomes, basically, his "trophy wife"—and she enjoys a period of stability and opportunity which she refers to as her time in the "kingdom of money." It was in the kingdom of money that she had the time and energy to think deeply. As she says, "what kept her in the kingdom was the previously unimaginable condition of not having to think about money, because that's what money gives you: the freedom to stop thinking about money" (90).

Vincent considers all the decisions she has made, and the alternate realities that would have sprung forth if she had chosen differently. Then, she extends this line of thinking to history and current events:

> Imagining an alternate reality where there was no Iraq War, for example, or where the terrifying new swine flu in the Republic of Georgia hadn't been swiftly contained; an alternate world where the Georgia flu blossomed into an unstoppable pandemic and civilization collapsed.... Or spin it back further: a version of history where the Korean peninsula was never divided, where the USSR had never invaded Afghanistan and al-Qaeda had never been founded, where Ariel Sharon died in combat as a young man. She could only play this game for so long before she was overcome by a kind of vertigo and had to make herself stop. (66-67)

Here, Vincent echoes early modern metaphysical deliberations over what it means to have free will, specifically Gottfried Leibniz's conception of freedom. For Vincent, as for Leibniz, the current state of the universe has materialized as a necessary result of all events leading up to the present. Even freedom itself is the product of this contingency. Despite all the latitude Vincent feels she has in her "kingdom of money," she senses she is not truly in control of her destiny, since any chance occurrence could spawn an alternate reality in which her life is radically different. As if to underscore this point, in *Sea of Tranquility*, Mandel references that Vincent started yet another new life as a cook on a container ship after her husband's fraudulent investments are brought to light. Then, after all that, she dies: "She just disappeared from the ship. Seems like it was an accident. No body" (51).

Mandel then introduces Olive Llewellyn, a novelist who hails from lunar Colony Two in the year 2203 and is in the midst of a dizzying book tour on Earth.[3] Nonstop readings, panels, book signings, and more than a few obtuse and patronizing questions about her work and family begin to wear Olive down. Still, she reminds herself she is fortunate and ought to enjoy the opportunities she has to travel the world and experience the glamor of artistic fame.

Nonetheless, Olive's storyline worries the relationship between opportunity, control, and freedom even more than Vincent's. Constantly in the public eye, badgered by reporters, drivers, and her own readers to be something she is not, Olive feels her grip on reality slipping. This is not the first time, since she, too, experienced the anomaly while walking through the Oklahoma City Airship Terminal. When pressed about her experience by Gaspery, who poses as a reporter for the conspicuously titled *Contingencies Magazine*, Olive responds: "I'm afraid I'll seem too eccentric if it makes it into the final version of the interview. Could we go off the record for a moment?" (99). For all her opportunity and access, Olive is prevented from being her authentic self by the constraints of public perception. Eventually, she and others on Earth and the lunar colonies face constraints more physical in nature when a deadly pandemic confines them to their homes.

Finally, Gaspery Roberts is the character most at the center of the novel's action and, curiously, the character who seems to evince the least control over his life. Raised on the same lunar colony as Olive, though two hundred years later, Gaspery grew up in the shadow of his older sister, saying that at the age of eleven "I already had the first suspicions that I might not be exactly the kind of person I wanted to be" (108). He struggles to find his way, until he is offered a job at the Time Institute.

In this new role, Gaspery becomes a time traveler, jumping back and forth in time to interview the characters who experienced the anomaly. Gaspery's sister, who also works for the Time Institute, suspects the anomaly may be evidence their world is a simulation, a sort of "file corruption" betraying the fact that reality is but a series of bits and bytes. Nonetheless, she is adamant Gaspery must do nothing to disrupt the timeline. Yet, unwilling to let Olive die in the pandemic or watch Edwin suffer from his perceived insanity, Gaspery contradicts the edicts of the Time Institute by convincing Olive to end her book tour early and assuring Edwin that what he saw in the forest on Vancouver Island had actually happened. These are remarkable acts of free will from someone who rarely feels in control of their life and who has reason to believe their very existence is less than real. What is more, Gaspery eventually discovers it is his interactions with Edwin, Vincent, Olive, and *himself* (at one point, a much older Gaspery disguised as an airship-terminal busker is interviewed by the time-traveling Gaspery, who is none the wiser) that precipitate the anomaly in the first place.

Whether encountering a supernatural event, grappling with their public image, responding to a pandemic, or simply musing on historical contingency, Mandel's characters all confront the fact that they have less control over their lives than they assumed. Indeed, their lives may not even be real. Any "control" they wield may be curtailed, if not actively directed, by the whim of an intelligence they sense but cannot understand. Of what value are material resources, access, and opportunities under conditions of such metaphysical uncertainty (or pandemic strictures, the vagaries of public perception, and questionable sanity, as the case may be)? Gaspery's response, which reads as Mandel's, is to dismiss the question: "If definitive proof emerges that we're living in a simulation, the correct response to that news will be *So what*. A life lived in a simulation is still a life" (246). In other words, freedom may not require *total* control over one's destiny. As Edwin, so distressed by his supposed insanity that all he can do is sit in a garden, puts it, "he could live here quietly, and care for the garden"—which, notably, is a simulation of natural flora—"and that might eventually be enough" (222). Faced with the possibility of unreality, and the questions about freedom-as-control that possibility raises, Mandel counsels living a life we find meaningful "might eventually be enough."

Simulations as Threats to Freedom

We now turn our attention from the relationship between freedom and simulation in the lives of Mandel's characters to what her novel might tell us about our own world. Ultimately, Mandel does not dwell on whether or not the world of *Sea of Tranquility* is a simulation. Instead, she supposes that it is, and uses the simulation as an analog for crises that threaten our sense of freedom in the twenty-first century. By emphasizing Gaspery's eventual ambivalence to the existential implications of the simulation hypothesis, Mandel invites us to consider the practical effects of a world built atop simulations. Specifically, she develops themes of personal environmental displacement, the erosion of individuals' social autonomy, and widespread ecological damage.

First, consider how the novel examines the limits of the characters' comfort with their environments. In addition to literally being set in a simulated universe, *Sea of Tranquility* is preoccupied with whether or not the modern world can be considered truly "real," given the many ways in which nature has been supplanted by technology. Olive and Gaspery both grew up on the Moon, where everything from the gravity to the weather is an artificial mimicry of Earth. Intriguingly, both characters find their lives quite ordinary. Olive describes it as "fine... she didn't grow up *longing for Earth* or experience her life as a *continual displacement*, thank you" (94). Neither exhibits signs of *solastalgia*, which Glenn Albrecht describes as "the distress that is produced by environmental change impacting on people while they are directly connected to their home environment" (95). Instead, they consider their lunar environment just as natural as Earth's. As Gaspery puts it, "I've always loved rain, and knowing that it isn't coming from clouds doesn't make me love it any less" (131). Mandel thus argues our intuition of what is real or natural, and how that affects our experience of a place, can stretch well beyond even what we might consider obviously manufactured.

However, Gaspery still values his sense of belonging to a specific environment. He begins to feel displaced as the likelihood of the simulation hypothesis dawns on him. He "stood there thinking of all the things around [him] that might not be real. The stone of the lobby floor. The fabric of [his] clothes" (Mandel, *Sea* 132). He becomes more rattled by the artificial weather and geography of his colony (147-48). Upon the discovery that both his sister and his old friend are in fact studying the simulation as agents of the Time Institute, he describes "the disorienting sense of one reality slipping away and being replaced by another" (141). Substitute "reality" with "environment" and we see how living in a simulation might trigger extreme solastalgia. It goes beyond the guilt and grief we feel today at humanity's failure to preserve its native habitat, and even beyond the indifference of postnaturalism. In a simulated world, the very notion of a habitat is meaningless. In *Sea of Tranquility*, no corner of our world, nor of any world, is unspoiled by mechanization, an idea that unsettles even someone accustomed to life in a lunar colony. The conclusion is sobering: no matter how totally we may adapt to modern life, humans will continue to feel the loss of habitats and of species as personal wounds. No matter how completely our sense of "home environment" drifts from its evolutionary and cultural roots, or is replicated with uncanny accuracy, we will mourn the loss of the real.

Broader social crises can be found in *Sea of Tranquility*, too. Consider the Time Institute, a secretive body at the intersection of government, academia, and law enforcement. Exercising a monopoly on time travel, it wields a power that the Party of *Nineteen Eighty-Four* (1949) could only dream of: the ability not just to rewrite history but remake it. The Time Institute does not appear to be accountable to any democratic body, yet its influence is immense. "Is there an unease that's specific to the sense of invisible bureaucracy at work around you?" Gaspery wonders during his experience applying to work at the Institute (148). We come to learn that many of the most severely punished criminals in Gaspery's world are rogue time travelers, and the Institute's criterion for whether to investigate an anomaly is whether the anomaly represents a direct threat to its existence. Thus, the state uses time travel primarily as a means of coercion, punishment, and self-preservation. One cannot help but think of facial recognition software's role as an instrument of party control in contemporary China, or of Amazon's brazen use of customer data to augment its algorithms.

However, while far from utopian, the Time Institute is not an allegory for totalitarianism. Somewhere between what behavioral economists call "nudging" and outright coercion, its influence represents the myriad ways in which we as twenty-first-century individuals are already being simulated, and the countless invisible bureaucracies that encroach on our agency. These bureaucracies are both public and private, physical and digital. Their blows to our autonomy are mostly subtle and behavioral, rather than absolute or legalistic. They are advertisers, predicting which video will catch our eye, continuously harvesting and processing elements of our personal realities to feed into the next generation of models; they are central banks, using macroeconomic simulations to shape our financial behavior; they are AI chatbots, feeding us advice from within black boxes. And, yes, they are health systems, whose epidemiological models informed recommendations and decisions around lockdowns, restrictions, and requirements during the pandemic, sparking a visceral debate around freedom that will doubtless be rehashed and relitigated on the campaign trail during upcoming election cycles. The Time Institute and the simulation it exploits take this idea to its logical extreme. In the world of *Sea of Tranquility*, you have been simulated fully. In fact, that is all you are. Gaspery's sister warns him of how hard it is to resist intervening in the lives of others once you know them in perfect detail. She says it "requires an... inhuman level of detachment" (136). Mandel might as well have been writing about our present-day techno-bureaucracy, which knows us so well and cares about us so little.

While Mandel's time travel and simulations provide an analog for the personal experience of environmental change and bureaucratic control, the spacetime anomaly at the heart of *Sea of Tranquility* functions as a metaphor for the harm wrought by humanity on entire ecosystems. In the novel, the anomaly is not formally "discovered" until the 2400s. By that time, the hubristic Time Institute hypothesizes that their observations are akin to a form of corrupted data in the simulation underpinning reality. Gaspery eventually discovers the anomaly was in fact created *after* the Institute sent him back in time. It arose from the computational burden on the simulation attempting to reconcile one individual's encounters with other versions of himself. In effect, the Time Institute triggered the very corruption it considered such a threat to humanity (and, perhaps more importantly, to itself).

In our own world, localized environmental catastrophes are a fact of everyday life. Twenty-first-century society is all too familiar with the threat of oil spills, toxic chemical leaks, and nuclear meltdown. And, of course, we are still only beginning to comprehend the global effects of anthropogenic climate change. What all of these ecological damages have in common is their basis in powerful technologies: the fuels that power our cities, the synthetic materials from which they are built, the emissions they disgorge. The anomaly is an example of how the powerful few employ technology to achieve mastery over their environment, only to discover they knew much less than they thought about that environment. In this way, Mandel uses the simulation hypothesis to envision an ecological disaster on a scale even grander than climate change. She imagines a simulation of reality that is not even safe from tampering by the people residing in it.

Freedom from the Simulation

Heretofore, we have examined how the freedom of the characters in *Sea of Tranquility* is troubled by the simulation hypothesis and how simulations can function as an analogy for unfreedom in the twenty-first century. In what remains, we examine some properties of the simulation hypothesis itself and suggest how these might be challenged. Before this, however, it is worth exploring how Mandel weaves into the novel a seemingly disparate theme: colonialism.

Since at least the fifteenth century, colonialism has radically remade the world many times over. This is not simply a florid way of saying colonialism has had "great effects." Rather, colonialism is a *world-making* phenomenon: it creates subjects and modulates relations between them, orients subjectivity and regulates standards of knowledge, and routes the flow of resources, wealth, and power. What makes colonization so destructive is that it never makes a world in a vacuum, but appropriates, attacks, or negates the worlds already existing in the spaces it penetrates. Its world-making power is simultaneously *world-ending*, and in more ways than one. In the shadow of colonialism's positive project—"gold, God, and glory"—is a more negative project. Anxieties of overpopulation and economic stagnation, an apoplectic social body, national decline, and dynamics that herald the "end of the world" in the colonial metropole are also motives for colonization. That is, to prevent the end of its own world, a colonial power remakes itself by ending others.

Two storylines in *Sea of Tranquility* illustrate these world-making and world-ending properties of colonialism. One of the first details the reader learns about Edwin is that he is a "remittance man" in British Canada, a status which communicates colonial anxieties of decline. To receive a remittance meant to be exiled from the metropole either because one was a social embarrassment (as in Edwin's case) or, more commonly, because the languishing British aristocracy could no longer sustain all its members. In Victoria, "a far-distant simulation of England," a fellow remittance man puts a positive spin on their situation, describing it as "building a new future... in a new and far-distant land. ... We can create our own world in this place" (19-20, 22). However, Edwin spots the ghostly negative in this image. Walking on a beach, he passes two indigenous women and is tempted to confess his abhorrence for colonialism before he realizes the "next logical question will be *Then what are you doing here?*" (26). "Building a new future... in a new and far-distant land" means denying the manifest present of the world that already exists there.

Olive's storyline is also intertwined with colonialism. Olive grew up in a lunar city "soothing in its symmetry and its order" that is a prototype of the intergalactic colonization that would allow humanity to survive the supernova of the Sun (76, 104-05). Each night on her tour, she delivers a lecture on the way empires throughout history have spread devastating disease and precipitated the ends of many worlds. She imparts the pervasiveness of colonial anxiety to her audiences, asking, "When have we ever believed that the world *wasn't* ending?" (189). Thus, Olive's reaction to news that the Far Colonies are under construction, the fulfillment of the project inaugurated by her lunar home, is surprising: "She would always remember this moment... When had she last experienced true awe? It had been awhile. Olive was flooded with happiness. She raises her glass. 'To Alpha Centauri,' she said" (90-91). Unlike Edwin, Olive does not see how her civilization's impulse to create a new world for fear of the present world's end might end yet another world elsewhere in the galaxy.

Why does Mandel embed these stories of colonial world-making and world-ending in a novel that is otherwise about time travel and computer-simulated reality? We suggest these same properties apply to the simulation hypothesis. First, the simulation hypothesis imagines a future in which simulators literally design numerous artificial worlds for their own benefit. Bostrom himself remains agnostic about the motivations of simulators, but commentators have speculated these could include nostalgia, social experimentation, testing artificial intelligence, and uploading all existence to a "cloud" to avoid apocalypse (Jenkins 24-26). It is an existential colonization rather than a spatial one. Second, while world-ending anxieties are evident in these motivations, they also animate Bostrom's own reasoning. Instead of "going crazy," the most sensible response to the simulation hypothesis, according to Bostrom, is to hope we are, in fact, simulated, as this would mean the scenario in which technologically-advanced societies cease to exist is false (Bostrom 255). To hope for simulation means to hope (naively) for a future in which our technological advancements—and their dense neocolonial entanglements—continue to end some worlds in order to remake others.

Colonialism's world-making and world-ending properties are emblematic of what Elizabeth Anker calls "ugly freedoms," or "a celebrated value of nondomination or uncoerced action [that] can be practiced as brutality, which also leaves this brutality discounted or disavowed" (6). If our comparison is plausible, then the simulation hypothesis also promotes ugly freedoms: the freedom to create entire realities for utilitarian exploitation or, at best, with cruel indifference toward the subjectivities that populate them; the freedom to continue ending worlds through resource extraction, with the hope that doing so will somehow assure the continuation of our own. If this is the freedom the simulation augurs, are there any alternatives? Can we be free *from* the simulation and its ugly properties? Mandel suggests we can, and *Sea of Tranquility* once again offers a model in the character of Gaspery Roberts.

We have already examined how Gaspery rejects any notion that the simulation alters his life in a meaningful way. In this sense, he remains free despite the metaphysical implications of the simulation hypothesis. We now want to demonstrate how Gaspery exemplifies another kind of freedom that is less a trait or attitude he possesses than an action he performs. Tasked with investigating the anomaly by the Time Institute, which wants only to solidify its world-making power, Gaspery does something else: he breaks protocol and liberates three individuals from ways of seeing their world that serve only the interests of the powerful. He gives Olive the information she needs to make a life-saving decision, even though the Time Institute and governments in her own era would choose to let her die in a "fairly well-contained" pandemic. He reassures Edwin he has not lost his grip on reality by confirming his "hallucination" and explaining that "reality" is not what it seems. Most interestingly, he encourages his younger self to continue probing his assumptions about the unreality of the world. One might call these acts a form of "consciousness-raising," or even *Matrix*-style "red-pilling."

To be sure, Gaspery's illicit acts do not topple the Time Institute or wreak vengeance against whatever intelligence is responsible for creating the simulation. However, by offering new ways of seeing the world, he helps three characters achieve peace, purpose, and, indeed, a certain level of control over their lives. On their own, they may not be able to halt the world-making and world-ending practices of the Time Institute and the unknown simulators, but they can at least see these "ugly freedoms" for what they are. Moreover, Gaspery's relentless examination of his world functions as the anomaly that disrupts, if only momentarily, the seamless functioning of the simulation. By questioning the world, he becomes an obstacle to the powerful few (be they colonizers or simulators) who seek to make, end, and remake worlds for their own benefit.

Conclusion

In this chapter, we have considered how the simulation hypothesis troubles freedom within the ambit of *Sea of Tranquility*, how it functions as an analogy for systems and crises of the twenty-first century, and how the assumptions of the simulation hypothesis parallel the "ugly freedoms" of colonialism. The novel shows us that simulations need not affect our subjective sense of freedom; it is possible to make choices and live a meaningful life within a simulation. At the same time, there are many things in our world that are simulations, or are simulation-like, and these tend to undermine freedom insofar as they shape or limit the decisions we are able to make. Like Gaspery, or one facet of his character, we are free to not care about this: "A life lived in a simulation is still a life." Yet, as our reality becomes increasingly simulated, we cannot count on self-serving institutions to protect and promote even this meager freedom. The novel conditions of the twenty-first century call us, also like Gaspery, to cast a critical eye on our worlds, to investigate the ugliness with which they are "freely" made and unmade. In so doing, we too might become the anomalies that disrupt our so-called "reality."

Notes

1. It's worth noting that Bostrom briefly considers something like this in his explanation of the simulation hypothesis: "a posthuman simulator would have enough computing power to keep track of the detailed belief-states in all human brains at all times… Should any error occur, the director could edit the states of any brains that have become aware of an anomaly before this spoils the simulation" (247).

2. It may be worth noting that the rigid constraints on aristocrats have once again been brought to the fore of popular discourse after the royal family pushed another "spare" son to leave England in favor of Vancouver Island, in this case to try to "carve

out a progressive new role within [the] institution" (The Duke and Duchess of Sussex).

3. Olive is clearly a stand-in for Mandel herself. Leading up to the COVID-19 pandemic, Mandel was on a book tour for her acclaimed pandemic novel, *Station Eleven* (2014). Likewise, Olive is traveling from podium to podium, reading excerpts about fictional pandemics even as a new, deadly pandemic begins to spread.

Works Cited

Albrecht, Glenn, et al. "Solastalgia: The Distress Caused by Environmental Change." *Australasian Psychiatry*, vol. 15, no. 1, 2007, pp. 95-98.

Anker, Elizabeth R. *Ugly Freedoms*. Duke University Press, 2022.

Bostrom, Nick. "Are We Living in a Computer Simulation?" *The Philosophical Quarterly*, vol. 53, no. 211, 2003, pp. 243-255.

The Duke and Duchess of Sussex. Photo of Harry and Meghan with announcement of role in the Royal Family. *Instagram*, 3 Jan 2020, instagram.com/p/B7EaGS_Jpb9/.

Jenkins, Peter S. "Historical Simulations—Motivational, Ethical and Legal Issues." *Journal of Future Studies*, vol. 11, no. 1, 2006, pp. 23-42.

Mandel, Emily St. John. *The Glass Hotel*. Alfred A. Knopf, 2020.

———. *Sea of Tranquility*. Alfred A. Knopf, 2022.

Virk, Rizwan. *The Simulation Hypothesis*. Bayview Books, LLC, 2019.

John C. Merfeld works as a programmer in Boston, Massachusetts, focusing on data-centric applications. His written work has appeared in NPR and a smattering of blogs, podcasts, scientific papers, open-source software projects, and indie rock albums. He is especially interested in the cultural impact of science and technology.

Tom Richards is a Ph.D. student in Comparative Biomedical Sciences at the University of Wisconsin-Madison. His current work focuses on the ecology and epidemiology of multi-host pathogens, especially those transmitted by ticks and mosquitoes. Among other things, this involves building simulations to explore disease transmission under varying scenarios.

Noah Stengl is a lecturer and Ph.D. candidate in Political Science at the University of Wisconsin-Madison, where he works on Indigenous political thought, American political thought, and environmental political theory. He is currently writing a dissertation on the political theory of land in nineteenth-century America. At least, such is the case in this simulation.

Caught in the Web: Freedom and Techno-Dystopia in *Mr. Robot*

Sony Jalarajan Raj and Adith K. Suresh

> "Control can sometimes be an illusion. But sometimes you need illusion to gain control."
>
> — *Mr. Robot*
> "eps2.5_h4ndshake.sme"

The idea of freedom has multiple meanings in different contexts. It is an integral part of discourses surrounding the functionality of societies, the nature of human relationships, and the operation of power structures. Ideologically conflated as "common sense" (Bogues 4) and universally recognized as a fundamental right, freedom in the abstract sense reflects a range of social, political, moral, cultural, and existential connotations. In the context of Western societies, the rhetorical nature of freedom implies the flexibility of its meaning, and the way people experience freedom not only affects the quality of their life but the characteristics of the social conditions that contribute to it. Measuring freedom in a globalized and technologically advanced world is extremely complex because the overproduction of information and the dissemination of knowledge are subjected to strategies of mind control. In the contemporary world, the crisis of freedom emerges from the production of contradictory meanings, which include contexts where freedom itself becomes a means of coercion (Han). Today, governments, corporations, media conglomerates, religious groups, and political parties construct specific narratives and false realities to assert their perception of freedom, which diminishes the understanding of what it means to be free in a complex system of communicative engagements.

Disruptions in the individualistic and collective aspects of freedom affect the thriving of modern democracies. Freedom faces new challenges in the age of the Anthropocene, where human activity has crossed both physical and cognitive barriers (Zajchowski, Dustin, and Hill). The environment-society relations in the Anthropocene have an "objective" dimension that refers to a concrete, observable transformation in the relationship between humans and the environment, and a "subjective" dimension involving how society perceives and comprehends the natural world (Stoner and Melathopoulos 22). According to Elisabeth R. Anker, different stories of freedom and subjectivity, even those exploring unpleasant aspects, can help foster the recognition and desirability of the essential actions needed for long-term planetary survival amidst environmental challenges (33).

Large-scale technology is identified as an important factor involved in the Anthropocene discourse where humans are inextricably tethered to the "technosphere" (Haff). Since freedom is relative to the restrictions that prevent its exercise, it is important to understand how catastrophic scenarios in the contemporary technological society redefine freedom as a concept, practice, and fundamental right. Media plays a major role in the portrayal of freedom through visual means and films and television series have represented dystopian imaginings and disasters where freedom is affected by human activities. Understanding the notion of freedom and its complex ruminations in a crisis is mandatory to discussions dealing with the ill effects of the Anthropocene.

This chapter examines this context by analyzing the American television techno-thriller series *Mr. Robot* (2015-2019), created by Sam Esmail. *Mr. Robot* has achieved critical as well as popular attention for its realistic treatment of themes such as cybersecurity, corporate power, political anarchy, radical protest, and clinical depression (Nellis). It portrays a technologically advanced world connected and controlled through the internet, where the boundaries between reality and illusion become arbitrary. The narrative follows the protagonist, Elliot Alderson (Rami Malek), and his attempts to break the barriers created by powerful authoritative figures hidden under the surface realities of technology.

This chapter analyzes how this series attempts to show the nature of freedom in a world where computer programs construct simulated pseudo-realities to propagate agendas. It argues that *Mr. Robot* presents a scenario of what can be called a "techno-dystopia in the Anthropocene," where technologically assisted human activity achieves a destructive power to undermine the futuristic aspirations of a free world. The emotional, psychological, and political borders of freedom emphasized in the show demonstrate characters trapped within and outside the realm of normative structures. This study discusses how the visual and narrative environment of *Mr. Robot* places the individual in this technosphere as a means to re-evaluate concepts of freedom and protest. In order to subvert the simulated natural order, characters have to adopt new radical strategies that transgress the normalized discourses of freedom.

Anthropocene and the Illusion of Freedom: The Rise of Technoscapes

The geological division that defines the contemporary global environment is the Anthropocene Epoch, in which human activity is observed to have overcome natural processes to reach a point of producing a maximum impact on the environment (Crutzen). The Anthropocene marks the "magnitude, variety and longevity of human-induced changes" that altered the relationship between humans and the Earth system (Lewis and Maslin). Human influence can be measured in terms of the changes happening in a range of areas including the atmosphere, Earth's surface, oceans, and biological life. Jedediah Purdy opines that the Anthropocene began as part of a threefold crisis—of ecology, economics, and politics. After agricultural and industrial revolutions skyrocketed human activity to new possibilities for exploitation in a new globalized context, the Anthropocene has become a category of narratives that reflect the disastrous effect on life not only on the ecological and biological levels but on the social, cultural, and political levels as well. The natural resources that helped human beings in their evolution to new dimensions of progress have now become agents of climate change in modern civilization, which is increasingly rendering geographical spaces uninhabitable for the human population and other species (Chakrabarty).

Anthropocene is a collective discourse that imagines the apocalyptic times in which humanity is reduced to its own consequences of expansion. Even though the Anthropocene is primarily imagined as a geological epoch that deals with humanity's problematic relationship with the environment and nature, the history of technology also reveals its significant influence on shaping this era (Jørgensen and Jørgensen). Slavoj Žižek notes that "ecological breakdown, the biogenetic reduction of humans to manipulable machines, [and the] total digital control over our lives" are the three levels of the apocalyptic end point where we are facing a phenomenon so entirely unfamiliar to our shared history that we often fail to recognize it, even in the face of compelling evidence (327). The exponential expansion of our freedom and power has led to the restriction of freedom itself in the technologically driven environment of the Anthropocene, where the new digital realities that control the human mind in the form of smartphones, social media, and artificial intelligence have already shown the potential to manipulate our physical realities into simulated meta-realities.

Cinema being the popular art of the technologically advanced and globalized world, it is possible to realistically visualize environmental disasters and their impact on the ecosystem. The ability to construct worlds in which disasters can be portrayed in their extremity makes cinema one of the useful mediums where one can make sense of the effects of the Anthropocene. In her book *Inhospitable World: Cinema in the Time of the Anthropocene* (2018), Jennifer Fay observes that "filmmaking occasions the creation of artificial worlds, unnatural and inclement weather, and deadly environments produced as much for the sake of entertainment as for scientific study and military strategy. Cinema's dominant mode of aesthetic world-making is often at odds with the very real human world it is meant to simulate" (4). Cinema as a creative medium stimulates the imagination to produce an aesthetic imitation of the Anthropocene:

> While no one film or set of films adds up to a totalizing explanation of climate change, cinema enables us to glimpse anthropogenic environments as both an accidental effect of human activity and a matter of design. Thus, not only is cinema like the Anthropocene in its uncanny aesthetic effects, but also, insofar as cinema has encouraged the production of artificial worlds and simulated, wholly anthropogenic weather, it is the aesthetic practice of the Anthropocene. Or, to put it more

> forcefully, cinema helps us to see and experience the
> Anthropocene as an aesthetic practice. (Fay 4)

The popular American television series *Mr. Robot* offers an aesthetic treatment of the Anthropocene by constructing a techno-disaster environment that serves as a haunting reflection of humanity's entanglement with technology and its consequences. The central discussion in *Mr. Robot* focuses on how large corporations that own the technology and data control the consumers by entrapping them within the bubbles of freedom and safety, two fundamental values that are essential to the working of the free world. The show contextualizes an American society that resembles a technological dystopia due to the impact of corporate power structures manipulating the economy and politics to control both the private and public lives of citizens. The notion of freedom of choice and expression are highly restricted in this version of America, where people are divided on the basis of class differences. The show emphasizes the lack of freedom in pursuing a social life outside the dominant ideology of capitalism and digital technology.

The pervasive role of digital technology creates a sense of "anonymous" freedom to do things that cannot be done in normal circumstances and therefore opens new possibilities for users to achieve their desires and imaginations in new ways. For example, in the first episode of the first season of *Mr. Robot*, protagonist Elliot Alderson, a brilliant cyber-security engineer and vigilante hacker suffering from social anxiety, confronts Rohit Mehta (Samrat Chakrabarti), a coffee shop owner, for secretly running a website that sells online child pornography. In this scene, Elliot addresses how people exploit the anonymity of freedom to do illegal activities in a technologically controlled world. While addressing Rohit, Elliot reveals why he decided to hack him:

> I like coming here, 'cause your Wi-Fi was fast. I mean, you're one of the few spots that has a fiber connection with gigabit speed. It's good. So good, it scratched that part of my mind, part that doesn't allow good to exist without condition, so, I started intercepting all the traffic on your network. That's when I noticed something strange. It's when I decided to hack you. ("eps1.0_hellofriend.mov" 02:15)

This scene gives specifics about why freedom in a technological world is problematic and susceptible to consequences. According to Elliot, Rohit worked really hard to keep his servers anonymous, but his "onion routing protocol" was not as anonymous as he thought it was. At this point, Elliot owns everything about Rohit: all his e-mails, files, and pictures because "whoever is in control of the exit nodes is also in control of the traffic." Here, it is evident that Elliot's intelligence and technical knowledge make him "the one in control." This type of control gives Elliot the power to unmask the "gentleman" façade of people like Rohit who are criminals freely operating under technology.

When Rohit offers money to Elliot to not destroy his personal life, the police arrive and Elliot walks away by saying: "That's the part you were wrong about, Rohit. I don't give a shit about money." In the series, Elliot continues to hack into computer systems, which reveals that the government, people, corporations, and society always have something to hide from others. Wendy Hui Kyong Chun notes that "freedom comes with no guarantees" and therefore it enables both good and evil (291). Elliot's freedom to explore the protected lives of others shows that freedom destabilizes the notion of protection. "The ideological conflation of freedom with safety—the idea that we are only free when safe defers freedom, and makes it an innocuous property of subjectivity" (291). The fragility of safety and protection offered by technology is criticized in this context by connecting it to the agendas of those who control technology in the Anthropocene.

Disaster Strikes: Techno-Dystopia in *Mr. Robot*

In the context of the politics of freedom in the Anthropocene, Wendy Brown notes that the foundational concepts and practices of politics in the Western world have inherent issues and shortcomings regarding both human and non-human activities. She argues that these understandings and practices tend to portray freedom in three problematic ways: "1) a practice of mastery and domination (freedom as the right to dominate, exploit, or subjugate charted by feminist, postcolonial, and critical race theory), or 2) against politics (freedom as the right to be let alone charted by liberalism), or 3) the dissolution of politics (freedom as the withering away of the state iterated in emancipatory Marxist and anarchist traditions)" (2).

In *Mr. Robot*, this perspective is reflected through the character of Elliot Alderson, who seeks to undermine and control the oppressive systems of power that dominate society. Elliot uses his skills to exploit and subvert the control mechanisms of corporations and government entities. His actions can be seen as an attempt to exercise freedom by challenging the dominant forces that oppress individuals.

However, to achieve this, Elliot has to fight his own psychological problems and release his identity from the traumatic forces that control his freedom. He embodies the perspective of freedom as the right to be left alone and lacks the social skills to execute his plans in a societal structure that works on discourses of communication. He is a highly introverted individual who prefers to live a secluded and detached life, avoiding personal connections and social interactions. Elliot's desire for solitude can be interpreted as a manifestation of this perspective, as he seeks freedom through isolation and the avoidance of external influences.

Mr. Robot also explores the perspective of freedom as the dissolution of politics. The series portrays a world in which the boundaries between political and corporate power are blurred, with corporations exerting significant control over society. The hacktivist group known as fsociety, led by Mr. Robot (Christian Slater), Elliot's revolutionary alter ego, aims to dismantle these power structures and bring about a state of anarchy. Their goal is to eliminate the existing political and economic systems, envisioning a society without hierarchical authority. This perspective aligns with the idea of freedom through the dissolution of politics.

Critics interpret that the historical context of the Anthropocene aligns with the modern capitalist society, which is characterised by alienated social relations (Stoner and Melathopoulos 22). Daniel Cunha argues that the Anthropocene is the "fetishized form of interchange" between humans and nature that is uniquely associated with capitalism, just as the concept of the "invisible hand" is an exaggerated representation of the idea of freedom in human interactions (65). Commodity fetishism, class differences, and market trends limit the concept of freedom in capitalism. Workers are considered "free" because they are not owned as slaves, but they lack ownership of the means of production and are deprived of their basic conditions of existence. Capitalists are "free" as long as they adhere to the objective rules of capital accumulation—otherwise, they face bankruptcy (65). Similarly, the relationship between individuals and technology is constrained and limited by the capitalist ideology inherent in the business models of the tech giants that operate on the basis of profit-based exploitation, commodity fetishism, and consumer culture. Žižek applies the Marxian view of machines dominating the human agency to observe that technological interactions have their own self-organization and freedom to undermine the control of human users over digital networks:

> The time is approaching when we will have to invert the standard complaint that our relations with other people are increasingly mediated by digital machinery, to the extent that, between every face-to-face contact, there always is an interface: the prospect for the near future is the explosive development of direct links between computers (and other media) themselves, which will then communicate, make decisions, etc., on our behalf, and simply present us with the final results of their inter-action. (For example, when we withdraw money from a cash machine, the machine informs our bank, whose computer sends the information to our PC via email.) Already today, there are more connections between computers themselves than between computers and their human users. (342)

The concept of the Anthropocene, which recognizes humanity's significant impact on the planet, coincides with a perception that the twentieth century was marked by the re-emergence of societal limitations, leading to a sense of helplessness in effecting transformative change (Postone). Digital realities in a capitalist environment can lead to a "techno-digital-post-human apocalypticism" (to borrow Žižek's term), which suggests an exploration of how the convergence of technology, digital culture, and post-humanist ideas can shape and inform beliefs, fears, or visions of an impending apocalyptic event or outcome. It reflects speculation on the potential consequences, risks, and transformative possibilities associated with these intersecting domains. In the modern digital world, we are trapped in networks that limit our freedom on both micro and macro levels (Berns and Aguilar). This means that, at a personal level, we become consumed by mobile devices and virtual games, isolating ourselves from real-life interactions. Meanwhile, corporations and governments have gained control over our personal data, further compromising our freedom and independence on a macro level.

Mr. Robot paints a bleak picture of a world where corporations hold immense influence and power over society, dominating every aspect of people's lives. The multinational conglomerate E Corp, often referred to as "Evil Corp" by Elliot, serves as a symbol of corporate hegemony. It embodies the unchecked greed and unethical practices that characterize the techno-dystopian landscape. Through Evil Corp's stranglehold on the economy and political system, the series illustrates the damaging consequences of unrestricted corporate control. In the digital age, the erosion of privacy and constant surveillance have become pertinent concerns. *Mr. Robot* confronts these issues head-on, highlighting the chilling implications of pervasive surveillance technologies. The show depicts a world where government agencies and corporations monitor individuals by collecting vast amounts of personal data. This omnipresent surveillance apparatus breeds paranoia, leaving citizens trapped in a state of constant vulnerability and suspicion.

Peter Haff reiterates that humans are not merely the creators and users of modern technology but they are part of the technological world of the Anthropocene, the technosphere.

> The Anthropocene is a product of human activities and of technology. Creation of technology is usually considered to be a consequence of those activities and therefore a derivative phenomenon. From a large-scale perspective a different picture emerges of the relation of humans to technology, that humans are parts of a dynamic and uncontrollable Earth system from which they cannot escape and in whose service they labor. (135)

Haff argues that the quasi-autonomous nature of the technosphere gives it a form of independence in the sense that humans cannot significantly control, alter or challenge the behavior of large-scale technological systems. In *Mr. Robot*, the existence of E Corp is an example of such a scenario where activities that pose a threat to the dominance of technological power only lead to a dystopic situation in which the characters need similar technical assistance to survive and reconstruct.

At the core of *Mr. Robot* lies the theme of hacking and cyber warfare. The series portrays hacking as a tool for rebellion and resistance against oppressive systems. Elliot employs his computer skills to expose the corruption that defines the corporate-controlled technosphere. He warns the audience about the techno-dystopia: "What I'm about to tell you is top secret. A conspiracy bigger than all of us. There's a powerful group of people out there that are secretly running the world. I'm talking about the guys no one knows about, the ones that are invisible. The top 1% of the top 1%, the guys that play God without permission" ("eps1.0_hellofriend.mov"). The show also examines the moral implications of hacking, as characters grapple with the consequences of actions that cross the fine line between liberation and chaos. The depiction of cyber warfare underscores the potential dangers of technological prowess falling into the wrong hands. In the techno-dystopian world of *Mr. Robot*, the prevalence of technology exacerbates social disconnection and alienation. The characters often find solace in virtual realms, detached from genuine human connection. Elliot, with his introverted nature and struggles with mental health, epitomizes this sense of isolation. The show emphasizes the toll technology takes on interpersonal relationships, serving as a cautionary tale about the dangers of prioritizing virtual interactions over genuine human connections.

Mr. Robot underscores the stark socio-economic divide that characterizes the techno-dystopian society. The show portrays a world where wealth and power are concentrated in the hands of a select few, leaving the majority to suffer in poverty and despair. The exploitation of vulnerable individuals by powerful corporations further widens this gap, emphasizing the inherent injustice and systemic inequality prevalent in the series' world. *Mr. Robot* serves as a stark warning about the perils of unbridled technological advancement and the dangers of unchecked corporate power. Through its portrayal of a techno-dystopian society, the series offers a thought-provoking critique of our own world, highlighting the potential consequences of disregarding ethical boundaries in pursuit of progress. The themes of corporate control, surveillance, social disconnection, and socio-economic inequality depicted in the show resonate with the anxieties and concerns of our contemporary society. As viewers, we are compelled to reflect on the impact of technology on our lives and the importance of safeguarding our freedoms in the face of ever-advancing technological crises.

Radical Subversions: Resistance and Hope

In *Mr. Robot*, the themes of freedom and resistance offer a glimpse into a world where individuals navigate oppressive systems and fight for a better future. Elliot's strong sense of justice is reflected in his anarchist views and pessimism. His disappointment toward society is described through internal monologues and narratives of introspection. In one scene, Elliot's therapist Krista (Gloria Reuben) asks why he is so cynical about society, to which he replies in his mind:

> Oh, I don't know, is it that we collectively thought Steve Jobs was a great man even when we knew he made billions off the backs of children? Or maybe it's that it feels like all our heroes are counterfeit; the world itself is just one big hoax. Spamming each other with our burning commentary of bullshit masquerading as insight, our social media faking as intimacy. Or is it that we voted for

this? Not with our rigged elections, but with our things, our property, our money. I'm not saying anything new. We all know why we do this, not because *Hunger Games* books make us happy but because we wanna be sedated. Because it's painful not to pretend, because we're cowards. ("eps1.0_hellofriend.mov" 12:19)

Mr. Robot goes beyond the mere portrayal of external resistance; it delves into the personal struggles and emotional complexities of its characters. Through Elliot's battles with mental health issues, the show addresses the internal obstacles that individuals face while striving for freedom. The scene where Elliot confronts his alter ego, Mr. Robot, who is the reflection of his own deceased father, represents the internal conflict and struggle for control. By intertwining the personal and the political, Mr. Robot underscores the notion that true liberation requires both external resistance and internal transformation.

Resistance in *Mr. Robot* is not limited to individual heroism but extends to collective action and alliances formed in pursuit of a common cause. The character Darlene (Carly Chaikin), Elliot's sister, plays a significant role in organizing and mobilizing resistance. She fosters solidarity among the marginalized and those affected by the actions of Evil Corp. Through these alliances, the show emphasizes the importance of collective action and the strength that lies in unity. Through his hacktivist actions, Elliot seeks to liberate others from the shackles of oppression by exposing the corporate agendas of exploitation. Hacktivism becomes a powerful tool of resistance throughout the series. The hacktivist group known as fsociety aims to dismantle the corporate power structure that dominates society. Their actions range from massive data breaches to crippling financial systems. The ideology of the fsociety aligns with the pursuit of freedom, as its supporters believe that only destabilizing oppressive institutions can bring change. For example, in the first season, fsociety successfully launches a cyber-attack on E

Corp servers and compromises their confidential data, forcing the corporation to shut down. Collaborating with the Chinese hacker group known as the Dark Army, fsociety orchestrates and executes the "Five/Nine hack." The main objectives of the hack were to destroy E Corp, one of the largest global conglomerates in the world, thus disrupting the stability of financial markets, obliterating financial records, and re-distributing wealth within the United States.

According to Rob Luzecky and Charlene Elsby, *Mr. Robot* does not bring destruction but "heralds a fascinating revolution where the very concept of limitation (more than any particular corporation or governmental institution) is an enemy to be attacked." By depicting these efforts to dismantle hierarchies, *Mr. Robot* offers hope for a future where freedom and equality can prevail. Through its depiction of radical subversions, acts of resistance, and the pursuit of freedom, the series offers a compelling vision of hope for the future. It highlights the transformative potential of individual and collective action, showing that liberation requires both external resistance against oppressive systems and internal transformation. Ultimately, the show encourages us to question the status quo and envision a future where freedom, justice, and equality triumph over oppressive forces. In a world yearning for change, *Mr. Robot* serves as a powerful reminder that the fight for a better future is worth pursuing and that radical subversions can pave the way toward a more liberated and just society.

Works Cited

Anker, Elisabeth R. *Ugly Freedoms*. Duke University Press, 2022.

Berns, Fernando Gabriel Pagnoni and Emiliano Aguilar. "Psycho-Politics in a Burnout Society." *Mr. Robot and Philosophy: Beyond*

Good and Evil Corp, edited by Richard Greene and Rachel Robinson-Greene, Open Court, 2017.

Bogues, Anthony. *Empire of Liberty: Power, Desire and Freedom*. University Press of New England, 2010.

Brown, Wendy. "Rethinking Politics and Freedom in Anthropocene." *Institute for Advanced Study*, 2022, ias.edu/sites/default/files/paper_68.pdf.

Chakrabarty, Dipesh. "Humanities in the Anthropocene: The Crisis of an Enduring Kantian Fable." *New Literary History*, vol. 47, no. 2 and 3, 2016, pp. 377–97.

Chun, Wendy Hui Kyong. *Control and Freedom: Power and Paranoia in the Age of Fiber Optics*. MIT Press, 2006.

Crutzen, Paul J. "The 'Anthropocene.'" *Earth System Science in the Anthropocene: Emerging Issue and Problems*, edited by Eckart Ehlers and Thomas Krafft, Springer, 2006, pp. 13-18.

Cunha, Daniel. "The Anthropocene as Fetishism." *Mediations*, vol. 28, no. 2, Spring 2015, pp. 65-77, mediationsjournal.org/articles/anthropocene-as-fetishism.

Fay, Jennifer. *Inhospitable World: Cinema in the Time of the Anthropocene*. Oxford University Press, 2018.

Haff, Peter. "Humans and Technology in the Anthropocene: Six Rules." *The Anthropocene Review*, vol. 1, no. 2, 2014, pp. 126–136.

Han, Byung-Chul. *Psychopolitics: Neoliberalism and New Technologies of Power*. Translated by Erik Butler, Verso, 2017.

Jørgensen, Finn Arne and Dolly Jørgensen. "The Anthropocene as a History of Technology: *Welcome to the Anthropocene: The Earth in Our Hands*, Deutsches Museum, Munich." *Technology and Culture*, vol. 57, no. 1, January 2016, pp. 231-237. doi: 10.1353/tech.2016.0026.

Lewis, Simon L., and Mark A. Maslin. "Defining the Anthropocene." *Nature*, vol. 519, no. 7542, 2015, pp. 171-180.

Luzecky, Rob and Charlene Elsby. "How to Become a Revolutionary." *Mr. Robot and Philosophy: Beyond Good and Evil Corp*, edited by Richard Greene and Rachel Robinson-Greene, Open Court, 2017.

Esmail, Sam, creator. *Mr. Robot*. Anonymous Content, 2015–2019.

Nellis, Allison. "Hello, Friend: Cybersecurity Issues in Season One of *Mr. Robot*." *The Serials Librarian*, vol. 71, no. 3-4, 2016, pp. 203-211, doi: 10.1080/0361526X.2016.1230533.

Postone, Moishe. "History and Helplessness: Mass Mobilization and Contemporary Forms of Anticapitalism." *Public Culture* vol. 18, no. 1, 2006, pp. 93–110.

Purdy, Jedediah. *After Nature: A Politics for the Anthropocene*. Harvard University Press, 2015.

Stoner, Alexander M., and Andony Melathopoulos. *Freedom in the Anthropocene: Twentieth-Century Helplessness in the Face of Climate Change*. Palgrave, 2015.

Zajchowski, Chris A. B., Daniel L. Dustin, and Eddie L. Hill. "'The Freedom to Make Mistakes': Youth, Nature, and the Anthropocene." *Journal of Outdoor and Environmental Education*, vol. 24, 2021, pp. 87-103.

Žižek, Slavoj. *Living in the End Times*. Verso, 2010.

Sony Jalarajan Raj is an assistant professor at the Department of Communication, MacEwan University, Edmonton, Canada. Dr. Raj is a professional journalist turned academic who has worked in different demanding positions as a reporter, special correspondent, and producer for several news media channels, including BBC, NDTV, Doordarshan, AIR, and Asianet News. Dr. Raj served as the Graduate Coordinator and Assistant Professor of Communication Arts at the Institute for Communication, Entertainment and Media at St. Thomas University Florida. He was a full-time faculty member in journalism, mass communication, and media studies at Monash University, Australia, Curtin University, Mahatma Gandhi University, and University of Kerala. Dr. Raj was the recipient of Reuters Fellowship and is a Thomson Foundation (UK) Fellow in Television Studies with the Commonwealth Broadcasting Association Scholarship.

Adith K. Suresh is currently associating as a research assistant at the Department of Communication, MacEwan University, Canada. He holds a Master's Degree in English Language and Literature from Mahatma Gandhi University. His research interest includes film studies, literary criticism, and South Asian cultural studies.

SECTION 3
Freedom for Whom?

Sonmi-451's Revolutionary Fight for Freedom in David Mitchell's *Cloud Atlas*

Martha Zornow

> "Unanimity Catechism Seven: A Soul's value is the dollars therein."
>
> — Orison of Sonmi-451
> *Cloud Atlas* (2004)

Freedom in the societies of the Anthropocene Global North is not what it seems at first glance. In the current neoliberal capitalist society of the United States, our freedoms are externally conditioned and then internally enforced. We are free to consume, to display our economic wellbeing to our neighbors, and to live with the nagging yet suppressed worry that what we are aspiring to and what we have achieved is not actually a product of our own free will. Our apparent comfort and ease have a dark underbelly in the persons of the less privileged inhabitants of our society who support our compulsive consumption. In my own New York City, for example, the streets are congested with e-bike *deliveristas* who serve the food whims of the apartment dwellers above by plying the streets in all weathers. Our restaurant kitchens and dishwashing rooms are staffed primarily by immigrants from the Global South working long hours for low wages. Similarly, in the future Seoul imagined by David Mitchell in two chapters of his *Cloud Atlas* (2004), "upper strata" citizens of that society experience apparent freedom, mind-blowing ease, and effortless convenience provided to them by the ruling corporate techno-culture, all made possible by rigidly enforced social strata and enabled in part by the enslaved labor of clone workers.

It is only a short leap from our current U.S. consumer culture to the "corpocratic" regime of Mitchell's future Seoul, now part of the mega-state of Nea So Copros.[1] There, the freedoms of the "pureblood" elites are possible only upon the backs of a permanent "down strata" human underclass along with a huge population of commoditized clones—"fabricants"—manufactured and sold to enable the pleasures of the elites. Less obviously, our current Western consumer culture as theorized by Szeman and O'Brien is "dependent on... the development of an enormous set of institutions that are geared toward the production and distribution of consumable objects and services" (133). They note especially that the "imperative for modern states to foster freedom and be open to global commercial flows persists along a preoccupation—heightened since 9/11—with security" (206). And in the neoliberal capitalist order, powerful corporate actors partner with and enable the controlling governmental regime to control its citizens: "The culture industry plays an important part in perpetuating the domination of human beings and nature under the guise of increasing their freedom" (99). Citing Horkheimer and Adorno's *Dialectic of Enlightenment* (1947), Szeman and O'Brien argue that industry intentionally produces a culture that functions "to reproduce incessantly the values of capitalist culture" by deceiving and misleading those living there. Those who live within the episteme built by the techno-corporate state experience the illusion that they are exercising free will in deciding what to buy and what to experience, yet they are in fact victims of manipulation.

Today's capitalist economies, while based on an idea of freedom equated with deregulation, exacerbate income inequality. Elizabeth R. Anker notes the privatization of public goods and social services that results from this so-called freedom for capitalist actors. She states, "[a]lthough it is commonly assumed that neoliberalism has diminished state power," it in fact "intensifies state power over the most insecure and marginalized segments of society" and "intensifies carceral and securitized power over a growing population of impoverished people excluded from capital flows" (113-14). Neoliberal capitalist regimes "shift governance to economization, erode public space, grant unregulated movement to finance, and spread market values to previously unmonetized spaces" (114). Anker's critique of the realistic Baltimore city of *The Wire* (2002-2008) also serves as an apt description of the so-called (by Mitchell) "corpocratic" forces at work in Sonmi-451's own failing post-industrial city.

Citizens of corpocratic states internalize and self-police themselves in enacting the discipline of the state as theorized by Byung-Chul Han. Han argues that the neoliberal capitalist state uses its power to brainwash its citizens and convert them to pure and compliant consumers through what he calls "psychopolitics." The state "has discovered the psyche as a productive force" which connects directly with "the mode of operation of contemporary capitalism... Physical discipline has given way to mental optimization" (25). As the citizens of such regimes go sheep-like to their malls and aesthetic surgery appointments, the voice of freedom moves to the "idiot": that is, the disfavored outsider who has the emotional distance to call foul on the cynical motivation of his fellow citizens. Anker notes that within coercive neoliberal regimes, often "freedoms [can only be] found in discarded and devalued spaces that can challenge neoliberal power" and by those devalued by the dominant social ethos (115).

Han theorizes, "In light of compulsive and coercive communication and conformism, idiotism represents a practice of freedom… The idiot is a modern-day heretic" (83). The role of the idiot—critical to human freedom—is to "stand opposed to the neoliberal power of domination: total communication and total surveillance" (83). A return to some kind of actual human self-determinism requires someone to play the role of idiot and call out the cynical moves by the modern corpocracy.

David Mitchell's Sonmi-451, existing in her devalued space, is just the so-called idiot Han cries out for. Sonmi-451 herself is a "fabricant," a wombtank-grown woman "genomed" to be a server in the red and yellow branded Papa Song's "dinery." In his fable-like chapters entitled "An Orison of Sonmi-451," Mitchell plays out to its logical end point the role of the "corpocratic" state in providing power for some on the backs of unfree others. Mitchell's futuristic political thriller serves as a parable and warning for how our own contemporary society can voraciously consume human products to feed insatiable consumer appetites. As Sonmi becomes aware of the insidious social structures keeping her people enslaved, she experiences a political awakening and becomes a revolutionary. Sonmi-451's tale—her "Orison" or radical declaration of rights—is her manifesto demanding that the underclasses rise up and claim their humanity. In this chapter, I will discuss the mechanisms by which Sonmi-451's enslavement is enforced, then the coercive structure of the Nea So Copros regime, including the merging of governmental and corporate impulses, and finally the role Sonmi plays as a revolutionary and martyr crying out for freedom. All of these aspects of Mitchell's tale shed a terrifying yet clarifying light on the prospects for freedom in the twenty-first century Global North.

Mitchell's novel consists of six narratives, each in a different genre, linked through time by texts from the prior narrative that play a role in the later one. The penultimate time-frame chapters take place in a post-Anthropocene dystopian future Asia; the two Sonmi-451 chapters take the form of an interview in which she, a captured political prisoner, tells her story to a government archivist prior to her execution for treason. Her tale is bisected in the novel by a chapter set even farther in the future in a post-apocalyptic Hawaii, in which rusticated subsistence-level survivors have obtained the device containing Sonmi's account and have made her their god, thus ensuring the continued influence of Sonmi as valorous "idiot" who speaks truth to power.

Sonmi-451's Constrained Existence

Sonmi-451 begins her existence as a quasi-human product, one of several in the branded line of Sonmis, a model that competes for shelf space with several other versions that consumers compete to acquire, much like sneakerheads in our world. Fabricant Sonmi-451's habitus, the corpocracy, is controlled by the powerful Juche Boardroom (an allusion to the current North Korean totalitarian regime). Her society initially maintains her as a docile body in an underground dorm and restaurant reminiscent of McDonald's, brainwashed by a commercial "Catechism" of servitude, and emotionally repressed by ingredients in her specialized foodstuff. She wears a collar that indicates her unprivileged station. Her unvarying schedule, constrained physical space, single synthetic food source, constant drugging, and lack of concept of the future or personal agency all make her a servile cog in a larger social machine over which she has no control.

Every day is identical to the last one for Sonmi; she tells her interviewer, "One twenty-four-hour cycle in Papa Song's is indistinguishable from any other" (Mitchell 185). She is awakened at 4:30$_{AM}$ by a stimulant in the dormitory ventilation system, bathes in a shower dehumanizingly named the "hygiener," dons a uniform denoting her servile status, and works straight for nineteen hours without a break. "For fabricants, 'rests' would be an act of time theft" (186). The workers are merely Papa Song's "investment," in other words, capital. At the end of a very long day, Sonmi imbibes one piece of manufactured food that also contains a drug that suppresses cognition and emotion (185-87).

The monotony of the single food source Sonmi as fabricant is able to ingest is another loss of freedom. It is bitterly ironic that her job is to serve foods to the entitled that she will never eat herself. Soap, which turns out to be biomatter collected from the reprocessed bodies of murdered retired fabricants (343), is the only nourishment her body is engineered to accept.

Sonmi's constrained circumstances deprive her of any meaningful concept of the world outside her workplace or a future outside the present. While she and her fellow servers realize that their customers come from somewhere else and constantly see advertisements set in places beyond the "servery," they "rarely wonder about life on the surface." Their concept of the long-term future features only the promised retirement reward—"Xultation" (186), which turns out to be a cynically-produced video montage of tourist sites they will never see. She later tells her ostensible benefactor, "I had no idea of fun," and the concept of relaxation is incomprehensible to her (225). She wonders what it would be like to be part of a family, a privilege denied her (227). Cloned humans like Sonmi have no freedom to conceive of future goals for themselves or of places outside the here and now. As she later realizes, "perpetual encagement endows any mirage of civilization with credibility" (193).

Describing her nineteen-hour days waiting on "pureblood" consumers, sleeping in a dormitory beneath the restaurant, and eating Soap, Sonmi notes that "every prison has jailer and walls" (188). Not only is her physical freedom constrained—she can never go up the elevator or "Outside" until she is removed by a rescuer—but the Soap she eats "represses… the xpression of an innate personality possessed by all fabricants" (187). Her situation mirrors that imposed upon the "docile bodies" described by Foucault, and the underground vertical bunker in which she lives and works resembles Jeremy Bentham's panopticon that enabled constant surveillance of the worker class subdued for the benefit of the more powerful.

Sonmi's body is the "object and target of power"; it is "in the grip of very strict powers, which imposed on it constraints, prohibitions, or obligations" (Foucault 136). She is subject to discipline, "a policy of coercions that act upon the body, a calculated manipulation of its elements, its gestures, its behavior" (138). Like Foucault's soldiers and workmen, her control requires enclosure, a "protected place of disciplinary monotony" (141).

Foucault speaks of regulation of tasks into timetables, which took on a religious cast (149). To this end, Sonmi's minutely scheduled days begin with the recitation of the consumerist "Six Catechisms" and a Sermon by the Logoman (a version of Ronald McDonald, actually) followed by a nonstop day of server work. The dinery holds a yearly, quasi-religious "Star Sermon" ceremony, during which the fabricants receive a star on their collars for each year of service at "Matins" and are shown images of their putative retirement destination (Mitchell 186). Sonmi's only religious rituals are cynical tools to justify and elevate her enslavement.

Overall, in the pre-"ascended" Sonmi-451, Mitchell has created a perfect embodiment of the docile body and controlled mind that characterizes the lower-tier humans of a neoliberal capitalist society run amok. But the privileged elites of such a society, fully in thrall to the commercial propaganda they constantly consume, are no more free than the clones they exploit.

Social Structure in Nea So Copros

The culture of Nea So Copros consists of three social classes: the upper strata "purebloods," the fabricants, and then the "untermenschen" who live in the slums of every "conurb." In her discussion of the Wachowskis' film version of Mitchell's novel, Raffaella Baccolini notes that "all the inhabitants [of Neo Seoul] are enslaved: the purebloods in their meaningless drive to consume, and—literally—the fabricants in working to fulfill the promise of freedom after 12 years of labour" (74). Mitchell's imagined society and its social classes hyperbolically illustrate Marcel Mauss's concept of habitus, expanded on by Pierre Bourdieu, in which "the way in which we conduct... basic activities should be understood not as natural, but as a series of 'body techniques' that are *learned* in particular social contexts and are hence culturally and historically specific" (Szeman and O'Brien 174). Individuals in each of the social classes in Sonmi's world express their social difference through comportment. Their habitus "describes the way in which particular social environments are internalized by individuals in the form of dispositions toward particular bodily orientations and behaviors" (175). Mitchell's upper strata "purebloods" "enjoy more privileged access to forms of economic, social, and cultural capital" than do their social inferiors (175). Sonmi notes that "a dinery server behaving like a pureblood attracts trouble" (190). The lower strata of the corpocracy, acting in their assigned roles, are essential for the elites to realize the consumerist paradise their government's propaganda promises them.

In Sonmi's time, most of the planet has been "deadlanded" and the cities that survive in Nea So Copros are run by a totalitarian government reminiscent of Kim Jong Un's North Korea, headed by the "Beloved Chairman" and overseen by the Orwellian "Ministry of Unanimity." The corpocratic government forces its upper strata citizens—here ironically renamed "consumers"—to spend a required amount from their implanted bank accounts. Those bank accounts also serve as identification and tracking devices and are called "Souls." In our own reality, materialism has replaced spirituality and religion, making "secular comfort seem not only possible but also morally good" (Szeman and

O'Brien 128). Sonmi notes explicitly that "corpocracy dissolved the pre-consumer religions" (Mitchell 329). Mitchell has literalized this by making the Soul an implanted device for consumerism.

The social order in Nea So Copros is enforced by a constant stream of commercial messages. The government has "shift[ed] governance to economization" (Anker 114). Citizen/consumers are required to support the corporate powers behind the state in a kind of near-religious civic duty. A privilege of belonging to the elite strata is to possess a Soul, which is in fact a kind of wearable Venmo. Freedom of travel within the country is surveilled and only those with positive balances in the Souls/bank accounts are free to move about. Beyond that, Mitchell has commoditized the work force, introducing an army of clones to service the upper strata consumers. These fabricants eat manufactured fuel and work without rights or rest. They do not have Souls —they are property.

Advertising and branding are important tools in a consumption-driven society, occupying "a position of unparalleled dominance, reflecting… the intensification of consumerism" and has become "the official art of modern capitalist society" (Szeman and O'Brien 131). In Mitchell's Neo Seoul, the AdV's are everywhere, a replacement for TV, and Seoul is a whole city of "corp logos." AdVs are even projected onto the moon (226). The names of common items in Neo Seoul are the brands of dominant producers, but consumption has become so acculturated that these names are lower case. Brand names have become common nouns. There are no shoes beyond "nikes" and no playback devices other than "sonys."[2] In this world, the items have lost their generic names because there is no product available beyond the corpocratically produced branded items. This branding metonymy serves as a "reminder that it is virtually impossible [for other producers] to compete with companies whose brands are so well known, whose product names have become recognized substitutes for everyday consumer goods, and whose corporate mission is to dominate the essential and discretionary spending of consumers" (Szeman and O'Brien 243). There are no competing producers left in Nea So Copros, a trenchant comment by Mitchell on the creeping monopolization in our own consumer culture. In Somni's world, nature has been branded as well, all in service of spurring the consumer/citizens to ever more frantic consumption.

Evidence of the branding of everything shows up every day in the United States of 2023. In the upper strata enclave of Miami's wealthy neighborhoods, for example, the *New York Times* real estate section recently highlighted the trend of enticing rich and famous condominium buyers by branding new residential buildings with luxury brands. Developer Gil Dezer boasts of his acumen in building a Porsche-branded apartment tower with attached glass garages served by an multi-million dollar auto elevator: "'The car brands of today want to be not just car brands, but also lifestyle brands as well,' said Mr. Dezer, who partnered with Porsche in 2012. 'The same goes for everything from golf clubs to sunglasses. And we were fortunate enough to be able to get in on it for real estate'" (Kamin). Dezer's over-the-top Miami condo tower would be right at home in NeoSeoul.

Creating an emotional connection between the hottest trend and the impulse to buy is a powerful tool used by capitalist actors with the support of the government. In Nea So Copros, the enabling by the government is even more expansive than in our own current culture. Advertisements are projected on the moon, and all of television has become solely a channel for advertising. Worship of corporate logos and symbols has replaced religion. The commercials portray a life of ease, beauty, and an aspirational free choice that does not exist. They parallel Szeman and O'Brien's analysis of the cynical subtext of advertising that features "images of cottages, beaches, or family settings: dealing with these institutions, these images suggest, will secure you with the freedom that your life otherwise so clearly lacks" (98). The center of town features the "Avenue of Nine

Thousand AdVs" and the 234th story of the Moon Tower offers the best view of the ads of the evening's sponsor projected onto the moon. Sonmi marvels at the advertisements projected on the moon's face: "tomatoes as big as babies, cauliflower cubes, holeless lotus roots. Speech bubbles blossomed from Seed-Corp's logoman's juicy mouth, guaranteeing that his products were 100% genetically modified" (226-27). Around Sonmi, "the consumers seethed to buy, buy, buy! Purebloods, it seemed, were a sponge of demand that sucked goods and services from every vendor, dinery, bar, shop, and nook" (227). Technology and human innovation have been fully harnessed to drive sales, the logical end result of the neoliberal capitalist project. The upper strata consumers of Nea So Copros are free only to spend to drive the economy.

Yet, feeding the machine of the corpocracy requires the existence of lower strata people even beyond the clones. On her informational tour of her city, Sonmi and her pureblood handler visit the slum of Huamdonggil, "A noxious maze of low, crooked ramshacks, flophouses, pawnshops, drug bars, and comfort hives" (315). The residents' "skin [is] inflamed by prolonged xposure to the city's scalding rain," from which the upper strata are protected (315). Sonmi's guide tells her that these slums are a necessary component of a capitalist society:

> "Every conurb… has a chemical toilet where the city's unwanted human waste disintegrates quietly, but not quite invisibly. It motivates the downstrata: "Work, spend, work," say slums like Huamdoggil, "or you, too, will end your life *here*." (316)

Untermenschen can sell healthy body parts to MediCorp and OrganiCorp. These lower-class people have also been commoditized.

As Sonmi grows in wisdom and is able to appraise the corrupt structure of her society, she realizes that clones like her are both enslaved labor and tradeable commodities.

Fabricants rise and fall in popularity as collectibles. For example, a newly released Kyelim is a "newly-created stemtype" that attracts "queues of fabricant spotters" (198). The fabricant producers even create a living fabricant toy, the Zizzi Hikaru Doll, which gets thrown out, that is, killed, when the pureblood child gets tired of her (335). Making humans into tradeable commodities is a logical extension of consumerist popular culture. It is not such a stretch to go from influencer culture—where would-be celebrities deliver up their aspirational life to thousands of slavish followers—to actually owning a collectible human.

On a more sinister note, it is also not a stretch to call Sonmi and her sister fabricants enslaved, despite the limited rights given them by the government. Sonmi explains to her interlocutor that the fallacy that fabricants don't have personalities is "propagated for the comfort of the purebloods. ... To enslave an individual troubles your consciences... but to enslave a clone is no more troubling than owning the latest six-wheeler ford" (187). The whole social organization rests on the assumption that these divisions among classes are natural and correct; her archivist insists "Corpocracy is the natural order" (234). And lest we feel too smug about our own moral high ground, we must acknowledge that own history is replete with rationalization of enslavement through dehumanization of the enslaved. Even beyond the shameful centuries of Western chattel slavery of captured Africans, modern-day privileged classes often look away when confronted with the human trafficking obvious at any truck stop or roadside motel, or at the essentially captive South Asian maids and construction workers in the Arab Gulf states.[3]

Sonmi as Revolutionary Martyr and Valourous "Idiot"

As Sonmi-451 becomes "ascended" into sentience, she gains an understanding of the evils of the consumerist society that enslaves her. Her growing awareness enables us to learn along with her the truth about the corpocracy in which she exists. It also motivates her to become a revolutionary. By choosing to "consume" a university education, Sonmi is signaling that she shares the tastes of the powerful classes. Her taste for higher learning positions her at a "site at which social power is produced and maintained" (Szeman and O'Brien 138). Her sponsor speculates, "What if the differences between social strata stem not from genomics or inherent xcellence or even dollars, but merely differences in knowledge? Would this not mean the whole Pyramid is built on shifting sands?" (Mitchell 222). Class mobility through education would undercut the hegemonic social order, echoing our own current resistance to abolishing legacy admissions at so-called elite universities. Learning the truth of how the cloned servants are recycled into "liquified biomatter" to feed the next round of clones, Sonmi becomes a rebel against the enslavement of her fellow clones and writes her own Declarations of the human right to free will.

Knowing the likely outcome of capture and death, Sonmi nonetheless braves the tyrannical regime to witness the injustices of her society and tell her story. Having gained a university education after being freed from a second captivity as an experimental subject in an investigation of "ascended fabricants," Sonmi-451 begins to understand the rigid class structure and totalitarian power of the ruling elite. She joins a long tradition of celebrated martyrs for justice, such as Che Guevara or Dr. Martin Luther King, who travel to learn of injustices against the disfavored and then to tell their story in a way that will live on after their capture and execution. Structurally, most of Sonmi's revelations about the cruelty of her society occur in the second interwoven Sonmi chapter, after we learn that the recording of her testimony—the "silv'ry egg what he named *orison*"—has become a sacred object of the primitive surviving Valley people in a ruined future after the time of Nea So Copros (309). Similarly, Che Guevara's image appears on the revolutionary insignia of many later struggles, almost as a form of worship. King's speeches and writings are quoted frequently. Sonmi's Orison likewise becomes an object of veneration. All these freedom fighters likely knew they would not survive to see the fruits of their struggles, yet they took great care in formulating a new doctrine for a better future. In Sonmi's case, her Declarations constitute rules for a fairer version of her world.

Ironically, it turns out that the whole false flag operation that positioned Sonmi-451 as revolutionary is a theatrical production by the Unanimity government to generate a show trial and make "every last pureblood in Nea So Copros mistrustful of every last fabricant" (348). Sonmi is about to be the subject of a meticulously-produced show trial followed by her execution. And yet, even knowing she is being manipulated and used to reinforce the very society against which she is rebelling, Sonmi forges ahead with her campaign to spread the truth of the rot at the heart of her culture. She has completed her manifesto and tells her interviewer that having it publicized, even as treason, will have the effect she desires:

> We see a game beyond the endgame. I refer to my Declarations, Archivist. Media has flooded Nea So Copros with my Catechisms. Every schoolchild in corpocracy knows my twelve "blasphemies" now... My ideas have been reproduced a billionfold. (349)

In the end, the brilliant, formerly enslaved Sonmi-451 has become the idiot hypothesized by Han. She is the disfavored outsider who is able to see what the privileged cannot—that the neoliberal capitalist culture in which she exists is rotten to the core.

With Nea So Copros, Mitchell has fully imagined a totalitarian, completely consumerist future society where free will does not exist and resistance is futile. His built world serves as an extrapolation and ominous warning for where our own Anthropocene capitalist culture may be headed. As the surviving Prescient in the ruined future after Sonmi's time tells her companion, "*human hunger birthed the Civ'lize, but human hunger killed it too*" (273). However, Mitchell leaves a bit of hope in the way Sonmi's Declarations survive into the future. As a last courageous act, quoting deposed Roman emperor Nero, she tells her interviewer, "No matter how many of us you kill, you will never kill your successor" (349).

Notes

1. This is a riff on the 1940s Japanese propaganda title for the region of the "Greater East Asia Co-Prosperity Sphere" (Windberger 159), implying colonization by an imperialist power.

2. See also "nikon" for camera (195), "ford" for vehicle (200), "marlboros" for cigarettes (331), "disney" for films (213), "exxon" for gas (326), and "starbuck" for coffee (324).

3. "According to the International Labor Organization, at any given moment in 2016 (the last year for which it has data), 4.8 million people were being forcibly exploited sexually worldwide" (Rosenberg).

Works Cited

Anker, Elizabeth R. *Ugly Freedoms*. Duke University Press, 2022.

Baccolini, Raffaella. "Utopia in Dystopia." *Science Fiction Film and Television*, vol. 9.1, 2016, pp. 73-76.

Foucault, Michel. "Docile Bodies." *Discipline & Punish*, Random House, 1977, pp. 135-169.

Han, Byung-Chul. *Psychopolitics: Neoliberalism and New Technologies of Power*. Verso, 2017.

Kamin, Debra. "The Latest Cool Amenity? A Name Brand. How About Porsche?" *The New York Times*, 15 September 2023, nytimes.com/2023/09/15/realestate/branded-real-estate-miami.html.

Mitchell, David. *Cloud Atlas*. Random House, 2004.

Rosenberg, Tina. "Fighting Sex Trafficking at the Truck Stop." *The New York Times*, 2 April 2019, nytimes.com/2019/04/02/opinion/fighting-sex-trafficking-at-the-truck-stop.html.

Szeman, Imre and Susie O'Brien. *Popular Culture: A User's Guide*. Wiley Blackwell, 2017.

Windberger, Eva-Maria. "Claiming Her Voice: 'An Orison of Sonmi-451'." *The Poetics of Empowerment in David Mitchell's Novels,* Routledge, 2023, pp. 159-170.

Martha Zornow studies dystopian and speculative fiction as a response to concerns about the distribution and exercise of power in contemporary society. She is presently a lecturer in the College of Arts and Sciences at Quinnipiac University in Hamden, Connecticut, and a Ph.D. Candidate at Old Dominion University in Norfolk, Virginia. She is a graduate of Harvard College and Harvard Law School and practiced media law before moving to academia. She also holds an Ed.M. in Education Leadership from Teachers College, Columbia University.

Seeing Environmental Crisis: Reproduction, Disability, and Climate Change in *Bird Box*

Tatiana Konrad

Images of parents worrying about their children's well-being in a world affected by climate change frequently appear on screen. Roland Emmerich's *The Day After Tomorrow* (2004), M. Night Shyamalan's *The Happening* (2008), John Hillcoat's *The Road* (2009), and many other examples focus on parents whose children's lives are directly threatened by environmental problems. Yet the ideas of pregnancy, childbirth, adoption, and child-rearing have been only sporadically and rather insufficiently explored in ecocinema.[1]

Susanne Bier's post-apocalyptic horror film *Bird Box* (2018) examines the intricacies of cis-gender single motherhood—from pregnancy to survival with children—in a new, hostile world. Reproduction in the age of extinction is tackled in the film through the issues of mothering, disability, and climate change. The only way humans can survive in the new world is by wearing a blindfold, for it keeps them from seeing their biggest fears and committing suicide. Blindfolded, the main character Malorie and two children are depicted on their way to a safer place. This chapter explores freedom in the age of extinction through the issue of reproduction. Specifically, it draws on the challenges that the single mother Malorie faces in the times of environmental crisis, trying to protect the children that are both her burden and a metaphor for humanity's future. It also addresses the symbolism of the blindfold in the film and how the blindfold challenges the idea of freedom, explicating the issues of motherhood, climate change, and survival in an era of crisis.

Mothering in the Era of Climate Crisis

Climate change is a paramount problem that humanity must address today. Establishing "new ways of being, belonging, and behaving" appears as the only right solution to the grave threat of environmental degradation and extinction (Szeman 46). The world as we know it is certainly changing, as climate change in a myriad of ways influences our practices and activities, as well as the human and nonhuman worlds at large. Parenting is one such practice that is dramatically challenged by climate change. One of the reasons for this is *climate anxiety*—a growing fear of the transforming and vanishing world (Jaquette Ray 5-6). How does one become a parent under conditions that are so uncertain, as the planet—our home—becomes unrecognizable and, in some parts, dangerous for living or even quite literally uninhabitable? To an already existing cluster of cardinal issues that surround parenting today, we must add climate change.

Motherhood has been socially, politically, and culturally constructed as something "natural" in every woman's life (Ortner 34). This construction, however, profoundly challenges gender equality and motherhood as a choice, reduces a woman to a mere biological incubator in which a baby can be grown (thus trivializing, among other issues, women's reproductive health as such and neglecting those women who, due to their health condition, might not be recommended/able to become pregnant), and undermines fathering as a significant practice, to name just a few consequences. *Bird Box* refutes the idea of mothering as a desirable experience for each cis-gender woman though the character Malorie (Sandra Bullock)—a single, pregnant woman. Malorie does not want to have this child, and, as is made clear in the discussion she has with her sister Jessica (Sarah Paulson), Malorie does not have any of the maternal instincts that are expected from her, based on the sole fact of her pregnancy and her being a cis-gender woman.

Nevertheless, soon the world plunges into chaos. Malorie joins a group of people who hide in a house from the supernatural powers that have allegedly attacked the Earth and is temporarily safe. She befriends another pregnant woman, Olympia (Danielle Macdonald). The presence of two pregnant characters reinforces human anxiety about the future. On the one hand, through the images of pregnancy, the film gives hope for the future and survival of humanity; on the other hand, pregnancy makes the women appear vulnerable and incapable of living through the times of crisis. For example, Malorie ends up in the house only because the wife of the owner of that house comes to help her. Prior to that, Malorie is shown falling down several times as she runs in a crowd. Malorie's survival, and the survival of her unborn baby, is thus possible, as the scene suggests, only because another woman feels sorry for her (importantly, *because* Malorie is pregnant, which is equated with weakness and vulnerability in the scene) and is ready to take the risk of coming closer, only to ultimately die. Pregnancy is seen as a drawback in a situation where a human body should be fit, strong, and enduring. In the end, helpless Malorie is assisted by a passerby who brings her inside the house.

The film's engagement with reproduction through pregnancy and mothering foregrounds the idea of freedom, and lack thereof, for women. Explicating the patriarchal, sexist visions of a woman whose body, essentially, does not belong to her, *Bird Box* reminds the viewer about the types of women's unfreedom against which feminists have been fighting. Feminism "question[s] the naturalized femininity that supposedly determines her [a woman's] social function" (Zerilli 8). Feminism has done much to detach the political, cultural, economic, and social understanding and treatment of a woman from the biological definitions of a woman based on sex and to reimagine a woman as a social being (9). Despite these important, gender-related developments, however, reproduction remains a complex issue through which women's unfreedom is vividly visible. Pregnancy deprives Malorie of freedom on the level of her body, but it is also through pregnancy that Malorie's unfreedom is further intensified. Malorie is forced to give birth and later to take care of the child. There is a certain moral tone attached to Malorie's mothering. The fact that she keeps the baby and later takes care of the child suggests that she is forced to do so due to social expectations, *because* she is a woman and a mother. Her detachment from the child throughout the film, however, illustrates Malorie's true feelings toward her offspring.

The representation of reproduction in *Bird Box* elucidates the ways in which practices and rhetorics of freedom are diminished in political, economic, social, and cultural spaces. Drawing on Simone de Beauvoir, Linda M. G. Zerilli emphasizes that "freedom can never be strictly a subject question, for freedom is only possible in a political community" (11). The obvious surveillance of Malorie's pregnancy and mothering foregrounds the lack of freedom for this woman. Borrowing from Beauvoir, Zerilli writes that "to be free is to be able to do" (11). This is exactly what Malorie is deprived of—the ability to do. Social expectations of how she should be treated, how she should behave, as well as what she should or should not do construct Malorie as a character but also create a specific archetype of a pregnant woman. This characterization, in turn, not only enforces a specific view of a pregnant woman but also promotes sexism through oppression in questions related to reproduction.

Both pregnant women, Malorie and Olympia, soon give birth. Yet while they are in labor, the film reveals that the mental condition of one of the individuals hiding in the house is affected as a consequence of not wearing a blindfold. His behavior leads to the death of several characters, including Olympia. Malorie is left with two newborn babies—as Malorie promised Olympia she would do, she takes care of Olympia's baby, too.

The only way humans can survive outside is by wearing a blindfold, for it keeps them from seeing their biggest fears and committing suicide—a peculiar type of "infection" spread by the supernatural powers that have attacked the Earth. Blindfolded, Malorie and the two children are depicted on their way to a safer place, as the film informs the viewer that five years have passed. Through the symbolism of the blindfold, *Bird Box* attempts to address the issues of motherhood, climate change, and survival.

The blindfold in the film is a powerful metaphor for human inability/unwillingness to face and find ways to address environmental and ecological degradation and destruction, including climate change. Scared of being deprived of the comforts that humans have and ready to sacrifice the planet for these comforts, including "speed, plastics, and the luxuries of capitalism," we, humans, refuse to fully open our eyes and thus *see* the true scale of the problem (Wilson, Szeman, and Carlson 15). The very uncertainty of what the future will bring us, and whether humans (and nonhumans) will become extinct, is illustrated through the image of Malorie—a blindfolded mother who, as the film suggests, cannot see her children (except for those short moments under a blanket when they can take off their blindfolds) or the road she is traveling, and, as a result, does not know if the place she is trying to bring the children to is, in fact, safe. Her children's future is unknown to this mother.

Through the images of Malorie trying to protect her children from the outside world merely with the help of a blindfold, the film seems to suggest that by refusing to face a certain problem, one can avoid it. Malorie employs this strategy of self-deception from the very beginning of the film, when she refuses to face the consequences of her pregnancy. Her sister Jessica sarcastically comments, "If you don't acknowledge a thing, it simply goes away." Yet, just as Malorie's pregnancy has not simply "gone away," leaving the woman with a child (or rather, with two children) to feed, protect, and take care of, so will climate change and the planet's destruction not stop if humanity, like Malorie, keeps refusing to face and effectively address the crisis.

The blindfold, however, also effectively contributes to the idea of Malorie's unfreedom, revealing how Malorie cannot even navigate through mothering herself, but rather goes through it as if it is an obstacle course. It is crucial that Malorie can only take her blindfold off and see her children if they are all under a blanket. In all other cases when they are together, Malorie merely tries to survive, making sure that the children are safe, too. This lack of freedom is symbolic, for it accentuates how women's reproductive rights and mothering as such are surveilled by others, thus depriving women of opportunities to make decisions on their own.

Disability, Mothering, and Environmental Crisis

Through the blindfold and the inability to see that it suggests, *Bird Box* includes disability into its discussion of mothering in the era of climate crisis. In doing so, the film supplies the viewer with explicitly ableist images. The ultimate sanctuary for Malorie and her children is the Janet Tucker School for the Blind. The only group of people who are unaffected by the film's apocalyptic events at the end of the film are individuals with vision impairment. On the one hand, this is a very empowering message: disability is not seen as "a flaw, lack, or excess," but, on the contrary, helps people survive (Garland-Thomson 1557).

Yet the film hardly celebrates disability. Instead, it uses disability as a lens through which to comment on motherhood in the era of environmental crisis. *Bird Box* moves from its metaphorical depictions of "blindness" with regard to climate change to very literal portrayals of blind people. While not visually impaired, Malorie is largely depicted as blind. Through this depiction, the film suggests that motherhood in this new, dangerous world makes Malorie disabled. Malorie is not the only character who must wear a blindfold to stay alive. Yet Malorie is the only character who experiences all these hardships while also trying to bring her children to a safer place. Supposedly, if she were alone, she could find a safe place to stay much faster and more easily. The responsibility that she has of being a mother forces her to do things she would hardly do if she were alone.

To film critic Natalie Reilly, Malorie embodies "the ultimate tiger mum," for she is "strict, uncompromising, focused, aggressive." Mothering in the times of crisis turns Malorie into a wild animal, waking up all necessary instincts that were not needed earlier. She is even capable of finding her children in a forest, going downstream on a river, and fighting those who try to attack them—all this with her eyes covered with a blindfold. Mothering thus not only animalizes, and thus de-humanizes, Malorie, but also appears to be a largely disabling practice. After all, her children's lives depend on whether Malorie will keep her blindfold on, thus remaining blind. Becoming blind is a sacrifice that Malorie makes to be able to deliver her children to safety.

Reilly concludes that, "*Bird Box* reflects a deeply insular, conservative and ultimately paranoid parenting philosophy." It conveys the idea that "all of us—mothers in particular—are not simply powerless against the horrors of the world, but deliberately blind to them." The film blames humanity for refusing to act now, despite the fact that climate change is destroying the planet, including its human and nonhuman inhabitants. But as it does so, it largely challenges, if not abuses, both motherhood and disability. Reproduction is one of the most difficult aspects of human life in the era of environmental degradation and climate change. Suggesting that motherhood disables women—consider the images of pregnant Malorie unable to deal with the crisis on her own, Malorie putting herself in danger trying to save the babies shortly after they were born and later traveling with her young children through wild places, and Malorie learning how to survive with her eyes closed)—*Bird Box* largely undermines and even critiques reproduction in the era of climate crisis.

The metaphor of disability in *Bird Box* is also directly connected to freedom, or lack thereof. Emphasizing how difficult it is to mother a child in the post–apocalyptic world depicted in the film, equating mothering to disability, and suggesting, in an ableist way, a certain kind of lack, limitation, and inability associated with mothering, *Bird Box* expresses that today's turbulent times might impact women's choice to become mothers as well as influence the role of being a mother.

Conclusion

Malorie and her children survive, as the film reveals in its final scene. Yet whether such survival is worth it is the question that every viewer will inevitably ask. Malorie will forever be worried for the safety and well-being of her children, ready at any moment to turn again into that "strict, uncompromising, focused, aggressive" mother. Her children are not allowed to see the world as it is; they are forced to remain in a building that seems to be safe. Is that the life that one wants to have, or wishes, for their children? Some viewers might conclude that parenting in the time of climate crisis is a life-threatening choice. The film's ambiguous references to disability—as a power that helps one fight evil but also as a sacrifice one has to make to stay alive—promote ableism, suggesting that living with disabilities means restricting oneself in multiple ways, such as, for example, by existing only behind the walls of the school that Malorie is lucky to discover. While the ostensibly happy ending of the film seems to deliver Malorie and the children to the safe haven of the school, the school's courtyard, with its rectangular enclosure housing a flock of birds, echoes the "bird box" of the film's title. The title of the film itself gestures toward this parallel, suggesting that, in the final moments of the narrative, Malorie has not attained any meaningful kind of freedom, but that she is merely trapped in a bird box of her own, with no choice but to cower in a beautiful but severely delimiting confinement. These references undermine reproduction, and mothering in particular, implying, in an ableist way, that in the times of environmental crisis, mothering is a challenging and limiting activity, as well as a practice that can only partially be fulfilled. Malorie's children are nameless for the most part of the film. She refers to them as Boy and Girl, which illustrates the deficient nature of the mother–child relationship. When Malorie finally gives them names—Olympia and Tom, in honor of the girl's dead biological mother and Malorie's dead lover—she hardly perceives these children as "the future," neither is the mother–child bond strengthened, for in these children she sees strangers, despite calling herself their mother. *Bird Box* thus unequivocally suggests that in the era of climate change, mothering is different and dangerous—if at all possible.

Note

1. For example, John Hillcoat's *The Road* (based on Cormac McCarthy's novel of the same name) only briefly refers to pregnancy through the main character's wife, who chooses to leave her family after having given birth to their son, thus rejecting motherhood as an option in an apocalyptic world. John Krasinski's *A Quiet Place* (2018) and *A Quiet Place Part II* (2020) are unique examples that directly explore how, first the father and the mother, and later only the mother, fight to protect their children (including their unborn baby) while also losing one of them. Krasinski's films explore the current environmental crisis

through sound, working with affect and emotion in unique ways. Like *Bird Box*, it thus explores environmental degradation and new ways of living through the senses.

Works Cited

Bird Box. Directed by Susanne Bier, Netflix, 2018.

Garland-Thomson, Rosemarie. "Feminist Disability Studies." *Signs*, vol. 30, no. 2, 2005, pp. 1557–87.

Jaquette Ray, Sarah. *A Field Guide to Climate Anxiety: How to Keep Your Cool on a Warming Planet*. University of California Press, 2020.

Ortner, Sherry B. *Making Gender: The Politics and Erotics of Culture*. Beacon Press, 1996.

Reilly, Natalie. "*Bird Box* Reflects a Deeply Insular, Conservative and Paranoid Parenting Philosophy." *The Guardian*, 4 January 2019, theguardian.com/film/2019/jan/05/bird-box-reflects-a-deeply-insular-conservative-and-paranoid-parenting-philosophy.

Szeman, Imre. "Energy, Climate and the Classroom: A Letter." *Teaching Climate Change in the Humanities*, edited by Stephen Siperstein, Shane Hall, and Stephanie LeMenager, Routledge, 2017, pp. 46–52.

Wilson, Sheena, Imre Szeman, and Adam Carlson. "On Petrocultures: Or, Why We Need to Understand Oil to Understand Everything Else." *Petrocultures: Oil, Politics, Culture*, edited by Sheena Wilson, Adam Carlson, and Imre Szeman, McGill-Queen's University Press, 2017, pp. 3–19.

Zerilli, Linda M. G. *Feminism and the Abyss of Freedom*. University of Chicago Press, 2005.

Tatiana Konrad is a postdoctoral researcher in the Department of English and American Studies, University of Vienna, Austria, the principal investigator of "Air and Environmental Health in the (Post-) COVID-19 World," and the editor of the "Environment, Health, and Well-Being" book series at Michigan State University Press. She holds a Ph.D. in American studies from the University of Marburg, Germany. She was a visiting fellow at the University of Chicago (2022), a visiting researcher at the Forest History Society (2019), an Ebeling fellow at the American Antiquarian Society (2018), and a visiting scholar at the University of South Alabama (2016). She is the author of *Docu-Fictions of War: U.S. Interventionism in Film and Literature* (University of Nebraska Press, 2019) and the editor of multiple books, including *Imagining Air: Cultural Axiology and the Politics of Invisibility* (University of Exeter Press, 2023) and *Plastics, Environment, Culture, and the Politics of Waste* (Edinburgh University Press, 2023).

Freedom in *Toy Story*: Reading Woody's Journey as a Post-Human Slave Narrative

Sutirtho Roy

The idea of freedom has adopted various connotations in the contemporary world, ranging from the liberation of the body and mind from the rules of an authoritarian entity to the realization of autonomy that breaks free from conditioned slavery. However, one form of twenty-first century American fiction that explores various dimensions of this autonomy beyond anthropocentric dimensions remains animated films. Whether it be the story of a fish struggling to break free of life in an aquarium (*Finding Nemo*, 2003) or a group of zoo animals trying to escape captivity in order to get in touch with their wild instincts (*Madagascar*, 2005) or even objects of waste attempting to escape their preordained destiny such as in the niche animated film *Trash* (2020), animation's use of anthropomorphism (Heise 304) lends itself easily to the portrayal of different dimensions of freedom.

Nowhere is this more evident than in the *Toy Story* quartet, which centers itself around the premise of toys coming to life in the absence of their owners and having their own adventures. While positing imaginative "what if" scenarios filled with a growing ensemble of characters, the four movies dramatize a shifting paradigm in the relationship between an owner and a toy as perceived through the protagonist's eyes. In *The Toy Story Films: An Animated Journey* (2012), Charles Solomon describes how Pixar filmmakers attempt to make a sequel feel like the next step in an overarching narrative (qtd. in Taylor), and the *Toy Story* sequels trace a natural progression in the protagonist's conception of his freedom. In each of the *Toy Story* films, Woody expresses an idealized notion about the toy-owner relationship. This idealized notion, voiced explicitly through the mantra "being there for a child is the most noble thing a toy can do," is challenged by the experiences of the characters around him, causing Woody's faith to weaken. This changing ideology makes for a slave narrative that gradually culminates in the characters realizing their latent agency and breaking free of servitude, achieving not only physical liberation in the form of bodily autonomy but also the self-conscious escape from the hegemonic dominion of an authoritative group.

Toy Story: **Being the Favorite Slave**

Widely regarded to be Pixar's *magnum opus*, *Toy Story* (1995) grounds its conflict, as well as the ensuing theme of its sequels, in the rivalry between two toys, a wooden pull-string sheriff named Woody (Tom Hanks) and a plastic space ranger called Buzz Lightyear (Tim Allen). Woody, who had occupied the role of Andy's (John Morris) favorite toy since kindergarten, is ousted from his privileged position by the arrival of Buzz, a birthday present who thinks he is a real space ranger as opposed to a plastic embodiment of the same. Buzz even seems to replace Woody as the de facto leader of the toys, who are immediately drawn to him, thereby re-enacting their owner's attraction to the new and cool "thing." The owned objects mirror their owner's humanistic temptations towards commodification culture, behaving as servants who microcosmically enact the power dynamics of their master and succumb to engendered biases of anthropocentric masculinity (Woody and Buzz are both militaristic "boy" toys). All the conflicts in the film stem from human negligence, ignorance, or outright abuse of power, which the toys re-enact among themselves or become victims to. It is Andy's nonchalant preference of the new toy that leads to Woody being relegated to a position of relative unimportance, thereby arousing the latter's jealousy. The narrative, however, establishes Andy as the good kid, as opposed to the bad kid, Sid (Erik von Detten), in a manner reminiscent of the politics of ownership in slavery. Gina Camodeca highlights this very issue by placing the "affective bond between the good slave owner and a faithful slave" (51) in opposition to a bad owner's disconnectedness "from the sympathetic capacity that slavery stands so ready to cultivate" (55). Andy's unintentional contribution to creating conflicts between his toys is overshadowed by Sid's intentional mutilation and destruction of his playthings. Sid's mutant, mutilated toys, created via parts in a Frankenstein-esque fashion, and the dark ambience of his playroom are opposed to Andy's cheery bedroom and brightly colored toys.

Woody's character arc in *Toy Story* involves his coming to terms with the fact that he might not be Andy's favorite toy anymore. For his part, Buzz fails to understand Woody's idealized notion of a toy's relationship with an owner. Buzz's belief that he is a real space ranger, and Woody's exasperated reaction to the same, make for several comedic exchanges:

                    BUZZ

    It looks as though I've been accepted
    into your culture. Your chief, Andy,
    inscribed his name on me.

                    REX

    With permanent ink, too!

This inscription of ownership, like a branding, is hardly enough to break Buzz free of his delusions. It is only his recognition of his own self in an advertisement in Sid's room—as one among many of mass-produced Buzz Lightyear figures—that breaks him, literally and figuratively, as his arm gets detached when his attempt to fly fails and he loses his sense of purpose. The discord between the real and the copy, and the implied hierarchy between these dualistic extremes, is rooted in Western epistemology from the Platonic notion of objects being inferior mimetic representations of an original idea. In this schema, toys, which are often copies of actual objects, are placed at the bottom of the hierarchy. This inferiority is implicitly echoed by the toys, as when Rex (Wallace Shawn) self-reflexively wonders whether his attempts to be scary make him come off as annoying.

Woody sardonically points out that Buzz's wings are plastic, that his laser is a simple blinking light, and that he is a toy—"You are an action figure! You are a child's plaything!"—illustrating Woody's understanding of the inherent inferiority of a toy to an actual space ranger. Woody finds compensation for this diminished ontological status, however, in his love for his master, explaining to Buzz that, while they might be toys, they are "*his* toys," referring to the joy and fulfilment of belonging to Andy. Woody's attempts to convince Buzz to return intersect with his own idea of loyalty: "What matters is that we are here for Andy when he needs us. That's what we are made for." This higher calling allows Woody to confront and overcome his jealousy of Buzz. Woody's words are enough to jolt Buzz into a newfound sense of purpose, even if said purpose is borne of an acceptance of his diminished role and endows him with less power than he would have possessed as an actual Space Ranger. In the contest of deciding who is the better slave (or toy), the human master always occupies a position of hegemonic dominance, allowing him to restore the status quo through the slaves' voluntary acceptance of their servitude.

Toy Story 2: **Slaves That Lose Their Value**

Toy Story 2 (1999) articulates themes of loss and disability through the depicted wear and tear of toys that have been played with and subsequently discarded. Woody is afraid that Andy will not take him to cowboy camp because he can't find his hat, and Bo-Peep (Annie Potts) reassures him otherwise. The concern with his hat becomes trivial, however, when Woody rips his arm and seemingly gets shelved. His belief in the previous movie that "no one's getting replaced" is ironically subverted here through the words of Andy's mother (Laurie Metcalf), who tells him that "toys don't last forever." The sustainability of a toy's relationship with an owner, already put into question by Woody's experiences in the previous movie, is further challenged through his interaction with Wheezy (Joe Ranft), a penguin with a defective speaker who has not been repaired yet or played with since becoming disabled. His fear of getting thrown out is conveyed in a series of montages and manifested visually through mental imagery of getting dropped in the trash.

The slippery relationship between "toy" and "trash" is introduced in this film and plays a recurrent role throughout the rest of the series. These teleological terms indicate the relative value of a toy (slave) from an owner's gaze. The human owners' perception of this value governs the narrative structure of the film, which places the two main human beings in opposition to each other. Whereas Andy's love for Woody stems from hours of play and imaginative regard for him as a friend without any regard for his "worth," Al (Wayne Knight) is only interested in the "buck, buck, bucks" that Woody will bring him as a collector's item. To Al, Woody is a simple commodity with exchange and use value, to borrow Marxist terminology. While Andy continues to be represented as the "good" toy-slave owner, Al is further vilified as the immoral businessman who had obtained Woody through theft.

This anthropocentric clash of ideologies pertaining to commodity culture is enacted on a microcosmic level between Woody and Stinky Pete (Kelsey Grammer), a conflict that intertwines the idea of freedom with the increasingly consumerist culture of the Anthropocene. Stinky Pete resembles Woody's past in his inherent jealousy of "space toys," which he blames for making him, a side character in a popular show, all the more irrelevant, leading to his embitterment. The other characters in the show, Jessie (Joan Cusack) and Bullseye (Frank Welker), also suffer because of anthropogenic negligence on the part of the owner, as both had been relegated to storage with Stinky Pete for eternity until the arrival of Woody signalled the completion of the toy "set," which can now be sold to a museum in Tokyo. Woody's already faltering faith in his owner's reliability is further challenged by Jessie's narration of her past:

> And when Andy plays with you, it's like... Even though you're not moving, you feel like you're alive because that's how he sees you. Emily was just the same... She was my whole world.

Jessie's narration is steeped in elegiac mourning and accompanied by poignant music, causing the audience to pity Jessie's experience of the unequal dynamic between a toy and an owner, where responsibility seems to be unidirectional. She further reiterates this imbalance—"You never forget kids like Emily or Andy. But they forget you."—to explicitly strike a chord at Woody's own preoccupation with ownership since the beginning of the movie. Becoming a permanent display item offers Woody an alternative to such a fate. As Stinky Pete remarks:

> How long will it last, Woody? Do you think Andy is gonna take you to college, or on his honeymoon? Andy's growing up and there's nothing you can do about it. You can go back, or you

```
can stay with us and last forever.
You'll be adored by children for
generations.
```

Woody's struggle to choose between possible fates as a "valuable property" and a "cool toy" reaffirms the slave-owner dynamic in that both options constitute an essential surrender of autonomy to the whims of a human owner. Woody's temporary desire to stay back stems from a selfless desire to prevent Jessie, Bullseye, and Stinky Pete from being put back into storage, but it is consequently overruled by the arrival of Buzz and Andy's other toys, who stage a rescue mission. Buzz reiterates Woody's words from the first film to convince him of his worth as Andy's toy—"Somewhere in that pad of stuffing is a toy who taught me that life's only worth living if you are loved by a kid"—and this leads to Woody's subsequent realization: "You are right, Prospector. I can't stop Andy from growing up. But I wouldn't miss it for the world." Such a restoration of the status quo represents an attempt to include his newfound friends in Andy's collection by providing them with a new purpose. Such a purpose seems to be a temporary solution to a long-running problem, as Andy's growing up would actually deny them their purpose again, but the slave mentality is hammered home for Jessie when Woody tells her, "Wouldn't you give anything just to have one more day with Emily? This is what it's all about, to make a child happy. And you know it."

Andy, to his credit, turns out to be a benevolent owner who not only embraces the new toys but also fixes Woody instead of abandoning him. However, Stinky Pete's outburst after his defeat—"You'll all be ruined, forgotten! Spending eternity rotting in some landfill!"—actually manages to critique the glorified servitude professed by Woody and to foreshadow the events of the last two films.

Toy Story 3: A Step Towards Autonomy

Stinky Pete's warning comes into effect after several years in *Toy Story 3* (2010), when the imminent danger of Andy's growing up becomes a reality. Exposition reveals that the toys have hardly been played with for several years, and, despite their efforts to gain Andy's attention, he consigns them to collecting dust in a huge box:

```
             TOY IN CHORUS#1

That kid's seventeen years old.

             TOY IN CHORUS #2

We ain't ever getting played with.

                  BUZZ

But we always said this job isn't
getting played with. It's about...

             TOY IN CHORUS #3

Being there for Andy. We know.
```

This exchange captures most of the toys' changing characterization of a child's ownership from a relationship that brings joy to both parties ("Life's only worth living if you are loved by a kid") to a thankless occupation ("job"). The conflicts between the toys in this film are, again, borne of human actions or negligence. Andy consigns the toys to the attic, but they are mistakenly dumped in the trash. As a range of misunderstandings ensues, the toys, despite attempts by Woody to convince them otherwise, realize that their best bet is to make their way to Sunnyside Daycare, where they will again be played with.

The series sticks to its mantra of painting Andy as the best among the depicted toy-slave owners, but, throughout *Toy Story 3*, being owned by a child takes on increasingly sinister dimensions. The narrative introduces human beings whose negligence and methods of play create tensions among the toys. Foremost among them is Molly (Bea Miller), Andy's sister, who nonchalantly drops Barbie (Jodi Benson) in the donation box. The kids at the Caterpillar Room are represented as being grotesque in their methods of play through close-up shots that depict them as monstrous. The filmmakers evoke an uncanny apprehension as the audience watches the children engage in rough play, throw the toys around, and even take the toys apart to stick them in their mouths, nostrils, and other orifices. The abject horror of watching hapless, animate toys becoming inanimate in the hands of gigantified children reaches its climax when one of the children sticks out her tongue to lick Buzz's helmet, with the saliva sticking to it in high-definition, 3D resolution. In this scene, the idealized conception of playtime represented in the previous films is subverted by a visceral representation of the bodily violation inherent in the toys' servitude.

Woody and Buzz gain the audience's sympathies through their empathy with other toys, evident in Buzz's refusal to adhere to the narrative of absolute loyalty to one's owner, as endorsed by Woody. Rejecting the idea that a toy's only priority is the whims of its owner, Buzz insists, "We need to figure out what's best for everyone." Woody, for his own part, chides everyone for this lack of "loyalty," calls their desire to be played with (as opposed to collecting dust or being thrown away) "selfish," and seems to walk out on them. However, his growing kinship with his fellow toy slaves shines through in his desire to return to Sunnyside to help them escape and even in his attempts to save Lotso (Ned Beatty) from being torn to shreds. Woody may have been subtly questioning his own ideology of ownership throughout, as suggested by his cryptic reply:

```
                    WOODY

          Don't worry. Andy's gonna take care of
          us. I guarantee it.
```

FIGURES OF FREEDOM

```
                BUZZ

    You guarantee it?

                WOODY

    I don't know, Buzz. What else could I
    say?
```

Whereas Woody clings to the idea of absolute ownership in *Toy Story* and reverts back to it after a brief period of self-doubt in *Toy Story 2*, he finally decides to let his own desire to be played with and love for his friends overrule the idea of being there for Andy through and through. He writes a small, anonymous note to Andy, the contents of which convince Andy to donate his toys to Bonnie (Emily Hahn). Bonnie is set up to be the new Andy, entrusted to "take care" of Andy's toys for him. As Andy and Bonnie play with all the toys in Andy's backyard, a symbolic end and renewal tinged with nostalgia, the credits roll. The toys become entities similar to Isaac Asimov's robots, who are unable to define themselves beyond their servitude to human beings and who do not know of or admit their sentience, but unlike in the novels—and *like* their film adaptation *I, Robot* (2004)—these toys surpass such imposed narratives of oppression. The toys, and especially Woody, overcome their adherence to the idea of loyalty to a single owner but do not do away with the idea of ownership altogether.

Toy Story 4: **Breaking Free of Voluntary Enchainment**

The continuous use of the terms "junk", "trash," and "garbage" in *Toy Story 3*, its recurrent imagery of landfills, packets for trash disposal, and garbage trucks, and a near-death experience near an incinerator set the stage for *Toy*

Story 4 (2019) and its theme of losing relevance, as well as its depiction of a rising kinship among toys (even antagonistic ones) that is complementary with the critique of the value-oriented system of the Anthropocene. Woody, who had desperately tried to convince his friends to be there for Andy despite his waning interest in them, faces a familiar dilemma when it becomes clear that Bonnie (Madeleine McGraw) is losing interest in him as well. Desperately trying to cling to the notion of loyalty, which he has transferred onto Bonnie from Andy, he tries to remain relevant in Bonnie's life by protecting her new favorite toy, Forky (Tony Hale), who is made from trash, craft supplies, and a spork. Woody and Forky (who achieves sentience after having been transfigured into a toy) undergo opposing character arcs in the film, made evident in Woody's attempts to convince Forky that he is a "toy" rather than "trash." These attempts not only reflect Woody's own belief in a selfless code of servitude beyond one's own happiness, a belief that he had temporarily overcome in the previous film, but they also bring to mind the very first movie of the franchise, in which Woody convinced Buzz of his role and responsibility as Andy's favourite toy. Woody explains to Forky, "You have to understand how lucky you are right now. You are Bonnie's toy. You are going to help create happy memories that will last for the rest of her life."

Gabby Gabby (Christina Hendricks), *Toy Story 4*'s antagonist, emerges as a misunderstood character who resembles Woody, even going so far as to echo his oft-repeated ideology: "Being there for a kid is the most noble thing a toy can do." Woody's ability to empathize with Gabby Gabby marks his own recognition of his past, as well as his own attempts to come to terms with his present. Her attempt to secure Woody's voice box develops out of different kinds of anthropogenic exercises of power. Firstly, her own manufacturing defect prevents her from becoming adopted by a kid, leading her to collect dust on the shelf of the antique store. Secondly, her own idealized view of Harmony (Lila Sage Bromley), the kid she wants to adopt her, echoes Woody's worship of Andy and, to a lesser scale, Bonnie. Her sentimental attachment to Harmony only increases the pathos of the scene in which Gabby Gabby is rejected by Harmony despite possessing a working voice box. Woody finds her curled up in a fetal position, a visual metaphor used earlier to depict Jessie and other toys, conveying the vulnerability of toys in the face of anthropocentric onslaughts.

The other new characters in *Toy Story 4* include a conjoined pair of duck-and-rabbit plush toys named Ducky (Keegan-Michael Key) and Bunny (Jordan Peele), a host of antique toys, and a Canadian motorist on a bike, Duke Caboom (Keanu Reeves), all of whom suffer from similar negligence. Duke Caboom's rejection by his owner Rejean is a result of his inability to fly his bike as far as the commercial for his toy promised. His attempt to come to terms with his reality both mirrors and contrasts Buzz's dilemma in the first film. While Andy had accepted Buzz for his limited abilities all along, it is Buzz who must come to terms with his status as a plastic version of a "Space Ranger"; conversely, while Duke Caboom is aware of his status as a toy inferior to the idea featured on television ("Canada's Greatest Stuntman"), it is his master who fails to negotiate this disparity. The idea of a toy's worth lying in servitude and ownership is a recurrent theme throughout the lives of all the *Toy Story* characters.

Bo-Peep regards her own sheep as more important than Forky, whom she views as a means to an end for pleasing Bonnie, and after a failed attempt to rescue Forky, she stands in opposition to Woody's decision to restage a rescue attempt through her assertive challenge, "Woody, look at us. Nobody is with you. It's over, okay?" The camera pans over the defeated faces of the toys, who are attempting to please a master who cannot even acknowledge their sentience. The film reaches its climax in a heated exchange between Woody and Bo:

FREEDOM IN *TOY STORY*

BO

Nobody wants this.

WOODY

I do!

BO

Why?

WOODY

Because!

BO

Why?

WOODY

Just because!

BO

Why?

WOODY

Because it's all I have left to do! I don't have anything else.

BO

So the rest of us don't count?

WOODY

That's not what I meant. Bonnie needs Forky.

FIGURES OF FREEDOM

               BO

> No. You need Bonnie! Open your eyes, Woody. There's plenty of kids out there. It can't be just about the one you're still clinging to.

The prioritization of these animate objects' own desires above those of a human being accompanies Woody's slow realization of his own slave mentality. The seeds of subtle dissent which had been sown long ago (Woody wistfully admits that Bo had handled the "lost toy" life better than he could) finally get a chance to sprout. Woody decides to become a lost toy and live a life with Bo instead of simply returning to Bonnie. His symbolic acts of passing over his voice box and sheriff's badge mark an end to his role as an object of play, though it would perhaps take some more time to wipe the mark of his owner's name from the bottom of his foot. The closing act rethinks the very definition of the word "lost" from meaning someone who has not found his purpose to someone who is simply living a life of freedom beyond ownership:

               REX

> Does that mean Woody's a lost toy?

               BUZZ

> He's not lost. Not anymore.

The film that marks the greatest development of kinship among different kinds of toys is not only the one where Woody finally overcomes his slave mentality but also the one that uses camera shots from the point of view of the antagonist to portray her before the audience in a sympathetic light. He voluntarily hands over his own voice box to Gabby Gabby, and after Harmony's rejection of her, convinces her of her own worth by borrowing Bo's words, "There are plenty of kids out there." In her own way, Gabby

Gabby does not let her experience mold her into a vengeful villain but accepts Woody's help and finds her own kid. Woody, Bo-Peep and her sheep, Ducky, Bunny, Duke Caboom, and Giggle McDimples (Ally Maki) become saviours to other toys who may have been stuck to carnival stalls, to help them realize their dream of being "with a kid."

Conclusion: A Post-Human Future

The *Toy Story* films attain metanarrative dimensions through their suggestion that these toys are the subalterns that are denied speech so as to leave the status quo undisturbed. Through a comparative reading of the *Toy Story* franchise with *Invisible Man* (1952), Imani Lateef notes the silence and invisibility that are used as tools of oppression by the authorities in power to deny the oppressed their rights. This dynamic is realized through a visual metaphor on screen in *Toy Story 3*, where Lotso literally takes away Mrs. Potato Head's (Estelle Harris) mouth to stop her from verbally assaulting him. Such acts of silencing occur throughout the *Toy Story* films, mainly through the toys' practice of becoming inanimate in the presence of owners. Woody challenges this status quo repeatedly, first by organizing Sid's toys into a resistance movement intended to scare him in *Toy Story* and again by writing an anonymous note to Andy in *Toy Story 3* in order to voice his fellow toy-slaves' collective desire. While the first act, culminating in a close-up of Woody's face as he tells Sid to "play nice," frightens a malevolent oppressor, the second establishes a bridge of communication between the faithful slave and his good owner. Both are acts of manifesting power that enable the films to juxtapose a narrative of subtle slave rebellion with a critique of commodity culture, asking uncomfortable questions regarding the idea of owning other autonomous beings.

Toys, in this regard, become less like familiar objects of play and more akin to marginalized life forms such as dehumanized people and domestic animals, who are exploited under the justification of their essential inferiority. Diane Nelson and Virve-Anneli Vihman describe several forms and degrees of agency that mediate the relationships in the *Toy Story* universe, most of which are enmeshed in a dualistic hierarchy, rooted in anthropocentric perceptions of the world of the other. The toys, with their own differences and divisions—of toy/trash, regular toy/mutant toy, owned toy/ lost toy, boy's toy/ girl's toy, human toy/ animal toy, Butterfly Room toy/ Caterpillar Room toy—manage to overcome such dualisms, adopt a post-binaristic approach, and restructure implicit power dynamics through a form of growing kinship among all kinds of toys. Post-human agency, as complementary to freedom, is realized over time. The toys are hardly powerless, and the films exhibit the latent agency which they embody, as manifested in Woody's aforementioned attempts to communicate with Sid and Andy. In each movie, the toys travel vast spaces beyond the confines of their room, and these spaces seem to widen with each film. In the first three films, the toys manage to subvert the gaze of human beings, find a way to return to Andy, save themselves from being incinerated, and leap off moving planes in order to return home. In a manner of speaking, they choose who they are owned by, as Woody rejects the ownership of Sid, Al, and even Sunnyside Daycare to return to Andy, suggesting the paradoxical dynamics of power in voluntary subjugation.

From being stuck as a "favorite" toy who could never have dreamt of being replaced to coming to terms with servitude because of loyalty to his owner to finally acknowledging the necessity of moving to another owner for the sake of his friends, Woody's story culminates in his liberation from ownership, all while he liberates his fellow toy-slaves. Taken as a whole, the films articulate a timely and relevant message for contemporary audiences in their portrayal of Woody as a role model that meta-narratively engages viewers in breaking free of mental constraints imposed upon them by bodies or institutions.

Works Cited

Camodeca, Gina. "Uncle Toy's Cabin: The Politics of Ownership in Disney's *Toy Story*." *Studies in Popular Culture*, vol. 25, no. 2, 2002, pp. 51–63.

Heise, Ursula K. "Plasmatic Nature: Environmentalism and Animated Film." *Public Culture*, vol. 26, no. 2, 2014, pp. 301–318, doi: 10.1215/08992363-2392075.

Lateef, Imani. "*Toy Story* is a slave narrative. Let me explain." TEDxToledo, *ted.com/talks/imani_lateef_toy_story_is_a_slave_narrative_let_me_explain*.

Nelson, Diane, and Virve-Anneli Vihman. "Bringing the Toys to Life." *From Culture to Language and Back: The Animacy Hierarchy in Language and Discourse*, vol. 5, no. 2, 2018, pp. 203–223, doi: 10.1075/ijolc.00007.nel.

Taylor, Blake. "Woody—The Character Arc of Pixar's Most Iconic Hero." *Rotoscopers*, 28 Oct. 2019, *rotoscopers.com/2019/10/28/opinion-woody-the-character-arc-of-pixars-most-iconic-hero/*.

Sutirtho Roy is an independent researcher who graduated from the University of Calcutta. His research interests converge at the intersection of popular culture, children's literature, post-humanism, and critical animal studies, the latter of which he has attempted to decolonize, highlighting Indian and Japanese perspectives. He has several existing and forthcoming publications with Routledge, BRILL, Palgrave, Cambridge Scholars, and Lexington, and has participated in various national and international conferences. He hopes to analyze popular texts to assess their efficacy as storytelling mediums for raising awareness and effecting tangible impacts on social welfare and wildlife conservation. To that end, he has contributed to websites such as *Wildlife SOS* and *Sportskeeda*, among others, which reflect his expertise in nature and entertainment writing and their interconnectedness for driving environmental change.

"Those Who Deny Freedom to Others Deserve It Not for Themselves":
Redefining the Content of Freedom in Colson Whitehead's *The Underground Railroad*

Beatrice Melodia Festa

Unfreedom, Slavery and the "Tradition of the Oppressed" in Antebellum America

According to a recent body of criticism, "Freedom is one of the most contested concepts in the history of political thought, referring both to principles and to the actions, conditions, and spaces motivated by those principles" (Anker 19). In his seminal study, Eric Foner has explained that "freedom" is the word that more than any other represents the entire history of the United States. Indeed, it is a concept that has run significantly through American history from the Revolution to the present and still lingers today as an essential and contested trait of American culture.[1] Cultural bind, dangerous line of tension, ambiguous term, and at the same time central element in the definition of American identity, freedom continues to be the subject of controversy and redefinition as it gradually takes on new meanings.

In light of this premise, this chapter intends to reassess the content of freedom through the lens of the neo-slave narrative genre and Colson Whitehead's novel *The Underground Railroad* (2016) as it reconfigures the value of liberty. By offering a personal reinterpretation of the antebellum period, the author reframes the meaning of the term to illustrate the need for black emancipation from oppressing white-centric supremacy. Above all, what this study seeks to draw attention to, precisely, is the growing attention in the liberty line—the route followed by slaves to freedom that has recently become the subject of renewed interest.

Despite its broad, rich, and varied significance, in the United States, liberty has a dual nature. On the one hand, it is related to a political and cultural ethos—defended even outside America's borders—and on the other, its relevance has been inevitably intertwined with the racial issue, specifically in the context of slavery and its repudiation of freedom as a natural right. In effect, the system of slavery oddly justified the negation of liberty to African Americans for whom it was a privilege effectively denied. Simply put, in the antebellum South, enslavement served to sustain white supremacy to the detriment of black inferiority. As such, in the American culture, slavery remains a useful investigative framework for understanding the importance of liberty and its undeniable association with the racial question. With respect to this dynamic, Jeffrey Ferguson claims, "As a dominant value in American life, freedom has always stood beside and competed with the idea of equality" (47).

As early as the 1830s, in the well-known study *Democracy in America* (1835), Alexis de Tocqueville stressed how in the United States democracy was based upon the tension between the freedom granted to white people and the perpetuation of inequality maintained by the stability of blackness.[2] As such, in antebellum America, freedom had an exclusive meaning as a privilege reserved for the white community. The very nature of slavery as a practice denied freedom as a status for enslaved people and served to reinforce the role of the white as an oppressor and the black as the victim, stigmatized by a condition of "unfreedom." Placing the concept in America's slave past, one must recognize that for black people, liberty, or rather its inaccessibility, defined itself in its absence.³

According to David Watkins, in the United States slavery served as a "paradigmatic example of unfreedom" (847). To this effect, for black slaves, freedom originated in the uncontrolled exposure to the wills of a dominant white race. Such thinking implies that the practice of slavery represented "a paradigmatic case of unfreedom, in part because it is the product of private and public domination" (848). Setting the concept within a fair balance between white supremacism and black inequality, as Watkins suggests, "dominium and imperium worked together to cut off any potential path to freedom for slaves" (853) who undertook unimaginable obstacles in their attempts to pursue liberation.

Needless to say, slavery is disturbing in itself as it limits the condition of the human being who is dependent upon another and is driven by a need to depart from a condition of captivity. Particularly of note is the fact that in the antebellum South, freedom-seeking strategies were common among slaves who were sustained by a system known as "the Underground Railroad," a safe and secret path to liberation supported by abolitionists who helped slaves escape through the South to reach the North and the free state of Canada.⁴ To this end, for black people, any potential attempt to freedom implied resistance against white domination.

By itself, the negation of liberty during slavery forced fugitive slaves to resort to engaging in clandestine escapes moved by the hope of achieving emancipation. For critics, through this flight to liberation, slaves challenged the standard white system, reclaiming their sense of freedom as a privilege to which blacks did not have access (859). As exemplified in the analysis conducted by Eric Foner, for slaves "[r]unning away, of course, constituted only one part of the spectrum of slave resistance that ranged from day-to-day contestation with owners and overseers to outright rebellion" (22). For this reason, the Underground Railroad soon became a well-organized network of passages to a forbidden promise of freedom (Gara 2). The secrecy of the Underground Railroad was made public with Stowe's novel *Uncle Tom's Cabin* (1852), which spread the word about the system and was followed by slave narratives that contributed to popularizing the importance of the organization as a gateway to black freedom.

Other theorists such as Anthony Bogues evidence how the notion of freedom concerning the African diaspora and the slave trade in the United States fall under what Walter Benjamin defined as the "tradition of the oppressed." As Bogues further remarks, in the American context, the concept is inevitably associated with the fight for oppression, and racial slavery, like colonialism, was historically catastrophic as it contributed to alter its meaning.[5] Frederick Douglass's well-known speech comes to mind at this point, as he contested the real meaning of the Fourth of July (the celebration of American freedom) for black people who in the United States have been denied any status of independence.

Drawing further attention to this issue, recent studies, such as that undertaken by Mimi Thi Nguyen, have traced the historical and current significance of the notion for minorities and African Americans in the U.S. For Nguyen, America liberty is a gift and a contradictory value, as the country was founded on the lure of freedom and was conceived as a land of opportunity. It is equally true, however, as Nguyen observes, that the United States was based upon a false promise of collective freedom (not accessible to all), becoming a country of contradictions that has always denied liberty to minorities and especially to enslaved African Americans, defining them as "unfree" (Nguyen ix).

(Neo)Narratives of Freedom in Colson Whitehead's *The Underground Railroad*

In investigating the content of freedom in contemporary African American literature through the (neo)slave narrative *The Underground Railroad*, let me first venture into a contextualization of the genre and its effective relevance for the issue of liberty. Slave narratives—also known as slavery fiction—became quite popular between the mid-1700s and the late 1800s and consisted of autobiographical stories written by former slaves recounting their own experience of slavery as well as the methods of their escapes. To this end, major fictional achievements of the genre dealt with the reconstruction of black endurance to slavery traumas and with the inhumane treatment of black people in the American slave past before the Civil War and the moral and spiritual blemishes it fostered. To such an extent, these texts grappled with the brutality of enslavement, illustrating the black struggle for resistance.

What is relevant to our current discussion is that fictional accounts belonging to this literary trend (one of the most influential traditions in American literature), mostly consisted of autobiographical stories of fugitive slaves.[6] Besides, studies have offered valuable insights into the quest for freedom as a central element of this narrative canon. In *Voices of Fugitives: Runaway Slave Stories and Their Fictions of Self-Creation* (2000), Sterling Bland suggests that slave narratives can be divided into non-fugitive texts (autobiographical accounts of the conditions of bondage), and fugitive narratives (stories of escapes to freedom). Implicit within such a distinction is the fact that the already mentioned system of the Underground Railroad, which is at the core of Whitehead's novel, falls within the category of fugitive slave narratives that hinge on the salience of freedom as an experience inherent in the condition of enslavement.

In *The Underground Railroad*, Colson Whitehead takes up this type of narrative, fictionalizing the escape of a runaway slave named Cora from a plantation in Georgia. Even though the novel dwells on America's slave past and its harsh consequences, the African American author departs from the original slave narrative. In fact, "the text veers away into the territory of counterfactual history" (Faith 147), going beyond a mere account of enslavement to adopt a new contemporary perspective that merges historical references with fantasy and reconceptualizes the racial question. Besides retelling the story of the Underground Railroad with historical imagination, Whitehead fictionalizes its function by turning it into a physical subterranean train that helped slaves cross the South to reach the liberal states of the North. For this reason, the novel pertains to the neo-slave tradition that is extremely popular amongst contemporary writers who have proven serious revisionist intentions of modernizing slave flights and runaway attempts. For Ashraf Rushdy, these texts are "contemporary novels that assume the form, adopt the conventions, and take on the first-person voice of the antebellum slave narrative" (3). Critics have recently come to the conclusion that among contemporary African American novelists, there has been a growing interest in the genre and a seemingly "widespread desire to reaffirm the historical value of the stories of the enslaved reimagining their subjectivity" (Addo and Anim 3).

Whitehead is known for the versatility of his work and his frequent revisitation of popular genres (Maus 1). Based on these assumptions, scholars have pointed out that Whitehead's fiction is in fact "a pastiche of narrative formulas" (Faith 146), a mixture of forms classifiable in Afrofuturism/black science fiction and in slave narratives (as in the case of the novel we are about to examine). As Derek Maus notes, "Whitehead parodies and appropriates the conventions of literary genres" (19). As said, in general, the neo-slave narrative conjures up the writing of mostly African American authors mainly invoking the memoirs of fugitive slaves.7 By renovating the black experience, these narratives grapple with the brutality of slavery and, as Natalie Crawford points out, "There is a push in the post and neo-slave narratives against time and space from slavery to freedom" (72). Stressing the importance of liberty as a recurring trope of these texts, Bernard Bell clarifies how neo-slave narratives "can be classified as modern narratives of escape from bondage to freedom" (qtd. in Smith 168).

Whitehead's Pulitzer Prize-winning novel *The Underground Railroad* has been defined as a beautiful, brutal, and heartbreaking portrayal of a journey to liberation. In the novel, Whitehead envisages the search for freedom of a black slave driven by her desire to escape as she abandons the plantation in the South and flees to the North. As the lure for freedom is perhaps the most salient theme of narration, the text unearths the effects of African American segregation in the U.S. and the black rebellion against white oppression, which in the novel takes the form of a physical flight. Bearing in mind these considerations, it is wise to remember that during slavery the boundaries between freedom and confinement were quite rigid, especially if we consider that African Americans were relegated to a condition of servitude, and breaking out from it meant subverting the traditional racist and hierarchical order. In this sense, scholars consider *The Underground Railroad* as "a narrative of emancipation steeped, in spite of the many trials and heartbreaks on the way, in the happiness of discovery" (Faith 157). To support this claim, in a recent study, Adam Kelly has underscored how freedom is an indispensable theme in Whitehead's fiction.

Nevertheless, one may legitimately conjecture that the achievement of freedom for the black community has always stood beside and competed with a form of liberation from white suprematism. As exemplified in a recent study conducted by Richard King, for the most part during the Civil Rights Movement, freedom, its signification, and its implication was at the core of black debates that claimed an aim to depart from a condition of social and physical bondage (16). It must be stressed, however, that discussions over the importance of black emancipation and the black freedom struggle in the U.S. have changed, receiving a boost of attention in recent years. As regards this increasing interest, Kelly invites us to more closely consider the context in which Whitehead wrote the novel: 2016.

By the time *The Underground Railroad* was published, issues such as race and racism became central to American culture. In this sense, Kelly remarks that Barack Obama's election in 2008 "seemed to many the mark of the culmination of the black freedom struggle" (17). But this event, an apparent accomplishment for African American culture, has been contrasted by the problematic murders of people of color by white law enforcement that "brought renewed attention to the precarious status of African American lives in US society" (Kelly 17). If, therefore, Whitehead's novel is situated precisely in the occurrence of these events, then the author's focus on freedom as a central element of the narrative and as a symbolic value to propose a new image of black emancipation should not be taken as casual. As a novelist who aims to dwell on the themes of black liberation and racial confinement, notably, the author took advantage of the slave narrative genre to draw on the historical background by reframing the significance of freedom, exploiting the importance of the theme in contemporary American society.

Let us, therefore, get to the core of the novel. From the outset, Whitehead highlights the brutality of the slave system through descriptions of the absolute violence employed to retrieve fugitives. In sharp contrast to the status to which African American people like the protagonist were ostracized, the novel offers the reader hope through escape, the only way to achieve idealistic freedom, given the dangers and risks involved in the fugue attempts. Overall, Cora's journey is undoubtedly fraught with difficulties, so much so that the author makes her travel through several states, highlighting the different treatment America exhibited toward black people. The narrator reports that

> Whites outnumbered slaves two to one in North Carolina, but in Louisiana and Georgia the population neared parity. Just over the border in South Carolina, the number of blacks surpassed that of whites by more than a hundred thousand. It was not difficult to imagine the sequence when the slave cast off his chains in the pursuit of freedom—and retribution. (142)

Given the unfortunate events of Cora's journey, *The New York Review* wrote, "In Whitehead's hands the runaway's all-American story becomes instead a subterranean journey through the uncharted epochs of unfreedom" (Lucas 56). The sense of unfreedom to which African Americans were condemned is at the root of a search for liberty that becomes evident in the text. As the protagonist manages to catch the fictional railway system that will enable her to reach Northern states, Whitehead makes it clear that the U.S. "plays down the trope of negative freedom in favour of a positive freedom many enslaved people actually sought" (Kelly 18-19).

By itself, the railroad becomes the utopian allegory to propound an achievement of freedom that originates precisely in its denial. This is confirmed by the numerous statements made by the characters who claim that "[t]he treasure of course was the Underground Railroad. Some might call freedom the dearest currency of all. Chattel slavery was an affront to God and slavers an aspect of Satan" (Whitehead 154). Characteristically enough, the quasi-realistic spirit of the railroad emerges a few chapters ahead as Whitehead writes, "Cora never told Royal to tell her about the men and women who made the underground railroad. The ones who excavated a million tons of rock and dirt toiled in the belly of the earth for the deliverance of slaves like her" (264). For *The New York Review*, "Whitehead's railroad is little like the emancipation superhighway imagined by abolitionists, an incomplete warren of provisional refuge" (Lucas 57).

To such an extent, Whitehead's fictional world proves how "a writer can add additional meaning to a symbol, and by doing so, create several layers of meaning condensed into one symbol" (Zabel 10). By proposing an allegorical image of the railway that embodies the importance of freedom over captivity, the writer makes clear how the train carries different meanings in the novel, being, on the one hand, a promise of hope and, on the other, an expressive vehicle of resistance and rebellion against white oppression. In this sense, the key to unravelling Whitehead's view of freedom as a prominent theme in the novel lies in the underground railroad, a concrete representation of a fanciful promise of liberty as well as the fulfilment of an American dream possibly accessible to the black community.

However, Darcy Zabel has pointed out how the railway is both a promise and a lie (3-4). From Whitehead's mind, the train becomes a literal threshold to the promise of black liberation. In effect, the destination of the train and the final achievement of emancipation is dubious, as Whitehead leaves the reader wondering whether Cora will finally achieve the much-suffered freedom. As Zabel further explains, "Many African Americans found themselves dubious about whether or not they were truly free" (20). Overall, there seems to be no effective achievement and positive outcome for Cora nor an effective liberation to reward the risks involved in escaping.

It is thus evident how Whitehead's text revolves around a desire for freedom that takes the shape of a never-ending fugue from racism. To this end, Whitehead's redefinition of this new freedom is only sought, never actually accomplished. This is also confirmed by Cora's thoughts, through which Whitehead articulates a profound reflection on the meaning of equality and liberation through the words contained in the Declaration of Independence:

> The whites came to this land for a fresh start and to escape the tyranny of their masters, just as the freemen had fled theirs. But the ideals they held up for themselves, they denied others. Cora had heard Michael recite the Declaration of Independence back on the Randall plantation many times, his voice drifting through the village like an angry phantom. She didn't understand the words, most of them at any rate, but *created equal* was not lost on her. The white men who wrote it didn't understand it either, if not *all men* did not truly mean all men. Not if they snatched away what belonged to other people, whether it was something you could hold in your hand, like dirt, or something you could not, like freedom. (103)

The position the novel takes seems clear: freedom is a right that African Americans have been deprived of at the expense of the false promise of nonexistent equality. As the narrative is strongly wedded to the importance of liberty, Whitehead's novel hinges on a sense of denial that continues to produce forms of unfreedom. As such, the ascension to self and property ownership traditionally marks the advent of freedom from slavery and it is narratively presented to lead only to a persistent confinement (Kelly 29).

Another intriguing aspect worth examining is that the question of violence in the novel is prominently embedded in the acquisition of liberty. Indeed, *The Underground Railroad* deals with the full spectrum of brutality. Cora is severely raped by four slaves and, in her attempt to escape from Randall plantation, she is responsible for the murder of a twelve-year-old boy. Whitehead exploits the tension between the perpetration of violence and the quest for freedom mainly illustrated through white indifference to the suffering of African Americans, which makes emancipation an even more desired value. As Cora observes, "The land she tilled and worked in had been the Indian land. She knew the white men bragged about the efficiency of the massacres, where they killed women and babies, and strangled their futures in the crib" (103).

For this reason, the novel could be read in light of Elisabeth Anker's recent theories as she draws attention to the emergence of a particular kind of liberty. Rejecting the positive significance of freedom, Anker argues that forms of freedom cultivated within uncomfortable environments, limited by economic, political, social, and violent conditions—as in the case of slavery—develop what she terms "ugly freedom" (11). The freedom Whitehead presents, cherished by slaves in antebellum America, corresponds to Anker's definition, which coincides with the development of forms of neoliberal and unconventional freedoms, such as that undertaken in the narrative. Anker adds that black slaves and women experienced "an ugliness enforced by white supremacy" (15). Taking up this thread, Whitehead proposes a form of (black) rebellion that subverts the traditional concept of liberty and at the same time dismantles the hierarchy of (white) power. The black protagonist challenges the boundaries of traditional freedom for an "ugly" utopian liberty that emerges from the harsh context of chattel slavery.[8]

Foregrounding a contemporary fugue to freedom, Whitehead develops what critics consider "Post-Black" or "new black aesthetic" concerning "that contemporary struggle for African-American self-delusion that contains great potential for artistic renewal and reinvigoration" (Maus 18) by proposing what Bertram Ashe defines "blaxploration" (qtd. in Maus 19). According to Maus, Whitehead's texts do not ignore the pertinence and importance of the racial question but somehow forge a new model of blackness characterized by non-conformity and a new attitude toward history (5).

In *The Underground Railroad*, Colson Whitehead reframes the content of freedom as a means necessary to highlight the dichotomy of bondage and liberty through the black struggle by contextualizing it from a contemporary perspective. With the presence of movements such as Black

Lives Matter exposing the systemic racism in the United States and urging public awareness on the question of race, there is a pressing need for literature to redefine the significance of freedom in light of the struggle for racial and social justice.

Notes

1. For a preliminary discussion on the history and meaning of freedom in the United States, see Eric Foner's *The Story of American Freedom* (1998) and *Give Me Liberty! An American History* (2004).

2. See especially Chapter 10, in which Tocqueville discusses the position the black race occupies in the United States and the dangers it exposes to the white community.

3. Although this status affected most slaves, some of them were in a condition defined by historians as "quasi-freedom." Quasi-free blacks were somehow free from the control of their owner and, in some cases, they could avoid detection. On this, see Loren Schweninger's essay "The Underside of Slavery: The Internal Economy, Self-Hire, and Quasi-Freedom in Virginia, 1780-1865" (1991).

4. It is wise to remember that enslaved African Americans could not free themselves under American law. This was further complicated by the promulgation of the Fugitive Slave Act of 1850, which made the federal government responsible for runaways who, if caught in a free condition, should have been returned to their owner.

5. Bogues also highlights how for black people freedom is a set of practices that differ from mere forms of emancipation.

6. The text considered to have initiated the genre is Frederick Douglass's text *Narrative of the Life of Frederick Douglass, an American slave* (1845), in which Douglass explains how he freed himself through literacy.

7. Among the texts considered part of the canon is William Styron's well-known novel *The Confessions of Nat Turner* (1967), which fictionalizes the story of the escape and rebellion of the notorious slave Nat Turner, compiled in the famous confessions he "fully and voluntarily" made in prison to Thomas Gray before his execution.

8. For a fuller discussion on violence, slavery, and freedom from a philosophical perspective, see Kistner and Van Haute's recent book *Violence, Slavery and Freedom between Hegel and Fanon* (2020).

Works Cited

Addo, Joan and Maria E. Lima. "The Power of the Neo-Slave Narrative Genre". *Callaloo*, vol. 40, no. 4, 2017, pp. 3-13.

Anker, Elisabeth. *Ugly Freedoms*. Duke University Press, 2022.

Bland, Sterling. *Voices of the Fugitives, Runaway Slave Stories and Their Fictions of Self Creation*. Greenwood Press, 2000.

Bogues, Anthony. "And What About the Human?: Freedom, Human Emancipation, and the Radical Imagination." *Boundary*, vol. 2, 2012, pp. 29-46.

Crawford, Natalie. "The Inside-Turned-Out Architecture of the Post-Neo Slave Narrative". *The Psychic Hold of Slavery: Legacies in American Expressive Culture*. Rutgers University Press, 2016, pp. 69-83.

Faith, Michel. "Tracking the Slave Narrative in Colson Whitehead's *The Underground Railroad*". *Revue D'Etudes Américaines*, vol. 4, no. 157, 2018, pp. 146-160.

Ferguson, Jeffrey. "Freedom, Equality and Race". *Daedalus*, 2011, pp. 44-52.

Foner, Eric. *Gateway to Freedom*. Oxford University Press, 2015.

Gara, Larry. *The Liberty Line*. University Press of Kentucky, 1996.

Kelly, Adam. "Freedom to Struggle: The Ironies of Colson Whitehead". *Open Library of Humanities*, vol. 4, no. 2, 2018, pp. 1-35.

King, Richard. *Civil Rights and the Idea of Freedom*. University of Georgia Press, 1996.

Lucas, Julian. "New Black Worlds to Know". *The New York Review of Books*, vol. 63, no. 14, 2016, pp. 56-57.

Maus, Derek. *Understanding Colson Whitehead*. University of South Carolina Press, 2021.

Nguyen, Mimi Thi. *The Gift of Freedom: War, Debt, and Other Refugee Passages*. Duke University Press, 2012.

Rushdy, Ashraf. *Neo-Slave Narratives: Studies in the Social Logic of a Literary Form*. Oxford University Press, 1999.

Schweninger, Loren. "The Underside of Slavery: The Internal Economy, Self-Hire, and Quasi-Freedom in Virginia, 1780-1865". *Slavery & Abolition: A Journal of Slave and Post-Slave Studies*, vol. 12, 1991, pp. 1-22.

Smith, Valerie. "Neo-Slave Narratives." *The Cambridge Companion to the African-American Slave Narrative*, edited by Audrey Fisch, Cambridge University Press, 2007, pp. 168-185.

Watkins, David. "Slavery and Freedom in Theory and Practice." *Political Theory*, vol. 44, no. 6, 2016, pp. 846-70.

Whitehead, Colson. *The Underground Railroad*. Fleet, 2016. Kindle edition.

Zabel, Darcy A. *The (Underground) Railroad in African American Literature*. Peter Lang, 2004.

Beatrice Melodia Festa is adjunct professor of American literature and English Language at the University of Verona, Italy. As adjunct professor she also taught American literature at the University of Bari and at the

University of Parma. Her main research interests are the intersection between American literature and new media, a topic she analysed in her monograph *The Evolution of Virtual Identity in American Literature* (Ombre Corte, 2022). Her fields of research also include William Faulkner—to whom she dedicated the book *William Faulkner sul grande schermo* (La Bottega Editoriale, 2023)—cyberfiction, and intertextuality in American literature and film. She has published on Faulkner, Wharton, cyberfiction, and Afrofuturism. She is a member of the editorial board of *Iperstoria: Journal of American and English Studies*.

The Struggle at the End of the World:
Black Freedom in Ta-Nehisi Coates's *Between the World and Me*

Sharmila Mukherjee

In November of 2016, in the wake of the election of Donald Trump as the forty-fifth president of the United States, I received many explicit and implicit assurances from my white liberal friends that all would be okay, that I would be okay, the potential for enduring a regime of racial anger, hatred, unease, racist swagger, and stoking of anti-immigrant sentiments notwithstanding. The assurances likely emerged from a place of historical naivety and faith in the state of the union as inherently pluralistic, democratic, and quintessentially free.

While I was appreciative of the liberal solidarity demonstrated thus with the colored body under these circumstances, my own thoughts veered in the direction of the precarity of the same. Have black and brown bodies been rendered vulnerable by what could be described as an instantiation of racialized sovereignty? But then again, I wondered whether the freedoms of black and brown bodies were ever guaranteed in a republic constituted in large parts by a process of racial othering? A watershed moment—

the "Unite the Right" rally in 2017—reinforced my concerns for my own vulnerability in a white nationalist moment of triumph. Between August 11th and 12th, marchers from a wide spectrum of race-baiting organizations marched toward Emancipation Park in Charlottsville, Virginia, manifesting, among other things, the speciously argued validity of the "Great Replacement" theory. "You (rhyming with "Jew") will not replace us" was the beat to which the Alt-Right-led posse of white nationalists strode, chanting variations of both the Confederate anthem "Dixie" and the Nazi ideology-bearing *"Blut und Boden."*

The march and its accompanying rhetorical violence, threatening to illegitimize bodies like mine that do not "matter" on white nationalist registers of an ideal of America, led predictably to real violence in which a counter protester was killed, leaving several others injured. What was witnessed was a twenty-first-century enactment of white supremacist menace, conjuring the specter of white violence of the Reconstruction era. But the public discourse on the event—including the media reporting—centered around concerns of Charlottsville being a disrupter of American "civility" and around fears that the disruptions might become a new normal under the Trumpian regime, threatening to rend the fabric of an otherwise equitable American polity.

However, neither Charlottsville nor its more ripened and consequently more vehement iteration—the January 6, 2021 insurrection—need be inferred as a racist power formation of the present, coined sensationally as the "whitelash," or a newfangled racist deformity. As Elisabeth R. Anker argues, these are recursions of "ugly" power paradigms that have been entangled continuously with white supremacy since the settler colonialism of American founding and slavery (15). Over time, "ugly" practices of brutality through disavowing, discounting, and sublimating of the attending "ugliness" of violence became consolidated in U.S. history as "freedom." If practices of freedom are really narrow-spectrum practices of liberty that serve the interests of white mastery, then white sovereignty is built, as Ta-Nehisi Coates contends, "on the back" of "Black" subjugation and minoritization (25).

To provincialize the iconic American praxis of the pursuit of life, liberty, and happiness as simultaneously a free practice of often exterminatory violence is not to wokishly decry American freedom in totality as gratuitously racist and violent but to insist that, as long as the practice of a predominantly white freedom and its infinite variations are produced within the matrix of power, it will always be imbricated in the "ugly" valence of domination and violence. In this chapter, I acknowledge white freedom's coercive ontology as a historical *fait accompli*, but I also delight in a Black thwarting of the same through practice of "beautiful"-because-authentic freedoms, or modes of self-preservation and self-actualization, outside the contingency of harm, exploitation, and domination.

I explore formations of authentic freedoms of Black thwarting in a seminal twenty-first-century (African) American text: Ta-Nehisi Coates's epistolary memoir *Between the World and Me* (2015). The text foregrounds mourning as the dominant condition of Black life in the U.S., the year 2015 having been marked by a tragically high incidence of Black death from police shooting and from the violence of white vigilantism. However, the mourning—a figurative staging of Black grievability—also occasions a disinterring of the structural conditions that make living while Black a precarious endeavor in America, because "death" is an immutable fact of Black life (Coates 12-15). The conditions more often than not are obliviated from the grand narratives of American nation-making, Dream, and citizenship. The exhumed structure of Black unfreedom is best captured by referencing Saidiya Hartman's "enclosure," the complex web of implicit and manifest spatial, social, psychic, and representational boundaries and strictures within which post-emancipation Black personhood is stymied, yet within which a unique version of personhood sprouts in the eye, as it were, of the disciplinary regime of white mastery and its afterlife (15).

"The enclosure is so brutal," sighs Hartman as she deciphers agency and "beautiful" living carved out by "wayward" early-twentieth-century black women within the brutality and poverty of gritty city tenements and their surrounding cartographies of streets, alleys, and by lanes (45). The black body, she claims, is in a perpetual state of fugue, volitionally so; the enclosure is white authorities' postbellum attempt to rein in the free black body, because white authority fears that in its formal freedom, the black body may escape into an altogether new grammar of self-possession, uncodified (and uncommodified) and uncodifiable, outside settler colonialism and racial slavery's figuration of an idealized Black American subject that's premised on propertied personhood. Black freedom, on the other hand, is driven by the singular energy of evading and escaping officially designated spaces. In other words, the black body resorts to marronage out of a fear of being propertied. Marronage refers to the practice of gathering in dark alleys, inside disreputable clubs, or in hallways of overcrowded apartments in states of unruliness and dishabille, in defiance of official regimens of proper living. To live "waywardly" is to refuse a handout of freedom with the bells and whistles of subjugation attached.

Just as the "wayward" black women in Hartman's configuration prefer marronage—at the risk of capture and punition—to the oppression of obedience and enclosure, so Coates's ideal of Black freedom can be explored through the lens/analytics of marronage or escape from the enclosures and limits sanctioned by whiteness, white freedom, and white knowledge that fosters specious hopes of a perfect union of universal liberty. In his letter to his adolescent son Samori, Coates predicates authentic black freedom on decolonized geographies of thought that are formed outside of the enclosures of white episteme. White episteme encodes popular freedom in strident patriotism and in the monolith of the American Dream. The stability of both, argues Coates, depends on a blind acceptance of "American innocence at face value" and a disposition of incuriosity (10).

The archives of white thought reveal America as "exceptional," a champion of unfettered democracy and freedom in the world, a lone defender of the white citadel of civilization against the terrorists, the despots, the barbarians, and other dark hued enemies of liberty. The archives of the white practice of freedom also reveal the American Dream as an equal opportunity pathway towards gaining parity in a post-racial America. But the American Dream, like the American claims to a perfect democracy and a perfect space of integrationist intent, is fraught with white abstractions, seductive in their suasive sheen, but fundamentally intransigent to "inquiry" and "interrogation." Were the fundaments of the American Dream, to be interrogated, a subtext of violence would likely emerge: "[The] Dream rests on our backs, the bedding made from our bodies. And knowing this, knowing that the Dream persists with the known world... I was sad for my country, but above all... I was sad for you" (11).

The peddlers of the White Dream have successfully immunized the Dream from doubt or from probing questions about the Dream's substructure and racialized history. Coates asks, or at least seems to ask, his son Samori and, by extension, the Samoris of America, to turn away from the fabulating snares of the practices of American patriotism and the American Dream and their coercive vacuities. If an escape from the American Dream of Coates's construing necessitates a vacating of white spaces in America, or a rhetorical defiling of America—a "killing field authored by federal policies" to "plunder" Blacks of their dignity, wealth, and lives (68-72) and a "crime syndicate" meant to sanctify and secure white bodies while evisceration of black ones (72)—then so be it. In this sense, the label of the unpatriotic or the unamerican would be a badge of honor for Coates.

In asking Samori to be skeptical of the assimilative practices of patriotism and the Dream, Coates is not asking the black sons of America to be anti-American or offend white sensibilities. He is clarifying that to raise an authentic Black dream built not on acceptance of white values but on "constant interrogation" and "confrontation" (12) of said values' codified brutality, Black bodies need to escape the tacit and overt enclosures of white power and grow their personhood on their own terms in the freedom of marronage, even if the freedom thus experienced, and the life thus lived, is provisional.

To be in marronage, the Black man does not necessarily have to abdicate American citizenship (and self-deport, for instance, to Haiti, historically the Western hemisphere's first Black Republic). He may revive the question ascribed to him by James Baldwin in *The Fire Next Time* (1963): "Do I want to be integrated into the burning house?" (45). He may pity the arsonists (white Dreamers) for their death drive through relentless extractive capitalism, pray for their sight to be restored (blinded as they are by the peremptoriness of white privilege), or simply leave them to self-combust because a pursuit of the Dream is ultimately a destructive pursuit with bleak ends (Coates 151). The stances that Samori can take are many. But these are merely attitudinal stances that will neither make nor break Samori in his passage through Black life in America. What, however, will be defining for Samori is the "struggle" or the process he uses to arrive at the crucial knowledge of how to live "free" under the constraints of pervasive antiblackness in America, for it is in America that he has to live and protect the sanctity of his body and of all Black bodies. In other words, no matter the provocation, the white imaginary must not be ceded the power to fetishize the Black body as property or possession all over again, not on Samori's watch (69). Yet it is "within the all" of America—the America of Black-breaking heritage and white disciplinary regime—that Samori must find "some way" to live (12).

How can the Samoris of twenty-first-century America live within the unyielding "all" of America's racial fracture? Coates's answer: through "struggle" (12). For Coates, "struggle" is an open-ended praxis, a critical thinking tool to pry open the opacity of "American history," primarily to make it speak to the continuing predicament of the "color line" in America. To "struggle" is also to historicize the sentience of the Black body, according to what Frantz Fanon describes as the sociogenic principle of black being (40). The end-goal of struggle is to "free" the black mind from "ghosts" and "gird" the black body "against the sheer terror of disembodiment" (Coates 12). The "struggle" is not the "struggle" of a Marxian ilk—a collective or public power tussle for the ownership of the means of material production. For Samori, it's an individualized and private endeavor that unfolds informally and perchance within the sovereign space of his inner life. Coates himself has "struggled" against magical thinking, the heresies, and the misprisions that the white world deliberately deploys to obfuscate its anthropocentric predations. The "struggle," Coates explains, is a placeholder for black thwarting of the white world's attempt to reduce Blacks into a "race" that can be flattened at will and whimsy and made to perform historical roles that are white-ordained. The "struggle," like charity, begins at home, in this case with the act of naming the self and the Black child meaningfully, so that the child becomes the name.

"Samori," writes Coates, is a name that portends for his son the struggle that Samori Toure, a black slave in French colonial captivity, undertook to thwart the colonizer's designs to own his body. The historical Samori died in prison, but he ensured that he did not die in vain, as a "face at the bottom of the well" (65). The "struggle" toward decolonizing the mind can be described as an essentially epistemic struggle, as advocated most fervently by Frantz Fanon in *Black Skin, White Masks* (1952), a treatise of Black thwarting of anti-Black racism in a colonial context. For Fanon, the black subject's struggle is both an *agon* against colonial rule and a more storied struggle for self-liberation from Europe's "suffocating embrace" (60). Coates similarly struggles against white America's asphyxiating enclosures that refuse Blacks the freedom to thrive as "we the people" (Coates 30-32).

The "struggle" is a reclamation of the particular from the universal, or of what Claudia Rankine calls the "self-self" from the "suffocating embrace" of black "historical self" (Rankine 25-28). Samori, claims Coates, must "struggle" to disentangle himself from white episteme's generalization of the black "race" as a faceless mass and individuate himself into a person, to avoid his body being entropied just as Emitt Till's body was, or Michael Brown's body was, or Trayvon Martin's body was. Samori must struggle/strive with equivalent agency to free his slave ancestors from a similar entropy and assign to them particularities of dreams, domesticities, and aspirations that are singular. Slavery, writes Coates, "is not an indefinable mass of flesh. It is a particular, specific, enslaved woman, whose mind is active as your own, whose range of feeling is as vast as your own, who prefers the way the light falls in one particular spot in the woods" (66). The remembering of the slave past "in all its nuance, error and humanity" (66) is intended to free the lives of those who have been amassed into an opaque collective and congealed into nodal points in a roadmap of American progress.

One of the lessons we learn from reading *Between the World and Me* is that the true liberatory gift of a Black dream is not possible to cultivate in the heart of whiteness—the "World" in the book's title—because the heart of whiteness is allergic to alternative visions that see America as an assemblage, a heterogeneity, instead of as a unified narrative, free of the need to be debated. A Black vision of America in a Coatesian vein is, on the other hand, informed by heterogeneity, scooped up in deep dives into the "unknown" of American history. What's "known" are the commonplaces of the greatness of America, among them being the city on the hill encomium. An "unknown" would be, per Coates, the radical knowledge that the hill rests on the "below" of Black America, and that the mountains of the "above" would not be mountains if there were nothing below. What sustains the mountain of white inviolability and gives it meaning is Black abjection. The landscape of racialism etched by Coates imparts a Manichean identity to America that cleaves into two Americas, in which the "Galaxy" of white suburban living is dependent on the privations—both literal and metaphorical—of black "ghetto" life for its "Dreams" to materialize:

> There is no them without you and without the right to break you they must necessarily fall from the mountain, lose their divinity, and tumble out of the Dream. And then they would have to determine how to build their suburbs on something other than human bones, how to angle their jails toward something other than a human stockyard, how to erect a democracy independent of cannibalism. (Coates 105)

White America, as Coates has argued in his forceful essay "The Case for Reparations" (2014), has built its ramparts by phagocytizing Black freedom to be success. Yet the coloniality of white success is not to be found in the "known" history of America. It can, however, be found in the "blooming consciousnesses" of black art, black music, and, above all, in the thoughts of Malcolm X. Furthermore, what's "unknown—that is, what is not made legible in the white archives of American stories about America—is the fact that the ecology of fear in which Black lives are perpetually shrouded, and within which black graves continue to be dug, is the handiwork of "men" who write Black lives out of contention from policies. What's "unknown" is the well-spring of Black-on-Black violence that Coates experienced daily growing up in West Baltimore.

A sanctioned explanation for Black-on-Black violence in dominantly Black neighborhoods of American cities is the failure of the Black to self-govern, to fulfill a stewardship of their own bodies, to relapse into a primordial state of violence when the white master is away at play. Following in the footsteps of James Baldwin, Coates posits Black violence as a white myth created by the white world to recuse itself from the crime of which the white world is the chief architect. The white world order's profession of innocence in the destruction of Black bodies is the real "crime", writes Baldwin (20).

The white crime of "innocence," of not knowing the unknown and not wanting to know the unknown, is reinforced by the schools Coates attended. The P.S.'s, ideally a space for pursuing "truth" over false narratives of redemption, were factories of passive pedanticism that institutionalized fallacious knowledge systems. Thus, as Coates reminisces, to educate was to discipline Black bodies into compliance such that they would stay off the streets, evade gangs, and believe that violence was a unique Black subculture. The academy would, if it had its way with Coates, consign him to the waiting room of a willed ignorance of history. The American academy, in other words, is breeding grounds for domesticated Black bodies that would happily pursue the white bourgeoisies Dream, believe in the glory of the white "Galaxy," and act in the world as white surrogates, if only to allay white anxieties by making the world safer from putative Black diabolism. The academy, the police, the Church (deifying Christ as white), the courthouse, the laws, the legislations, the stock market, in short, the entire social, ideological and economic apparatus of America, or to be more precise, white America, Coates claims, reproduce and reinforce power structures and relations in which the Black body is infantilized, disregarded, "jeopardized" (20), "erased" (25), imperiled, "lost" (35), "exploited" (40), subjected to violence, both quotidian and spectacular (the lynching of Mary Turner in 1918), warred against, torched, truncated, enslaved, stolen, broken, rendered fungible and unfree, "Blackened" into an object, possessed, plundered, and assaulted. These are the modern American states' enclosures of anti-blackness that preclude the possibility of Black autarky.

In a blistering speech on white America's refusal to grant political freedom to blacks on conditions of equality and mutuality, human rights activist Malcolm X thundered that the Black man should seize his freedom by "any means necessary," even if it meant that the means are violent. Believing that Black separation from whites was a necessary precondition for authentic Black freedom to gain traction in America—because, simply put, integration would logically lead to a subsumption of the particularities of Black thought by the tentacles of white universalism—Malcolm X further declared that to secure Black freedom from a diluted presence in an integrated democracy, Blacks should opt for a severance from white America, if not in action, then definitely in thought (15). It could be argued that Malcolm X was rooting for Black freedom in marronage.

It is to Malcolm X that Coates says he turned when he was seeking answers to questions of how to "live" freely *in* his body and *with* his body in an America that treats the black body as whitedom's "essential below" (50). Yet, at a glance, Malcolm X reserves the right to seize freedom through the "bullet." However, it is not the element of violence in Malcolm X's politics that Coates disseminates to Samori, but the belief that X's free-standing thoughts were germinated in marronage, in prison. In prison, Malcolm "struggled" to gain perspective on Black abjection in America, as he read deeply. While prison encased his body physically, it paradoxically afforded him the freedom of infinite study, of epistemes and knowledge architectures that were heterogenous and international in their scope. "He had found himself while studying in prison," writes Coates of his choice of Malcolm X as the unparalleled arbiter of human freedom and human truth.

> I loved Malcolm because Malcolm never lied, unlike schools and their façade of morality,

unlike the streets and their bravado, unlike the world of dreamers. I loved him because he made it plain, never mystical, or esoteric, because his science was not rooted in the actions of spooks and mystery gods but in the work of the physical world. Malcolm was the first political pragmatist I knew, the first honest man I'd ever heard. He was unconcerned with making the people who believed they were white comfortable in their belief. If he was angry, he said so. If he hated, he hated because it was human for the enslaved to hate the enslaver, natural as Prometheus hating the birds. He would not be a better man for you. He would not be your morality." (36)

The long poetic paean to one of America's most reviled and most loved (sometimes in secrecy because of Malcom's supposed tirades against the ineffectuality of a non-violent democratic world order) political rhetors is Coates's way of telling Samori that Malcom spoke intrepidly and freely because he spoke from inside his body, whose sanctity was not merely a talking point in a larger theory of race but a viscerally felt truth, an unfiltered emanation of the black body's "lived experience" of becoming an object amongst other objects, of being transformed from the dynamic synergy of a mind-body-world system into property by the power of the white gaze. The discovery of Malcolm X holds a key to reclaiming the black body "through books, through my own study and exploration" (Coates 63), though Coates throws into the individualized epistemic mix of Black liberation such vernacular sources of wisdom as his grandmother, his father, his mother, his wife, Kenyatta, and the "house of humans" he visits while at Howard University, the eclectic "Mecca" of Black internationalism.

Writing in the aftermath of the "breaking" of the body of Michael Brown in Ferguson, Missouri, and the acquittal of white police officer Darren Wilson, Coates tells his son to not push back against patent misassumptions of the innate diabolism of the black body (Officer Wilson evidently defended his shooting of Brown on grounds that he saw Brown not as a person but as a "demon" to be slayed), or tear up about miscarriages of a racialized judiciary—that's a futile task, as the misassumption and injustice of Black personhood as property, demon, wayward evil fairy (anything but person) is baked into the white episteme that informs the racist logic of citizenship in America. Samori must "live with" that, though Malcolm would not. However, Malcolm's world order has passed and Samori's world order is less virulent, though not any less antiblack in its essence. Besides, Samori is halfway crossed over into the green zone of the white Galaxy, thanks to Coates's upward mobility along the echelons of the Dream. Nonetheless, Coates advises his son to be wary of drinking "from the poison" of colorblindness and individualized social responsibility and of mistaking the appearance of racial progress in a post-civil-rights, multiracial America for substantive change to the racial order. Samori, Coates writes, must "struggle" to survive, not necessarily the onslaught of white body snatchers, but the siren call of Circe-like absolvers of the white crime of "innocence" (145).

The complexities of the current racial moment in America demand greater vigilance on the part of the Samoris, vigilance against the persistence of indiscriminate antiblackness at the expense of grappling with its new and differential expressions. In the last segment of the twentieth century and the early twenty-first, the grammar of post-racial justice used by Michael Brown's killer(s) strikes a familiar note: "You can't perform the duties of a police officer and have racism in you" (qtd. in *Whose Streets?*). Coates's figuration of the Dream indicates that Wilson may well be stating what he believes to be true. Antiblackness can be opaque, not only to those who practice it, but also to those who suffer it.

The deep study to which Coates dedicated himself to help him "struggle" with the deviousness of the Dreamer's rhetoric in the '90s has to be further deepened in the case of Samori. He must study with an eye to attain knowledge of

American "crimes," not to absolve them of it, but to gain radical consciousness of white history and white maneuverings such that the possibility of "losing" his body is foreclosed in an environment where Samori needs to worry about Black loss embodied in sly legislations rather than through direct policing of his body. According to Coates, the forfeiture and imperilment of the Black body is one constant in the shifting ontogeny of white America, though the loss can manifest in markedly quotidian forms. Samori should know the world in which he is coming of age, he should know the antiblack tenets of the world, he should, in a way, arrive at the radical knowledge that America is not a Dream factory, that the portal to the American Dream may be inlaid with landmines that can, if not carefully navigated, revert the black body to property in the blink of an eye. It's not that Michael Brown, Tamir Rice, and Eric Garner, among others, "lost" their bodies from ignorance of the tenet of "white America's progress" but that they died within the epistemic enclosure built by white America's progress, or rather, the progress of those Americans who believe they are white. Said enclosure, Coates states, was founded on "looting and violence," and a systemic "breaking" of the black body (125).

Indeed, as many theorists of antiblack racism contend, the so-called "freedom-caucus" of white American ideology imagined the official declaration of emancipation and the subsequent constitutionalizing of Black-freedom-as-an inalienable right to be markers of progress in and of itself. Likewise, the legislation in 2020 of Juneteenth as a recognition day is a hot air balloon of effete symbolism that does not address the continued endemicity of Black death. As argued, or rather pleaded, by Keeanga-Yamahtta Taylor, real progress is imbricated with freedom that's embodied, not simply ratified in Congress. If one applies the understanding of real freedom as the enabling of a fluid movement through the world in unconditional self-possession, and not just as the conditioning of freed people for the human scrum for clothing, housing, and food, then the entire project of American freedom is a failure (46). The Black body's transition from property to person remains incomplete without making substructural efforts to heal the deformation cast into Blackness that had legitimized and rationalized post emancipation enclosure of Black bodies.

While Coates does not signal a failure of American freedom, he (bitterly) attributes its stellar success to white America's cynical ploy of predicating said freedom on Black demolition. In other words, the historical omissions and occurrence of Black unfreedom that shape Black entry into personhood in the U.S. are not examples of innocent oversight, unfortunate slips, and accidental erasures born out of ignorance and guilelessness. They are a product of white machination and the historical perjury of whiteness. As Coates reminds us, the process of becoming "white" was...

> not achieved through wine tastings and ice cream socials, but rather through the pillaging of life, liberty, labor, and land; through the flaying of backs; the chaining of limbs; the strangling of dissidents; the destruction of families; the rape of mothers; the sale of children." (26)

This is to say that the enclosure, or the "policy"-scripted pen within which Black subjectivity is disallowed to breathe freely, is white-made, of white provenance. The enclosure's persistence as a penumbra of freedom in twenty-first-century America is owing to the enduring power of white supremacy's "tradition" and "legacy."

Works Cited

Anker, Elisabeth R. *Ugly Freedoms*. Duke University Press, 2022.

Baldwin, James. *The Fire Next Time*. Vintage, 1992.

Coates, Ta-Nehisi. *Between the World and Me*. One World, 2015.

Fanon, Frantz. *Black Skin, White Masks*. Grove Press, 2008.

Hartman, Saidiya. *Wayward Lives, Beautiful Experiments: Intimate Histories of Social Upheavals*. W.W. Norton & Company, 2019.

Rankine, Claudia. *Citizen: An American Lyric*. Graywolf Press, 2014.

Whose Streets? Directed by Sabaah Folayan, Magnolia Pictures, 2017.

Sharmila Mukherjee is an associate professor of English at Bronx Community College at the City University of New York (CUNY), where she teaches a variety of courses ranging from Composition to Afro-Caribbean Literature to Creative Writing. Her areas of interest are the intersection of globalization and literature, postcolonial and South Asian literature, and global discourses of poverty. She received her Ph.D. from New York University and has published essays on the contemporary South Asian novel and is currently working on a book on narratives of poverty and empowerment in global South Asia. Dr. Mukherjee is also a fiction writer.

INDEX

1619 Project, 21
28 Days Later (2002), 27

Aboulafia, Mitchell, 107
Adorno, Theodor W., 158, 234
Afrofuturism, 284, 294
Afterglow (2023), 154
Ahn, Sunyoung, 107
Albrecht, Glenn, 200
Alderson, Elliot, 213, 216, 218
Allen, Tim, 262
Alpha Centauri, 205
Amazon.com, Inc., 68, 171, 202
American Dream, 31, 39-52, 298-99, 308
Anker, Elisabeth R., 23-24, 34, 76-77, 88, 206, 209, 212, 225, 235, 241, 247, 279, 290, 292, 296, 309
Anthropocene, 32, 118, 132, 135, 157-158, 170-171, 212-21, 226-27, 233, 236, 247, 266, 271
Appalachia, 174-82, 187-88
Appalachian Trail, 146
Arendt, Hannah, 85
Arlington National Cemetery, 46
Armstrong, Jonas, 64
Ashe, Bertram, 290
Ashman, Nathan, 80
Asia, 77, 237, 247, 310
Asimov, Isaac, 270
Atwood, Margaret, 29

Baccolini, Raffaella, 240

Bachelard, Gaston, 185
Baldwin, James, 300, 304
Balliro, Matthew, 107
Baltimore, Maryland, 235, 303
Barad, Karen, 119, 126, 135
Barbour County, Alabama, 22
Batman, 27, 48
Batman v Superman (2016), 27
Beatie, Ann, 106
Beatty, Ned, 269
Beauvoir, Simone de, 252
Bell, Bernard, 285
Bellow, Saul, 106
Benjamin, Walter, 282
Benson, Jodi, 269
Bentham, Jeremy, 239
Berlin, Isaiah, 94
Between the World and Me (2015), 33, 297, 302, 310
Biden, Joe, 19, 72
Bier, Susanne, 249, 258
Bird Box (2018), 33, 249-58
Birke, Lynda, 135
Black Lives Matter, 21, 291
Black Skin, White Masks (1952), 301, 310
Blackwood, Algernon, 116
Bland, Sterling, 283
Blunt, Emily, 60
Bogost, Ian, 134
Bogues, Anthony, 170-71, 211, 226, 282, 291-92
Bonca, Cornel, 83
Bostrom, Nick, 192
Bourdieu, Pierre, 240

Boym, Svetlana, 113
Brady, Amy, 154
Braidotti, Rosi, 135
British Empire, 195
Bromley, Lila Sage, 271
Brontë, Charlotte, 106
Brown, Michael, 302, 306-08
Brown, Wendy, 218
Bullock, Sandra, 251
Burn, Stephen J., 96, 108
Bush, George W., 17

California, 42, 49, 52, 258
Camodeca, Gina, 263
Canada, 110, 195, 205, 227-28, 272, 281
Capgras syndrome, 29
CBS, 24
Centers for Disease Control and Prevention, 187
Chaikin, Carly, 224
Chakrabarti, Samrat, 216
Charlottsville, Virginia, 296
Chelyabinsk, Russia, 79-81
Chen, Mel Y., 135, 137
Children of Men (2006), 26
China, 202
Chun, Wendy Hui Kyong, 21, 76, 217
Civil Rights Movement, 45, 285, 293
climate fiction, 145, 154
Cloud Atlas (2004), 10, 33, 233-34, 248
Coates, Ta-Nehisi, 297
Coca-Cola, 50
Cold War, 21, 44
Colebrooke, Claire, 135
Commonwealth of Nations, 195, 228
Communist Manifesto, The (1848), 144, 155
Confessions of Nat Turner, The (1967), 292
Conrad, Joseph, 106

Constitution of the United States, 18, 176
Control and Freedom (2006), 21, 34, 88, 226
Coon, David R., 43
Cowart, David, 77
Cowrie, Malcolm, 22
Crawford, Natalie, 285
Cruise, Tom, 59
Crutzen, Paul, 170
Cullen, Jim, 40
Cunha, Daniel, 219
Cusack, Joan, 266

Darwin, Charles, 114, 117
Daston, Lorraine, 134
Day After Tomorrow, The (2004), 249
Day of the Triffids, The (1951), 116
Day, Charlie, 57
Declaration of Independence, 18, 288-89
DeLillo, Don, 71, 88-89, 95, 107-08, 321
Democracy in America (1835), 280
DeSantis, Ron, 72, 89
DeWitt, Rosemarie, 39
Dezer, Gil, 242
Dickens, Charles, 106
Dobbs v. Jackson Women's Health Organization, 73
Donovan, Christopher, 104
Dostoyevsky, Fyodor, 106
Douglass, Frederick, 282, 291

Echo Maker, The (2006), 29, 34
Egan, Jennifer, 29
Elba, Idris, 58
Elsby, Charlene, 225, 227
Emergency Skin (2019), 159, 166, 170-71
Emmerich, Roland, 249
Encanto (2021), 28
England, 110, 195, 205, 208, 226
Esmail, Sam, 213
European Space Agency, 88

INDEX

Fanon, Frantz, 301
Fay, Jennifer, 215
Feminism and the Abyss of Freedom (2005), 23, 34, 258
Ferguson, Jeffrey, 280
Ferguson, Missouri, 306
Fifth Season, The (2015), 159, 161, 164-65, 171
Finding Nemo (2003), 261
Fire Next Time, The (1963), 300, 309
First Amendment, 18
Foner, Eric, 279, 281, 291
Franzen, Jonathan, 31, 91-109
Frozen (2013), 28
Fugitive Slave Act of 1850, 291

G.I. Bill, 43
Gaddis, William, 92, 98, 102, 109
Game of Thrones (2011-2019), 26
Garner, Eric, 308
Georgia, 197, 284, 287, 293
Ghostbusters (1984), 28
Gift of Freedom, The (2012), 23, 34, 293
Glass Hotel, The (2020), 196, 209
GLQ, 135, 137
Godzilla, 55
Gorman, Burn, 58
GQ, 47, 53
Graeber, David, 176
Grammer, Kelsey, 266
Gray, Thomas R., 292
Green, H. Richard, 50
Greenwich Village, 39, 50
Greyhound Lines, 102
Grist, 154
Groos, Karl, 177
Grosz, Elizabeth, 135
Guardian, The, 34, 47, 258
Guevara, Che, 245
Gurry, Kick, 64

Haff, Peter, 221
Hahn, Emily, 270

Haiti, 300
Hale, Tony, 271
Hamm, Jon, 39, 47
Han, Byung-Chul, 21, 57, 86, 143, 235
Hanks, Tom, 262
Happening, The (2008), 249
Haraway, Donna, 112, 121, 126, 135-36
Harbach, Otto, 47, 53
Harman, Graham, 134
Harris, Estelle, 275
Harris, Sharee Renee, 154-55
Harris, Thomas Anthony, 99
Hartman, Saidiya, 297
Hawaii, 237
Hendricks, Christina, 271
Hensley, Nathan, 93
Herren, Graley, 77
Hershey Company, The, 48, 52
Hidalga, Jesús Blanco, 96
Hillcoat, John, 249, 257
Hồ Chí Minh, 30
Hodge, Edwin, 65
Horkheimer, Max, 234
Houle, Karen, 135
Howard University, 306
Hugo Award, 166
Humes, Edward, 43
Hunnam, Charlie, 58
Huxley, Thomas, 133

I Am Legend (2007), 27
I, Robot (2004), 270
Independence Day, 282
India, 138, 195
Industrial Revolution, 170
Invisible Man (1952), 172, 275
Ivanchikova, Alla, 83

JR (1975), 102
Jameson, Frederic, 76
January 6th United States Capitol attack, 296
Jemisin, N. K., 32, 157, 159, 160
Jones, January, 39

Juneteenth, 308

Kakutani, Michiko, 100
Karate Kid, The (1984), 28
Kartheiser, Vincent, 40
Keetley, Dawn, 117
Keller, Julia, 92
Kelly, Adam, 285
Kennedy, John F., 45-47
Kent State University, 45
Kermode, Frank, 62, 68
Kern, Jerome, 47
Ketterer, David, 56
Key, Keegan-Michael, 272
Kikuchi, Rinko, 58
Kim Jong Un, 240
King, Martin Luther, Jr., 245
King, Richard, 285
Kistner, Ulrike, 292
Knight, Wayne, 265
Koja, Kathe, 116
Konstantinovka, Russia, 74, 80-82
Korean War, 39, 43-44, 49, 53
Krasinski, John, 257

Laist, Randy, 134
Lamb, Meghan, 10, 32, 173, 178, 188
Lateef, Imani, 275
Le Guin, Ursula K., 111-12, 137, 155
Lincoln in the Bardo (2017), 29
Lost (2004-2010), 25
Louisiana, 287
Luciano, Dana, 135
Lukács, György, 158
Luzecky, Rob, 225

Macdonald, Danielle, 251
MacIntyre, Jeffrey, 71
Madagascar (2005), 261
MaddAddam Trilogy, 29
Mahon, Áine, 97
Maki, Ally, 275
Malcolm X, 303, 305-06
Man of Steel (2013), 27

Mancuso, Stefan, 134
Manifest Destiny, 52
Marder, Michael, 117, 120, 134-35
Martin, Trayvon, 302
Martini, Max, 63
Marvel, 28
Marx, Karl, 144, 155, 176, 186, 188
Marxism, 171, 176-77, 183, 188, 218-19, 265, 301
Matrix, The (1999), 191-93, 207
Maus, Derek, 284
Mauss, Marcel, 240
McCarthy, Cormac, 257
McCaughrean, Mark, 88
McGraw, Madeleine, 271
Meeker, Natania, 111
Meillassoux, Quentin, 134
Melathopoulos, Andony, 157, 171, 227
Metcalf, Laurie, 265
Miami, Florida, 60, 242
Mill, John Stuart, 154
Miller, Bea, 269
Miller, T.S., 117
Millett, Lydia, 10, 32, 143, 145
Milton Hershey School, 48
Ministry for the Future (2020), 154
Minnesota, 90, 96, 103, 138
Mitchell, David, 33, 233-48
Mittman, Greg, 134
Morries, John, 262
Morse, Robert, 41
Moses, Mark, 41
Moss, Elisabeth, 42
Mr. Robot (2015-2019), 32, 211-25, 227
Musk, Elon, 72, 87, 89, 192
Myers, Natasha, 132, 134

Nancy, Jean-Luc, 85
Nelson, Camilla, 108
Nelson, Diane, 276
Nelson, Joel, 173
Nero, 247
New York, 42, 44, 52, 74, 103, 107-09, 233, 242, 248, 287, 293, 310

INDEX

New York Review, The, 287, 293
New York Times, The, 108-09, 242, 248
New York, New York, 233
New Yorker, The, 92, 107, 109
Nguyen, Mimi Thi, 23, 282
Nguyen, Viet Thanh, 30
Nimona (2023), 28
Nineteen Eighty-Four (1949), 202
Nixon, Richard Milhous, 45
North Carolina, 287
North Korea, 237

O'Brien, Susie, 234, 240-42, 245
Obama, Barack, 286
Obelisk Gate, The (2016), 159, 166, 171
Offill, Jenny, 10, 32, 143, 145
Oklahoma City, Oklahoma, 198
Operation Enduring Freedom, 17
Ossining, New York, 39, 43
Oswald, Lee Harvey, 46

Pareles, Jon, 108
Park, Hong-Kyu, 44
Pastoor, Charles, 108
Patriot Act, 17
Paulson, Sarah, 251
Paxton, Bill, 63
Peele, Jordan, 272
Pennsylvania, 39, 48, 173, 178-79, 185
Pentagon, The, 17
plant studies, 116, 321
Porsche, 242, 248
Postone, Moishe, 158
Potts, Annie, 265
Powers, Richard, 29
Pratt, Chris, 60
Psychopolitics (2017), 21, 34, 68, 89, 145, 153, 155, 226, 247
Purdy, Jedediah, 214
Purple Heart, 43
Putin, Vladimir, 81
Pynchon, Thomas, 95, 98-99

Quiet Place Part II, A (2020), 257
Quiet Place, A (2018), 26, 257

Rankine, Claudia, 302
Raya and the Last Dragon (2021), 28
Reagan, Ronald, 174
Reconstruction era, 296
Reeves, Keanu, 272
Reilly, Natalie, 255
Republican Party, 72, 175, 182
Reuben, Gloria, 223
Rice, Tamir, 308
Richardson, Sam, 65
Road, The (2009), 26, 249, 257
Robinson, Kim Stanley, 154
Rockwell, Norman, 104
Rocky (1976), 28
Rushdy, Ashraf, 284
Russia, 74, 79, 81
Russo-Ukrainian War, 74, 81

Salon, 71, 89
Sardar, Ziauddin, 60
Sartre, Jean-Paul, 62
Saunders, George, 29
Schweninger, Loren, 291
Scott, James C., 176
Sea Beast (2022), 28
Seitz, Matt Zoller, 45
Seoul, South Korea, 234, 240-41
September 11th Attacks, 17, 19, 71, 92, 94-95, 104, 107, 110, 234
Shaviro, Steven, 134
Shawn, Wallace, 264
Shreck (2001), 28
Shyamalan, M. Night, 249
Siff, Maggie, 40
Simmons, J. K., 65
Slater, Christian, 219
Slater, Philip, 41
Slattery, John, 39
Smith, Clark Ashton, 116
Solomon, Charles, 262
South Carolina, 155, 287, 293

317

Southern Reach Trilogy (2014), 31, 111-37
St. Paul, Minnesota, 96
Star Wars (1977), 28
Station Eleven (2014), 209
Stead, Christina, 106
Stein, Howard F., 67
Stoermer, Eugene, 170
Stone Sky, The (2017), 159, 162, 171
Stoner, Alexander M., 157
Stovall, Tyler, 22
Stowe, Harriet Beecher, 282
Strahovski, Yvonne, 61
Styron, William, 292
Sun, Jiena, 87
Superman, 27, 68
Superman Returns (2006), 27
Supreme Court of the United States, 73
Survivor (2000-), 24-27
Sympathizer, The (2015), 30, 34
Szabari, Antonia, 111
Szeman, Imre, 234, 240-42, 245

Tanenhaus, Sam, 95
Taylor, Noah, 60
Thatcher, Margaret, 99
Thoreau, Henry David, 41
Till, Emitt, 302
Tocqueville, Alexis de, 280
Tolstoy, Leo, 103, 108
Tondeur, Anaïs, 135, 137
totalitarianism, 202
Toure, Samory, 301
Toy Story (1995), 33, 261-77
Toy Story 2 (1999), 265, 270
Toy Story 3 (2010), 268, 270, 275
Toy Story 4 (2019), 270-72
Trash (2020), 261
Truman, Harry S., 44
Trump, Donald, 19, 72, 90, 295-96
Tsing, Anna, 135
Turner, Mary, 304
Turner, Nat, 292
Twitter, 72, 89, 189

Tyson, Neil deGrasse, 192

Ugly Freedoms (2022), 23, 34, 88, 209, 225, 247, 292, 309
Ugolini, Luigi, 116
Uncle Tom's Cabin (1852), 282
Underground Railroad, The (2016), 280, 283-93
Underworld (1997), 95
Union of Soviet Socialist Republics, 82
United States of America, 18-19, 21-24, 31, 40, 44-47, 50-51, 66, 71-73, 82, 87, 89, 91-92, 97, 109-10, 173-74, 177, 180, 182, 187-88, 194, 210, 216, 225, 233-34, 242, 259, 279-82, 284-87, 290-91, 295-99, 300-09

V. (1963), 98
Van Haute, Philippe, 292
Vancouver Island, British Columbia, 196, 199, 208
VanderMeer, Jeff, 31, 111-33, 137-38
Vermont, 187
Victoria, British Columbia, 195
Vietnam War, 45
Vihman, Virve-Anneli, 276-77
Viola, Alessandro, 134
Visit from the Goon Squad, A (2011), 29
Voelz, Johannes, 103
von Detten, Erik, 263

Wachowskis, The, 240
Walking Dead, The (2010-2022), 26
Wallace, David Foster, 92, 107
WandaVision (2021), 28
Wandrei, Donald, 116
War on Terror, 96
Watkins, David, 281
Weiner, Matthew, 40, 53
weird fiction, 115
Welker, Frank, 266
West Virginia, 187-88

Whitehead, Colson, 279-80, 283-93
Williams Institute, The, 187
Wilson, Darren, 306
Wire, The (2002-2008), 26, 235
Wood, James, 100, 106
World Trade Center, 17, 321
Wulfres, Roger, 116

Wyndham, John, 116

Zabel, Darcy, 288
Zerilli, Linda M. G., 23, 252
Žižek, Slavoj, 23, 26, 34, 159, 171, 214, 219-20, 227
Zola, Émile, 101
Zombieland (2009), 27

ABOUT THE EDITORS

Randy Laist, Ph.D., is a professor of English at the University of Bridgeport in Bridgeport, Connecticut. He is the author of *Rethinking Writing Instruction in the Age of AI* (2024), *The Twin Towers in Film: A Cinematic History of the World Trade Center* (2020), *Cinema of Simulation: Hyperreal Hollywood in the Long 1990s* (2015), and *Technology and Postmodern Subjectivity in Don DeLillo's Novels* (2009). He has also edited volumes of essays on college movies, plant studies, Indiana Jones, retro-representations of the 1980s, and inclusive educational design. He lives in New Haven with his wife, two kids, and Sigmund the cat.

Brian A. Dixon, Ph.D., is a cultural studies scholar and media critic who serves as a professor of English at Goodwin University. His academic writings include studies concerning nineteenth-century American literature, detectives in film and fiction, ethnic humor in British sitcoms, archetypes in comic books, the works of Ian Fleming, and the James Bond films. He is the author of *Sex for Dinner, Death for Breakfast: James Bond and the Body* (2024). With writing partner Adam Chamberlain, Dixon has edited *Columbia & Britannia: An Alternate History* (2009), nominated for the 2010 Sidewise Award for Alternate History, as well as the acclaimed television retrospective *Back to Frank Black: A Return to Chris Carter's* Millennium (2012).

www.ingramcontent.com/pod-product-compliance
Lightning Source LLC
Chambersburg PA
CBHW051600230426
43668CB00013B/1925